Our Search for Meaning

Our Search for Meaning

A Humanistic Anthology

Katherine Oubre
Phillip Schoenberg

With an Introduction by Jack Crocker

MIMBRES PRESS
of Western New Mexico University

Mimbres Press of Western New Mexico University is dedicated to advancing the University's mission by publishing works of lasting value that reflect the intellectual, creative, historical, natural, and cultural heritage of the southwest region and state of New Mexico, as well as selective works of national and global significance.

FIRST EDITION, 2022
Request for permission to reproduce material from this work should be sent to:

Permissions
Mimbres Press
1000 W. College Avenue,
Silver City, NM 88061

Cover and Layout Design:
Paul Hotvedt, Blue Heron Typesetters, LLC

Cover Photo Credits:
Top row: L–R.
Photograph by Paul Hotvedt
Public Domain
Photo courtesy of Pixabay
Photo courtesy of the Indiana State Museum and Historic Sites

Bottom row: L–R
Portrait of Mary Shelley by Richard Rothwell. c. 1840. National Portrait Gallery, London. Public Domain
From first page of *Beowulf* in Cotton Vitellius A. xv. British Library, London. Public Domain
Antigone. Detail from illustration, 1892. Artist unknown. Retrieved from Wikimedia Commons
The Droeshout portrait of *William Shakespeare*, 1623. Copper engraving print. Public Domain

Our Search for Meaning / Katherine Oubre and Phillip Schoenberg

ISBN - 978-168489269-3 (Hardcover)
ISBN - 978-168564297-6 (Paperback)

MIMBRES PRESS OF WESTERN NEW MEXICO UNIVERSITY
Western New Mexico University
P.O. Box 680
Silver City, New Mexico 88062
mimbrespress.wnmu.edu

Acknowledgements

Katherine Oubre

The development of this Applied Liberal Arts and Sciences curriculum, as well as the opportunity to publish this anthology, would never have been possible without the support and assistance of Jack Crocker, Western New Mexico University Provost, and our collaboration with John Gist over the past six years.

Many thanks go to those who have taught this Humanities course and worked to bring the course's vision to life over the years: Roberta Brown, Benjamin Cline, Casey Dickens Frentzen, John Gist, Jacquie Nichols, Phil Schoenberg, and Heather Steinmann.

This anthology began as a course pack of Creative Commons source materials compiled first with the assistance of Casey Dickens and then edited and formatted by Jacquie Nichols. Susan Hasse compiled and formatted our various drafts of this manuscript and provided great assistance in proofreading. Katie DeLong also assisted in the proofreading of the manuscript.

As noted in the anthology, on behalf of a new generation of humanities students, thanks to Ian Johnston for allowing us to use his modern translation of *Antigone*.

I am deeply appreciative of the Mimbres Press of Western New Mexico University for its support, encouragement, and work in the publication of this anthology. A special thanks goes to Marvel Harrison, whose sheer force of will and attention to detail and process made this all possible, and J.J. Amaworo Wilson, who provided insightful and thorough editorial feedback on a very strict deadline.

Many thanks as well to my husband Nick Varner and our two canine companions, Bjorn and Betty, for their assistance in helping me maintain some semblance of work-life balance. A jaunt in the Gila National Forest solves many of life's woes.

Phillip Schoenberg

I'm a late-comer to this project in many ways. The course was the result of a lot of work by many people before I showed up at Western New Mexico University. I'm grateful to my co-editor, and department chair, Katherine Oubre for inviting me to share this work, her inspiration, vision for the course, and persistence in bringing this project to fruition. None of this would have been possible without the support and encouragement from our Provost, Jack Crocker. I've taught the course now for four years, and I love teaching it. I'm also grateful to everyone who worked on the pilot course, and the development of the curriculum for the initial humanities focused version, especially Katherine Oubre, John Gist, and Jacquie Nichols.

The many conversations about teaching the texts with Benjamin Cline, Roberta Brown, Scott Smith, and Jacqueline Nichols continue to be important to me. I'm especially thankful to Roberta for reading an early draft of my contribution to this project.

I owe a huge debt to the many students who have either taken philosophy or this course from me in the past four years, from whom I continue to learn. I can't list them all here, but Emma McKinley, Michael Dirmeyer, Oscar Oehlsen, and Raymond Cressler all stand out. I rely very much on the hope that they inspire.

My teacher John Himelright changed my life by introducing me to the study of philosophy nearly twenty-five years ago, and his continued support, conversation, friendship and laughter are dear to me.

Finally, I am thankful to my wife, Amanda Schoenberg, for her patience and encouragement, and to my children Robert and Madeline for being awesome kids and helping me lead a good life and strive to be my best self.

Table of Contents

The Age of Discovery, The Rise of the Atlantic Slave Trade, and The Age of Revolutions

Late Modernity

Afterword

Introductions

Introduction

Questions you cannot answer are usually far better
than answers you cannot question.
—Yuval Noah Harari
From *21 Lessons for the 21st Century*

Dear Student:

I welcome you into what is going to be an exciting adventure in thinking. Before you jump in, let me provide some information that should help you understand what we are doing.

The curriculum is structured around four fundamental questions: (See the addendum for details.)

What is truth?
What is justice?
What does it mean to be human?
What is the "good" life?

When asked *Why are you at university?*, the most common response from students was to obtain preparation for a job, a career, to make a good salary. There is absolutely nothing wrong with this answer. Such preparation is an essential part of the mission of any institute of higher education.

But we also think a university education should have knowledge *and* meaning, and indeed "usefulness," along with vocational preparation. This means pursuing a deeper understanding of your "self," your values, and your humanity. Your life goes beyond what you do for a living.

Why These Four Questions?

Questions are the roots of human learning and advancement. From the time a primitive ancestor first consciously wondered *why*, we have searched continuously for meaning and knowledge— and thus the birth of language, numbers, myths, religion, art, songs, poems, stories, philosophy, science, and ultimately, universities.

Like many people, you may not have thought seriously about these specific questions. They may seem only the sort of non-practical things that philosophers and professors argue about. But this course will ask you to apply what you are learning as a way to think more consciously and deeply about these questions. They have essential relevance to our academic disciplines, to our time—and to you.

The four big questions cut across the disciplines—sociology, psychology, political science, anthropology, government, literature, history, communications, philosophy, math, computer science, art, etc.—and are intended to be a connecting thread in a web of knowledge. This approach to learning is not perfect, but if you give it a chance, it can make your college experience more connected, coherent, memorable, and relevant.

Although they use a variety of methods, all of the courses and disciplines taught at universities share a common purpose: to explain and demonstrate who we are as humans—how we relate to each other and to the natural world, why we do what we do, what we believe and know, where we are now, and where we are headed.

When you start to think about these questions in the context of your courses, you will at first naturally rely mostly on your experiences in life so far. Your thinking will be influenced by your race, ethnicity, belief systems, gender, upbringing, and even where you are from. As you engage in the act of critical thinking, your answers will ultimately help determine who you are, how you relate to others, how you conduct yourself in the world, and how you live your life.

The Stories We Live By

In his book *Sapiens,* Yuval Noah Harari connects the beginnings of the universe to what were to become the scientific disciplines that emerged to study and understand it:

> About 13. 5 billion years ago, matter, energy, time and space came into being in what is known as the Big Bang. The story of these fundamental features of our universe is called physics.
>
> About 300,000 years after their appearance, matter and energy started to coalesce into complex structures called atoms, which then combined into molecules. The story of atoms, molecules and their interactions is called chemistry.
>
> About 3. 8 billion years ago, on a planet called Earth, certain molecules

combined to form particularly large and intricate structures called organisms. The story of organisms is called biology.

About 70,000 years ago, organisms belonging to the species *Homo sapiens* started to form even more elaborate structures called cultures. The subsequent development of these human cultures is called history.

Notice Harari's use of "story." Although he refers primarily to science and by inference the "scientific method," we humans did not start with natural sciences as the basis for "stories" to describe our understanding of the universe and our place in it. We used myth, religion, and philosophy to explain things and created literature, music, and art for dramatic, aural, and visual representations. Each narrative has its own way of determining "truth," "reality," and "human experience." These "ways of knowing" became the search engines driving the evolving human quest for meaning and knowledge.

These disciplines trace their ancestry to what came to be called the "liberal" arts. Available to free citizens since antiquity, the liberal arts are intended to "liberate" us from ignorance and unveil reality and truth. And while science and the scientific method buttressed by mathematics opened up a new world of empirical truths and continue to provide astonishing facts and technological magic, our original narratives continue to inform and influence our experiences and views of ourselves in moral, ethical, and humanistic terms.

The topics may be diverse, but at the center of all these ways of knowing and believing is the *human* brain and the consciousness that is creating all the stories we live by. Universities historically have collected these stories, created many of them, continue to debate and add to them, and now we offer you the opportunity to participate in this uniquely human endeavor.

And as an individual *Homo sapiens*, your thoughts, beliefs, ethnicity, nationality, culture, heritage—your history and condition—spring from *everything that has happened from the beginning of time*. YOU are a character in this story.

A Little Learning Is a Dangerous Thing

While all of us are characters in this universal play, we are primarily engaged in the drama of our own daily lives, following the stories we grew up with and were handed down to us. Your education so far has probably been mostly "passive"; that is, information was fed to you with the expectation that you would ingest it and remember enough of it to repeat it successfully on tests. It's the "will-this-be-on-the-test" model. This is one way to learn. But we are asking you to move to the next level—taking more responsibility for thinking about what you are learning. In fact, learning that requires thinking is hard and can be dangerous. It can be especially threatening when the learning calls for unlearning. For example, when humans had to unlearn the proofs that "explained" how the sun and planets revolved around the Earth and had to accept new evidence that the Earth and planets orbit the sun, our whole place in the universe was upended.

Not only did Copernicus' theory refute Ptolemy and question the unquestionable observation of one's own eyes standing on Earth, it also challenged interpretations of Holy Scripture (and caused Copernicus trouble with the church). It changed the "story." We humans were no longer the center of the universe. Those who believed the new findings had to accept a new, downgraded understanding of our relationship to the natural world and "unlearn" what had been "scientific" (and divine) Truth.

Even more so now than ever, what we think we know is changing. As you participate in the course and engage the four big questions, you may have to decide whether to "unlearn" or at least question what you think you know. This process may be unsettling. But it does not necessarily mean that *you* have to change. It does help you to know better who you are and where you stand on basic human values. In turn, knowing yourself, your values, with the ability to think independently and to communicate your thoughts, establishes a strong ethical and philosophical foundation for whatever you choose to do in life.

Knowing the Past; Understanding the Present; Becoming the Future

We live in a world of tweets, Snapchat, Instagram, TikTok, and layers of social media where the internet connects us constantly and instantly to information, people, places, and things on a global scale. Information floods and manipulates our daily lives.

On the employment front, it is predicted that in the next 10 to 20 years, 40% or more of jobs existing today will be automated—performed by machines/robots programmed with artificial intelligence. Sixty to seventy percent of today's jobs will no longer exist. Self-driving cars are here. 3-D printers are making replacement body parts. Robot bricklayers are building houses. Software exists that recognizes faces better than humans can. And with the gene-editing tool CRISPR humans now have a simple way of manipulating our DNA. We are becoming more and more controlled by and dependent on *algorithms.*

Rapid and Radical Change

These examples only touch the surface of how science and technology are affecting the ways we live now, and changing the ways we will work and live in the future. Just as in all major transformative changes in our history—from agricultural to industrial societies, and now from industrial to technological—we are having to rethink not only our work but also what it means to be human. The changes are perhaps radical enough to cause our current geologic epoch—the Holocene, in effect for the past 10,000 years—to be given a new name: *Anthropocene*. This change is being proposed based on evidence of effects that humans are having on the planet.

The Past Is Still with Us

Yet, on the flip side, this sci-fi reality is taking place on a wounded planet threatened by overpopulation, human-induced climate change, racial and ethnic conflict, political disunity, economic inequality, religious divisiveness, and nuclear stockpiles that raise questions about our very survival as a species.

While astronomers are showing us unbelievable pictures of black holes millions of light years away in the universe, and artificial intelligence may be on its way to surpassing human intelligence, we are still engaged in the cultural, racial, social, religious, and political conflicts of our distant ancestors.

A Closing Note on the Possibility of Joy and Awe

As you engage in the adventure of thinking about the four big questions, we hope you will find time to appreciate the feelings of joy and awe that you will experience in being part of this human journey.

Consider the human genius we are heir to:

Letters abcdefghijklmnopqrstuvwxyz

26 squiggly signs the combination of which contains all of literature in English; all writings created or translated into English—the basic way we have to explain our thinking and converse with each other. You can find your own beauty and truth not only in knowledge but also through your imagination in the creation of words and their combinations.

Numbers 0123456789

Think about the genius of the invention of zero. Ten digits basic to all mathematical processes. And now it is the arrangements of one (1) and zero (0) that create the algorithms by which our lives are changing. So simple. So revolutionary. And growing so powerful in your digital life.

Cosmos *Passengers in the universe*

As you read this, you may not realize that you are on a planet traveling about 67,000 miles an hour through space in orbit around the sun, and that you are spinning at about 900 miles an hour.

Moon Shot

Planet Earth going 67,000 miles an hour in orbit around the sun; spinning at over 1,000 miles an hour at the equator. Moon going 2,288 miles an hour in orbit around planet Earth. Your assignment: Create a manned spacecraft and then do the calculus it takes to hit "that" spot on the moon. The human mind at work!

Beauty and Emotion

A poem's effect; shapes of paint on a canvas; a philosophical idea that challenges or inspires; lyrics set to music; music alone; a medieval cathedral; a beach sunset; a spirit wind in a chapel of trees....

The adventure awaits you. Enjoy.

JACK CROCKER
Provost and Vice President of Academic Affairs, Western New Mexico University

ADDENDUM:
Applied dimensions of the four questions

WHAT IS TRUTH?
Applied Dimension:

In a constant flow of information from multiple media and other sources, how do I determine what is "factual," what is "true"? In an age that is being called "post-truth"—populated by "fake news," hacked by unknown sources, manipulated by pernicious bots, harassed by seductive marketing, and threatened by environmental if not nuclear catastrophe—the need for students (and all of us) to recognize and analyze dogma, propaganda, lies, bias, hidden agendas, and falsehoods in general is more important than ever. Not only are these challenges the daily bread of 21st century life in politics, society, and global complexities but also in the "paradigm shifts" of cosmological reality evidenced by the empirical processes and mathematical equations of science.

But students cannot live by content alone. If we are serious about "seeking truth," we academic people have an obligation to nurture curiosity, motivate questioning, and develop the intellectual skills needed to support independent thinking.

WHAT IS JUSTICE?
Applied Dimension:

How do I judge and define fairness and equity in complex social, cultural, political, economic, racial, ethnic, and environmental issues? What are my values and beliefs? Where do they come from and how do I express and apply them? The idea of justice becomes integral to the moral and ethical decisions I make that affect me personally, the community, and society in general. This includes my responsibility as a citizen. While a perfect condition of justice may be unattainable, how do I participate in its pursuit?

WHAT DOES IT MEAN TO BE HUMAN?
Applied Dimension:

Who am "I" in the context of my heritage and personal history, in relation to human and natural history across time, in concert and co-existence with the natural world and other living beings, and probable future interactions with humanoid robots cognitively empowered by artificial intelligence? According to Socrates, "The unexamined life is not worth living." But exposure to the new ideas, broader vision, and critical insights that may be part of that examination carries threats, creates value conflicts, and confronts our given identity with uprooting choices toward deeper self-knowledge. It transcends the "selfie" by which the smartphone knows more about us than we do about our "selves." How are science and technology affecting how I live? As evolving beings, how did we get to where we are today and in what direction are we headed? As new genetic research gains information of our DNA across time, will we move toward no longer defining ourselves by race? In addition to AI robots, will we come to accept "customizing" human beings by manipulating our DNA with gene-editing tools like CRISPR? If evolution is still at work, what will be next for me and the rest of Homo sapiens?

WHAT IS THE GOOD LIFE?
Applied Dimension:

What does it mean to me to have "life, liberty, and the pursuit of happiness"? In a future of possible diminished opportunities, what is the balance of material, social, and spiritual well-being that will provide me with the most happiness? How does the future of work in a world of constantly advancing technology fit into this balance? What are my career choices, and what preparation do I need to make a "good living"? What skills do I need to be successful? These decisions are fluid across time, and education can help you to make them. It generates personal, informed decisions that balance both short-term and long-term ideas about achieving a successful career and happiness.

The four big questions provide a common connective tissue across the credit hours of area content courses. By applying their content to these questions and to your experiences during the course, you will learn and demonstrate essential skills and will not only better comprehend how the disciplines are related to human understanding but will also reach a deeper understanding of yourself.

Our Search for Meaning

"We are the storytelling animal. " —Salman Rushdie

This course examines the intellectual history of western civilization as it is portrayed in literature and philosophy within the context of the four big questions: *What is truth? What is justice? What does it mean to be human? What is the good life?* History, literature, and philosophy seek to help humans as a species explain the world, the world around them as well as the world within. And they all do so through narratives, stories that help us try to understand and explain our purpose in our very mortal existence.

In this course and in this anthology, we examine texts within the western literary tradition in conversation. First and foremost, these stories act in dialogue with one another in meaningful ways. Secondly, they are texts that still speak to us in the modern age. While societies have changed over time, due to internal as well as external influences, we owe it to ourselves to understand where we've come from, how far we've come (if and how we have progressed at all), and how to make sense of the past and present in relation to the future.

For some of you, the purpose of this examination might be to avoid the mistakes of the past. Some of you might be more interested in understanding the past in order to see how we have developed as a species or as a society—and perhaps consider where and how we might improve. For others, it might be to understand the way the human mind and/or community works. And some of you, well, you might just be in it for the story as future storytellers yourselves in literature, television, movies, or video games.

The fact is, we read, listen to, and watch stories every day; whether those get classified as fiction or non-fiction, scientific article or sci-fi series, nightly news or political blog, we understand the world through the ways that we hear, see, and tell within a narrative structure—a beginning, middle, and end, with characters (people, animals, corporations), symbols, and themes (meaning).

As far as we know, our sense of history, of self-consciousness, of story, is unique among biological species on the planet. We could be wrong about that, as we can't see inside the minds of creatures besides ourselves. However, we don't see dogs contemplating their purpose and goals in life or planning out their future. This self-consciousness includes an awareness of our own mortality and our attempt to understand our purpose within the larger cosmos.

Within western civilization, stories contain a nearly archetypal idea of progress, of building on the past in order to create a better future. That is a storyline that not every society—much less every individual—would agree with, but to some degree it's become part of our cultural genetic code.

In the intellectual history of ideas, for example, we need the oral tradition of storytelling in order to set the groundwork of print storytelling, which is necessary before we can begin to imagine digital storytelling. In the discipline of Philosophy, we need Plato before St. Augustine can re-conceptualize his ideas in a Christian context, and then St. Augustine to set the stage for thinkers like Thomas Hobbes, whose fundamental philosophy was questioned as other Enlightenment philosophers begin to re-imagine the individual's liberation of the mind. In literature, archetypal stories from long before written literature existed still inform the "bones" of our stories, so that instead of creating a brand-new plot and characters, we're generally improvising on a common theme; for example, the *Odyssey* and Odysseus' hero's journey turns into the modern road trip novel...or the Coen brothers' *O Brother, Where Art Thou?*.

Our core texts were written between 3500 BCE and the mid-20th century, and that means that they were predominantly written, composed, or told by those who had enough power to have their stories told and memorialized. They reflect the biases of their time and place. It's imperative that in a university setting we question assumptions, biases, and judgments held by others, both in the past as well as in the present. Critical thinking and an open mind help to prevent us from repeating the mistakes and misjudgments of the past.

While a number of you may be majoring in fields outside of humanities or even outside of the Liberal Arts, the texts and themes in this book, as well as the different perspectives we bring to the four big questions, are designed to help you think critically about these questions in relation to your life's purpose and goals.

Here is just a snapshot of the ways that you and your classmates may consider the questions in this course:

What is Truth?

Many people today, even the devoutly religious, say they believe that truth is relative—that my truth and your truth might be different and both can be "true."

Perspective has become very important to us, and we know, for example, that the narratives of historical events are skewed in perspective based on the storyteller and that the "truth" might not appear in the historical record. However, many people don't realize that they believe in some form of ultimate Truth. In this course, we examine our underlying assumptions about truth and where those assumptions come from so that our individual "answer" to "What is Truth?", even if that answer doesn't change, is grounded and that we know where belief, faith, reason, and social upbringing come into play in our minds. In the Liberal Arts, as Dr. Crocker's Introduction explains, our goal is to help you liberate your mind, and while that may often be uncomfortable, you must seek and find your own answers to live a fully engaged life.

What is Justice?

If you're a Criminal Justice major, this question might seem fairly simple. We have systems of justice in place that could potentially give us straight answers to the question. Follow the rules, and if you don't, expect an appropriate punishment. If you're a Psychology or Sociology major, the question becomes more complicated as we examine people's motivations and the circumstances under which they committed wrongs or crimes; these disciplines focus, in addition to legal justice, on mitigating circumstances. In this course, we examine complex situations where it's difficult to determine justice "for all." In literature and philosophy, we're allowed to view scenarios or case studies so that while we aren't directly involved with a "case," we see more than we would in real life cases and can therefore examine our own assumptions, as well as the assumptions of our community and perhaps our religion. In a democratic society, building a better system involves everyone, not just those in power.

What does it mean to be Human?

While it is absolutely true that we can define humanity by our genetic markers, it's also true that we at least assume that we are unique as a species in terms of our self-awareness (though some animals have been proven to possess self-awareness), our emotional and psychological make-up (again, some animals have pretty strong emotional responses), or our capacity through our biology and culture to fundamentally alter our environment. At a time when we have the capacity to artificially alter DNA, considering what it is that makes us fully human and what we might consider to be the limits of humanity have never been more complicated. How do our past stories about ourselves, about power, about using technology to improve our species, inform how we think of our own humanity and the ways that we treat others who may be slightly or perhaps radically different from us?

What is the Good Life?

In the humanities, the good life can't be a life of blind acceptance, belief, or even faith. As Dr. Crocker mentions in the Introduction, we still abide by Socrates' maxim, "The unexamined life is not worth living." Many of us come to the course with a basic outline of what a good life looks like, whether that includes family structure, career goals, and/or expectations about social/economic success. By reflecting on the lives and ideas of others, we indirectly examine who we are and who we can become, both individually and collectively. Ultimately, your search for meaning is your own; it is our job as instructors not to impose our answers upon you but rather to help guide you towards both an informed search and an informed meaning. You are both the storyteller and the main character of your own story.

Early Civilizations

Early Civilizations: Overview
3rd Millennium BCE–6th Century CE

History as we know it couldn't begin until the technology of writing came into existence to leave us a record. Up until sometime around 3200 BCE, history and literature existed only in verbal form and were passed down through the oral tradition. In many cultures, professional historians and storytellers made their living memorizing the ancient tales and details of life that were important for both survival and entertainment. While these stories were passed on from generation to generation, they evolved and changed with the times and audiences, so we can't look back and document any single "original" story.

The development of early civilizations closely paralleled this new technology along with many other innovations and inventions that made it possible for humans to live in larger and more permanent communities. Prior to this time, most humans lived in relatively small groups that were often quite mobile to ensure sufficient resources necessary for survival.

The earliest civilizations formed in the Fertile Crescent of Mesopotamia (in the Middle East), Egypt, the Indus River Valley (in India), and in China. All four civilizations developed in major river valleys, where water was plentiful. Natural flooding cycles provided irrigation to support the development of agriculture necessary to sustain larger, permanent human populations.

As people settled in ever increasing numbers, they had to invent social systems and technologies to avoid constant conflict and to thrive. While cultures developed differently in their respective river valleys, they shared a number of things in common that began to define and form the seeds of civilization as we know it today.

Government, laws, law enforcement, and systems of justice were developed and implemented. Generally, the leader of the people was an authoritarian one, sometimes viewed as a god or demi-god, while some were simply monarchs ruling from their position as priests or warriors. Hammurabi's code from ancient Babylon (also in the Fertile Crescent) in the 1700s BCE was the first written legal document that established clear and prescribed standard punishments for specific crimes.

Economic systems of exchange and trade had to be established both for people living within the river valley civilization as well as those outside of the community. The barter system (for example, trading a goat for five pairs of shoes) in a large society becomes quite difficult, both tracking exchange and finding equal relative value of items to be exchanged. Writing was actually invented more for accounting purposes rather than history and literature, since records had to be kept surrounding trade and systems of exchange. Agricultural tools and methods had to be invented, as did the processing and storing of foods.

While evidence of rituals surrounding death, fertility, and agriculture have been found in prehistoric art and archeological digs, the development of writing allows us a much more detailed description of the religious beliefs of these early peoples. The different cultures of the river valleys held different beliefs, but all were animist. Animism is the belief in a wide variety of spiritual beings, who were often associated with nature, who involved themselves in human life, and who could help and/or create challenges for people. Three of these cultures, the Sumerians in Mesopotamia, the Egyptians, and the Chinese, were also polytheistic, believing in multiple gods who could interact directly with and influence the people in their daily lives.

While all of these civilizations developed innovations in writing and in agriculture, each developed special technologies unique to their culture. The Sumerians in Mesopotamia developed sophisticated irrigation systems, cast bronze, and invented tools like the wheel, sail, and plow. The Egyptians created the pyramids and medicine. The Indus Valley civilization invented plumbing and sewage systems that weren't even dreamed of in the west for centuries, and in some cases millennia. The Chinese invented silk and coined money for trade.

If you are interested in learning more about early civilizations, you might consider taking a World Civilization course in your General Education requirements. All four civilizations are fascinating individually as well as comparatively, but our focus here will be on the Sumerian culture of *The Epic of Gilgamesh*.

Introduction to *The Epic of Gilgamesh*
The World's First Written Text

The Epic of Gilgamesh is the first written narrative that has survived the test of time—5000 years! Even today, readers find it to be an entertaining, enjoyable, and in some ways very relatable narrative.

The epic comes down to us originally in cuneiform, the first written language of ancient Mesopotamia that was either chiseled onto stone or pressed into clay tablets. Over time, these tablets have cracked and broken, and some were lost, so what remains of the epic is a set of 11 tablets, with some pieces missing.

Most versions of the story are broken down by tablet and indicate the missing places with blank spaces or ellipses (. . .). The version we're using, *Gilgamesh* by Stephen Mitchell, a modern American writer, takes some liberties to fill in the gaps so that the story doesn't feel so fragmented and also adapts the translation of the original for modern readers.[1]

Gilgamesh is set in Ancient Mesopotamia, which in Western culture has been called "the birthplace (or cradle) of civilization." One of the four ancient river valley cultures, Mesopotamia developed in the river delta between the Tigris and Euphrates Rivers, famously known as the Fertile Crescent, centered in modern day Iraq and the surrounding region. Much of Western history and culture begins right here, and Gilgamesh was one of the great kings who ruled the city-state of Uruk somewhere around 2750 BCE. The people who lived in Mesopotamia were known as the Sumerians.

Gilgamesh was a legendary historical figure, appearing in the official King's List as the builder of the walls of Uruk. However, apparently he wasn't always a great king. In fact, he's a tyrant at the beginning of our narrative.

In the text, Gilgamesh appears larger than life. He's more god than human, a 9-foot man with thighs the size of tree trunks. He interacts with gods, monsters, and men, and while he's presented as physically ferocious, he's such a violent and vicious

---

1. Stephen Mitchell, *The Epic of Gilgamesh* (New York: Atria, 2006).

king at the beginning of the epic that the gods have to intervene to save the people of Uruk from their own leader.

Mesopotamia was both an animistic and polytheistic culture where gods and humans interacted quite directly and actively and where gods had both natural characteristics and often human personality traits. Gilgamesh's father, Lugulbanda, was an Uruk king who became a god, and his mother, Ninsun, was a demi-goddess, making Gilgamesh himself two-thirds divine and only one-third mortal. Gilgamesh interacts with the gods, who are sometimes in his favor and at other times against him.

The Sumerian gods are difficult to differentiate at first, but the following table includes the major players in the epic, along with a comparative Greek god for general reference.

Sumerian god	Divine traits	Comparable Greek god
Anu	Father of the gods	Zeus
Aruru	Goddess of nature, involved in creation of humans	Gaia
Ea	Creation god, creator of humans with Aruru, trickster God	Prometheus
Enlil	God of water and war	Poseidon/Ares combination
Ishtar	Queen of Heaven, Patron god of Uruk, goddess of love and war	Aphrodite
Ninsun	Minor goddess—Gilgamesh's mother	Nymphs in Greek mythology, who often bore human children (like Achilles' mother Thetis)
Shamash	God of the Sun and Justice	Apollo

The epic is quite short—eleven brief "chapters" or episodes that correspond to the eleven tablets. Despite its brevity, however, *Gilgamesh* provides us with a glimpse into the ways of gods and men within the first written hero's journey, complete with a journey to and return from the underworld.

The first chapter describes Gilgamesh's behavior towards his people, so dangerous and wicked that at the request of the people, the gods create a perfect companion and equal, Enkidu. Chapter 2, Enkidu's creation, the process by which he becomes civilized, and the way that Gilgamesh and Enkidu become friends, gives

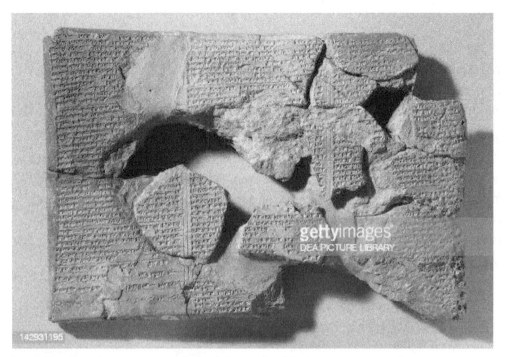

https://media.gettyimages.com/photos/gilgamesh-tablet-written-in-cuneiform-script
-artefact-from-nineveh-picture-id142931195? s=594x594

us a glimpse into the ways that the Sumerians thought about the relationship between the non-human and human worlds and about the very nature of this new
entity called civilization. In Chapters 3–7 the two friends embark upon adventures
together and become so powerful that they threaten to overpower the gods.

Tragedy strikes in Chapter 8, and we see the first narrative description of Sumerian funeral rites as well as Gilgamesh's deep grief and concern over his own mortality.

In Chapters 9 through 11, Gilgamesh travels to the underworld in search of his
relative Utnapishtim to determine how he, like his relative, can defeat death and
gain immortality. Utnapishtim's story recounts one of the most universal pre-history
narratives that exists across cultures and across the globe—a flood story. Gilgamesh's
journey to the underworld, the tests of his worthiness, and his return to Uruk set the
stage for hero stories that still resonate with us across space and time.

Gilgamesh Questions

What is Truth? Gilgamesh is not a philosophical character; rather, he is a warrior who must learn truths about the human condition and about our human role within the cosmos, if not necessarily about himself.

What is Justice? Gilgamesh is a terrible king, and in a society where one person dictates justice, that's not a set-up for a just society. Additionally, in an animistic religious structure, gods are often inconsistent in their treatment of humans, so for ordinary humans, their decisions often appear quite arbitrary. In this epic, we can think about justice in relation to Gilgamesh, to Enkidu, and to the people of Uruk. How do you attain justice in a world that appears to be against you?

What does it mean to be Human? Gilgamesh is not fully human but is part god and part human; however, he is still mortal, which ultimately makes him one of us. The epic as a whole is an extended exploration of how Gilgamesh comes to terms with his own humanity and the larger philosophical question of what it means to be human.

What is the Good Life? At the beginning of the epic, Gilgamesh is clearly living what he believes to be the good life in much the same way we'd like to think about it—What's good for me? What gives me pleasure? How can I enjoy my own life to the fullest? However, is that way of living good for society? Does it give purpose and meaning to our lives? How does Gilgamesh's perspective on this change from the beginning of the epic to the end—to the degree that we can see change or the possibility of change?

Gilgamesh. Questions for Discussion

1. *Gilgamesh* can be read as a series of lessons in leadership, though it's not always clear that he actually learns these lessons. Examine Gilgamesh's adventures and consider what he could learn as a leader, what he does learn as a leader, and what he perhaps fails to learn as a leader. How do those lessons speak to us today even if we lack the genetics and leadership positions that he is granted by birth?

2. Ancient Mesopotamia followed an animistic religious structure, with many gods, goddesses, and semi-divine beings who were closely connected to the natural elements and who influenced the daily lives of humans in ways that were sometimes unexplainable. Examine the ways that the gods influence Gilgamesh's life and journeys, and consider what that might show not only about Gilgamesh's character but also what we can learn about Mesopotamian culture and values.

3. The story of Enkidu from his creation to his death gives insight into the ways that the ancient Mesopotamians thought about companionship, friendship, love, the process of civilization, and even life and death. In many ways, the relationship between Gilgamesh and Enkidu mirrors a relationship between husband and wife perhaps even more than it does a fraternal or brotherly relationship. What do you think is the significance of this relationship in understanding human behaviors and relationships?

4. The flood story is one of the most archetypal of all stories. An archetype is a universal or nearly universal pattern, structure, symbol, and/or story. Many cultures across the globe have within their tradition some kind of story of a global flood, and they have many common elements. Compare Utnapishtim's story of the flood with others, perhaps the Bible's Old Testament story of Noah and the Ark, and consider both the similar elements as well as the unique ones in this story that help us understand the Sumerian relationship between gods and humans.

5. Consider how and why the epic ends in the way that it does. In some ways, it might seem like a bit of an anti-climactic ending, and it is very abrupt. One explanation of that, of course, is the fragmented nature of the tablets. But how and why does this ending "work" in this particular case?

The Golden Age of
Classical Greece

The Golden Age of Classical Greece: Overview
(8th Century BCE–6th Century BCE)

The flourishing of Greek culture, especially in the city of Athens, during the fifth and fourth centuries BCE is today referred to as the classical age of ancient Greece, or the Golden Age. This period of about two hundred years saw the development of most of the things that we now look back on with gratitude to the Greeks: philosophy, art and architecture, comedy and tragedy, and the foundation of Western democracy.

Greece of the Classical period was not a single political unit, and nothing like modern nation states. The many, mostly small, Greek cities were semi-autonomous.[1] Each city had its own form of government, and in the best of times was self-governing, although larger cities often bullied smaller ones. Still, the Greek cities shared a common language and religion, traded with each other, and had a strong sense of a shared culture. The two most powerful cities were Athens and Sparta, although they were very different, in spite of their common culture. Athens was a democratic city, and Sparta was a militaristic oligarchy.

In 478 BCE they banded together on the island of Delos and formed the Delian League to defend themselves from invasion by the Persian Empire, the greatest power in the Mediterranean world at the time. The Persian War ended in 449 BCE with the conclusive defeat of the Persian army at the battle of Plataea.

Athens dominated the Delian league from the beginning, however. Over time the League would devolve into an Athenian empire, as Athens began to demand tribute from other members. After many years of peace following the defeat of the Persians, increasing tension with Athens' powerful neighbor Sparta eventually led to a war, which split Greece between two loyalties, the Peloponnesian League, led by Sparta, and the remnants of the Delian League, led by Athens. The resulting Peloponnesian War lasted twenty-seven years, from 431 to 404 BCE, and ended with a decisive victory for Sparta.

1. The Greek word for city is *polis*, meaning "city," and is sometimes translated as "city-state," but this is misleading; the *polis* was more than a city and less than a state, in our sense. Note, too that *polis* (plural *poleis*) is the root of all our words cognate with politics.

Sparta did not destroy the defeated Athens, however, as might have been expected. Instead they set up a puppet government of thirty tyrants, all Athenians, who were Spartan collaborators, or sympathizers who hated the democracy. The rule of the thirty was brutal, and they used state power to inflict great injustices on personal enemies. Although democracy in Athens was eventually restored, the power and might of the Athenian empire was never the same. The final unification of Greece would come from Macedonia through Alexander the Great. He conquered Greece with little resistance, which gave him the opportunity to cross over to Persia and extend his empire throughout Asia and Africa. After his death in 323 BCE the Classical period of Ancient Greece ended, and his empire was divided among his generals. The cultural dominance of Greece, however, continued for centuries throughout the Mediterranean.

The period of Greek cultural dominance and its decline in political power is called the Hellenistic Age (the Greek word for Greece is *hellas*). The Mediterranean world continued to look to Greece for standards of high culture for several centuries, even after the rise of Roman political dominance in the region.

Introduction to Pericles' "Funeral Oration"

The Athenian historian and general Thucydides (c. 460–c. 400 BCE) wrote a first-hand account of the war between Athens and Sparta, the Peloponnesian War (431–404 BCE). His *History of the Peloponnesian War* includes an account of one of the most famous speeches in history, the funeral oration of Pericles. The oration has inspired many through the centuries. Abraham Lincoln (1809–1865 CE) even relied on it when drafting the Gettysburg Address. [1]

Pericles (c. 495–429 BCE) was an Athenian general and political leader. He was extremely popular in the democratic city. Xenophon, a follower of the philosopher Socrates, compares the power of his speech over the people (*demos*) to a love spell. [2] He also served as a *stratēgos*,[3] or general, in the first year of the Peloponnesian War. Pericles' career, however, ended with his death from the plague that wracked Athens about a year after he delivered this speech.

The occasion of the Funeral Oration was a ritual funeral commemorating all of the war dead at the end of the first year of that very long war. It was one of the very few public events at which women were present. The public funeral was itself an expression of Athenian democratic values. It meant that the wealthy would be buried alongside the poor, and aristocratic families would not be allowed extravagant funerals or monuments for their sons alone. Everyone in Athens would have been present. Indeed, it is not unreasonable to suppose that Sophocles and Socrates would have been present along with their fellow Athenians.

---

1. James V. Morrison, "Interaction of Speech and Narrative in Thucydides," in *Brill's Companion to Thucydides*, ed. Antonios Rengakos, and Antonis Tsakmakis, (Boston: Brill, 2006), 261. For more on his influence see also Vincent Azoulay, *Pericles of Athens*, trans. Janet Lloyd (Princeton, NJ: Princeton Uni. Press, 2014).

2. Ibid.

3. The role of *stratēgos* was an elected position, and a great honor. Sophocles and Thucydides also held this position during the Peloponnesian War.

"Funeral Oration" Questions

What is Truth? It is important to keep in mind that this is a political speech given in a democracy. Pericles is provoking an emotional response, not a critical reflection. As such it raises important questions about when, if ever, it is okay for democratic citizens to suspend their critical thinking and settle into a comfortable acceptance of political claims. The complicated relationship between rhetoric, truth, and democracy was as salient in ancient Athens as it is for us today.

What is Justice? Pericles makes this speech at the end of the first year of the war. The war would drag on for another twenty-six years, and end in the defeat of Athens. This speech is given at the height of Athenian power and culture and at the height of their commitment to the values celebrated by Pericles. They are especially proud of their democracy, and Pericles is proud that Athenians "look to the laws" and "afford equal justice" to all citizens. This is in stark contrast to Sparta, a military state.

In *The History*, Thucydides is critical of what Athens later becomes – an empire interested in material gain and power. In many ways it fails to live up to the ideals Pericles celebrated, and embodied, at the beginning of the war. The contrast with the idealism of the funeral oration is striking: the city of Athens comes to behave like a tyrant in its dealings with weaker cities.[4] Pericles' funeral oration of 431 BCE invites us to reflect on the political disjunction between ideals of justice and the reality of power in a democracy.

What does it mean to be Human? The ancient Greek philosopher Aristotle (384–322 BCE) famously defines the human being as the political animal (*zoön politikon*). For the Athenians, citizenship was central to their identity. All citizens (adult males) were expected to take part in the public life of the city, including politics and the military, regardless of class or wealth. Although citizenship was limited to adult men, all citizens were expected to participate in the political and military life of the city. Pericles' funeral oration invites reflection on the importance of the political community in the identity of the individual. The speech offers an opportunity to reflect on the importance of group identity in an age of individualism, and the importance of others in our individual identity.

---

4. Rosalind Thomas, "Thucydides' Intellectual Milieu and the Plague," in *Brill's Companion to Thucydides*, ed. Antonios Rengakos, and Antonis Tsakmakis (Boston: Brill, 2006), 86. See also the so-called "Melian Dialogue" in Thucydides' *The Peloponnesian War*.

What is the Good Life? This speech is Pericles' celebration of the Athenian way of life. He celebrates those who have paid the highest price for their devotion to the ideals of the city. He then exhorts his listeners to follow the example of the dead and risk their own lives for those ideals, which make life worth living. Pericles provokes us to reflect on what, if anything, is worth dying for, and why.

The Funeral Oration of Pericles According to Thucydides[1]

Most of those who have spoken here before me have commended the lawgiver who added this oration to our other funeral customs. It seemed to them a worthy thing that such an honor should be given at their burial to the dead who have fallen on the field of battle. But I should have preferred that, when men's deeds have been brave, they should be honored in deed only, and with such an honor as this public funeral, which you are now witnessing. Then the reputation of many would not have been imperiled on the eloquence or want of eloquence of one, and their virtues believed or not as he spoke well or ill. For it is difficult to say neither too little nor too much; and even moderation is apt not to give the impression of truthfulness. The friend of the dead who knows the facts is likely to think that the words of the speaker fall short of his knowledge and of his wishes; another who is not so well informed, when he hears of anything which surpasses his own powers, will be envious and will suspect exaggeration. Mankind are tolerant of the praises of others so long as each hearer thinks that he can do as well or nearly as well himself, but, when the speaker rises above him, jealousy is aroused and he begins to be incredulous. However, since our ancestors have set the seal of their approval upon the practice, I must obey, and to the utmost of my power shall endeavor to satisfy the wishes and beliefs of all who hear me.

I will speak first of our ancestors, for it is right and seemly that now, when we are lamenting the dead, a tribute should be paid to their memory. There has never been a time when they did not inhabit this land, which by their valor they will have handed down from generation to generation, and we have received from them a free state. But if they were worthy of praise, still more were our fathers, who added to their inheritance, and after many a struggle transmitted to us their sons this great empire. And we ourselves assembled here today, who are still most of us in the vigor of life, have carried the work of improvement further, and have richly endowed our city with all things, so that she is sufficient for herself both in peace and war. Of the

---

1. Thucydides, *Thucydides*, vol. 1, ed. and trans. Benjamin Jowett, (Oxford: The Clarendon Press, 1900), 125–135. For ease of reading I have changed British spelling to American standard spelling.

military exploits by which our various possessions were acquired, or of the energy with which we or our fathers drove back the tide of war, Hellenic[2] or Barbarian, I will not speak; for the tale would be long and is familiar to you. But before I praise the dead, I should like to point out by what principles of action we rose ~ to power, and under what institutions and through what manner of life our empire became great. For I conceive that such thoughts are not unsuited to the occasion, and that this numerous assembly of citizens and strangers may profitably listen to them.

Our form of government does not enter into rivalry with the institutions of others. Our government does not copy our neighbors', but is an example to them. It is true that we are called a democracy, for the administration is in the hands of the many and not of the few. But while there exists equal justice to all and alike in their private disputes, the claim of excellence is also recognized; and when a citizen is in any way distinguished, he is preferred to the public service, not as a matter of privilege, but as the reward of merit. Neither is poverty an obstacle, but a man may benefit his country whatever the obscurity of his condition. There is no exclusiveness in our public life, and in our private business we are not suspicious of one another, nor angry with our neighbor if he does what he likes; we do not put on sour looks at him which, though harmless, are not pleasant. While we are thus unconstrained in our private business, a spirit of reverence pervades our public acts; we are prevented from doing wrong by respect for the authorities and for the laws, having a particular regard to those which are ordained for the protection of the injured as well as those unwritten laws which bring upon the transgressor of them the reprobation of the general sentiment.

And we have not forgotten to provide for our weary spirits many relaxations from toil; we have regular games and sacrifices throughout the year; our homes are beautiful and elegant; and the delight which we daily feel in all these things helps to banish sorrow. Because of the greatness of our city the fruits of the whole earth flow in upon us; so that we enjoy the goods of other countries as freely as our own.

Then, again, our military training is in many respects superior to that of our adversaries. Our city is thrown open to the world, though and we never expel a foreigner and prevent him from seeing or learning anything of which the secret if revealed to an enemy might profit him. We rely not upon management or trickery, but upon our own hearts and hands. And in the matter of education, whereas they from early youth are always undergoing laborious exercises which are to make them brave, we live at ease, and yet are equally ready to face the perils which they face.

---

2. Hellenic is another word for Greek. *Hellas* is the Greek word for "Greek." The contrast in this sentence is between those who speak Greek and those who do not speak Greek.

And here is the proof: The Lacedaemonians come into Athenian territory not by themselves, but with their whole confederacy following; we go alone into a neighbor's country; and although our opponents are fighting for their homes and we on a foreign soil, we have seldom any difficulty in overcoming them. Our enemies have never yet felt our united strength, the care of a navy divides our attention, and on land we are obliged to send our own citizens everywhere. But they, if they meet and defeat a part of our army, are as proud as if they had routed us all, and when defeated they pretend to have been vanquished by us all.

If then we prefer to meet danger with a light heart but without laborious training, and with a courage which is gained by habit and not enforced by law, are we not greatly the better for it? Since we do not anticipate the pain, although, when the hour comes, we can be as brave as those who never allow themselves to rest; thus our city is equally admirable in peace and in war. For we are lovers of the beautiful in our tastes and our strength lies, in our opinion, not in deliberation and discussion, but that knowledge which is gained by discussion preparatory to action. For we have a peculiar power of thinking before we act, and of acting, too, whereas other men are courageous from ignorance but hesitate upon reflection. And they are surely to be esteemed the bravest spirits who, having the clearest sense both of the pains and pleasures of life, do not on that account shrink from danger. In doing good, again, we are unlike others; we make our friends by conferring, not by receiving favors. Now he who confers a favor is the firmer friend, because he would rather by kindness keep alive the memory of an obligation; but the recipient is colder in his feelings, because he knows that in requiting another's generosity he will not be winning gratitude but only paying a debt. We alone do good to our neighbors not upon a calculation of interest, but in the confidence of freedom and in a frank and fearless spirit. To sum up: I say that Athens is the school of Hellas [Greece], and that the individual Athenian in his own person seems to have the power of adapting himself to the most varied forms of action with the utmost versatility and grace. This is no passing and idle word, but truth and fact; and the assertion is verified by the position to which these qualities have raised the state. For in the hour of trial Athens alone among her contemporaries is superior to the report of her. No enemy who comes against her is indignant at the reverses which he sustains at the hands of such a city; no subject complains that his masters are unworthy of him. And we shall assuredly not be without witnesses; there are mighty monuments of our power which will make us the wonder of this and of succeeding ages; we shall not need the praises of Homer or of any other panegyrist[3] whose poetry may please for the moment, although his

---

3. The term "panegyric" means a public speech in praise of someone.

representation of the facts will not bear the light of day. For we have compelled every land and every sea to open a path for our valor, and have everywhere planted eternal memorials of our friendship and of our enmity. Such is the city for whose sake these men nobly fought and died; they could not bear the thought that she might be taken from them; and every one of us who survive should gladly toil on her behalf.

I have dwelt upon the greatness of Athens because I want to show you that we are contending for a higher prize than those who enjoy none of these privileges, and to establish by manifest proof the merit of these men whom I am now commemorating. Their loftiest praise has been already spoken. For in magnifying the city I have magnified them, and men like them whose virtues made her glorious. And of how few Hellenes [Greeks] can it be said as of them, that their deeds when weighed in the balance have been found equal to their fame! I believe that a death such as theirs has been the true measure of a man's worth; it may be the first revelation of his virtues, but is at any rate their final seal. For even those who come short in other ways may justly plead the valor with which they have fought for their country; they have blotted out the evil with the good, and have benefited the state more by their public services than they have injured her by their private actions. None of these men were enervated by wealth or hesitated to resign the pleasures of life; none of them put off the evil day in the hope, natural to poverty, that a man, though poor, may one day become rich. But, deeming that the punishment of their enemies was sweeter than any of these things, and that they could fall in no nobler cause, they determined at the hazard of their lives to be honorably avenged, and to leave the rest. They resigned to hope their unknown chance of happiness; but in the face of death they resolved to rely upon themselves alone. And when the moment came they were minded to resist and suffer, rather than to fly and save their lives; they ran away from the word of dishonor, but on the battlefield their feet stood fast, and in an instant, at the height of their fortune, they passed away from the scene, not of their fear, but of their glory.

Such was the end of these men; they were worthy of Athens, and the living need not desire to have a more heroic spirit, although they may pray for a less fatal issue. The value of such a spirit is not to be expressed in words. Any one can discourse to you for ever about the advantages of a brave defense, which you know already. But instead of listening to him I would have you day by day fix your eyes upon the greatness of Athens, until you become filled with the love of her; and when you are impressed by the spectacle of her glory, reflect that this empire has been acquired by men who knew their duty and had the courage to do it, who in the hour of conflict had the fear of dishonor always present to them, and who, if ever they failed in an enterprise, would not allow their virtues to be lost to their country, but freely gave their lives to her as the fairest offering which they could present at her feast. The sacrifice which they collectively made was individually repaid to them; for they received again each one for himself a praise which grows not old, and the noblest of all tombs, I speak not of that in which their remains are laid, but of that in which their glory survives, and is proclaimed always and on every fitting occasion both in word and deed. For the whole earth is the tomb of famous men; not only are they commemorated by columns and inscriptions in their own country, but in foreign lands there dwells also an unwritten memorial of them, graven not on stone but in the hearts of men. Make them your examples, and, esteeming courage to be freedom and freedom to be happiness, do not weigh too nicely the perils of war. The unfortunate who has no hope of a change for the better has less reason to throw away his life than the prosperous who, if he survive, is always liable to a change for the worse, and to whom any accidental fall makes the most serious difference. To a man of spirit, cowardice and disaster coming together are far more bitter than death striking him unperceived at a time when he is full of courage and animated by the general hope.

Wherefore[4] I do not now pity the parents of the dead who stand here; I would rather comfort them. You know that your dead have passed away amid manifold vicissitudes; and that they may be deemed fortunate who have gained their utmost honor, whether an honorable death like theirs, or an honorable sorrow like yours, and whose share of happiness has been so ordered that the term of their happiness is likewise the term of their life. I know how hard it is to make you feel this, when the good fortune of others will too often remind you of the gladness which once lightened your hearts. And sorrow is felt at the want of those blessings, not which a man never knew, but which were a part of his life before they were taken from him. Some of you are of an age at which they may hope to have other children, and they ought to bear their sorrow better; not only will the children who may hereafter be born make them forget their own lost ones, but the city will be doubly a gainer. She will not be left desolate, and she will be safer. For a man's counsel cannot have equal weight or worth, when he alone has no children to risk in the general danger. To those of you who have passed their prime, I say: "Congratulate yourselves that you have been happy during the greater part of your days; remember that your life of sorrow will not last long, and be comforted by the glory of those who are gone. For the love of honor alone is ever young, and not riches, as some say, but honor is the delight of men when they are old and useless.

To you who are the sons and brothers of the departed, I see that the struggle to emulate them will be an arduous one. For all men praise the dead, and, however

---

4. In this context, "wherefore" means "for that reason."

preeminent your virtue may be, I do not say even to approach them, and avoid living their rivals and detractors, but when a man is out of the way, the honor and goodwill which he receives is unalloyed. And, if I am to speak of womanly virtues to those of you who will henceforth be widows, let me sum them up in one short admonition: To a woman not to show more weakness than is natural to her sex is a great glory, and not to be talked about for good or for evil among men.

I have paid the required tribute, in obedience to the law, making use of such fitting words as I had. The tribute of deeds has been paid in part; for the dead have them in deeds, and it remains only that their children should be maintained at the public charge until they are grown up: this is the solid prize with which, as with a garland, Athens crowns her sons living and dead, after a struggle like theirs. For where the rewards of virtue are greatest, there the noblest citizens are enlisted in the service of the state. And now, when you have duly lamented, everyone his own dead, you may depart.

Thucydides' account of Pericles' Funeral Oration.
Questions for Discussion

What does Pericles think of those citizens who do not take part in the democratic process in Athens? How well do you think this sentiment would be received today?

Pericles thinks that the democracy of Athens, their way of life, is worth dying for. What are the reasons he gives? Do you think democracy is worth this high price? Why or why not?

Is there anything in the features of Athenian democracy that Pericles praises that you can find in your own country? Are there features of your country's government that are not mentioned, but that you believe deserve such high praise? Explain your answer.

Pericles offers a definition of democracy. What is that definition, and is it a good definition, or would you add to it?

What is democracy, and why is it important according to Pericles? Is he right? Why or why not?

Introduction to Antigone
Sophocles (441 BCE)

Ancient Greek theater was religious. As part of the annual festival of Dionysus (god of wine, ecstasy and theater), a competition was held in Athens for the best playwright. Competitors would write a set of three plays to be performed during the multi-day event. Very few of the many plays performed during these events have survived the centuries and come down to us. *Antigone*, one of eleven tragedies by Sophocles (c. 497–c. 406 BCE), is one of the best. Sophocles was also an influential public figure in Athens, and served with Pericles as a general (*stratēgos*) in the Peloponnesian War (431–404 BCE).

Antigone was probably produced around 441 BCE at the Theater of Dionysus, which could seat some 20,000 people. As a tragedy, the play has a specific structure. The play would begin with a prologue followed by a *parados*, or entry of the actors. A series of acts would then unfold, with occasional choral odes. The actors wore long gowns and heavy masks that covered their faces. The masks would have required actors to face the audience and deliver their lines at high volume, as well as exaggerating their movements to convey the action of the play. The chorus of twelve to fifteen actors would have danced while they sang the odes,[1] while only one member would occasionally interact with other actors directly. The chorus was usually representative of ordinary people (and the audience to some extent). In *Antigone*, the chorus is made up of elderly men called together by Creon for their counsel.

Ancient Greek Tragedy

Why were the Greeks of the classical age so wild about tragedy? What did they get out of watching a play about bad things happening to people? These are difficult questions, and scholars disagree about how to answer them. Aristotle, who was, after all, himself a contemporary Greek, defines tragedy as, "an imitation of an action that is serious and also, as having magnitude, complete in itself... with incidents arousing

---

1. An ode is a poem intended to be sung, similar to lyrics. The chorus sang and danced to the odes.

pity and fear, wherewith to accomplish its catharsis of such emotions."[2] The word *catharsis* here is key. It can be translated as purgation, or a cleansing. But in what sense a tragedy offered an opportunity to the spectator for a "cleansing" of emotions is not at all clear.

The emotions in question, however, are specific: pity and fear. The central figure of a tragedy is the tragic hero. Tragic heroes are victims of fate. The tragedy that befalls them is the result of their own free action, and so somehow their own fault. They could have done otherwise. But in another sense, they could never have done anything but the great error that leads to such terrible consequences because of the kind of person they are, or their character. The tragic flaw is often seen only in retrospect, when it is too late, and all is already lost. In a Greek tragedy fate differs from strict determinism in that fate is when someone freely acts according to who they really are. If they had the whole story ahead of time, choices would have been different, but no one has the whole story ahead of time.

Mythic Background to the Play

Antigone is a dramatic portrayal of one episode of the tragic myth of the cursed family of Oedipus, king of Thebes. Greek religion had no sense of orthodoxy, and there were no doctrines, and no official version of the myth of Oedipus and his family. Indeed, Sophocles introduces novel elements into the story. It was natural for myths to change with retelling. Still, there is a basic storyline for the background of *Antigone*, which Sophocles could count on his audience knowing well.

Oedipus was the son of Laios and Jocasta. When he was an infant, the Oracle at Delphi prophesied that Oedipus would one day kill his father and marry his mother. To avoid this fate Laios leaves Oedipus exposed in the wilderness to die, but he is found by a shepherd and then raised by the king and queen of Corinth as their own son. As a young man Oedipus is travelling to Thebes, gets into a fight with a stranger on the road, and kills him. The stranger was Laios, his father. He then defeats the Sphinx by answering her riddle correctly, and triumphantly enters Thebes. Creon, next in line to rule Thebes, is grateful to Oedipus for saving the city from the Sphinx. As a reward, he offers Oedipus the throne and the hand of his widowed sister-in-law, Jocasta, in marriage.

Unbeknownst to Oedipus, the prophecy had been fulfilled. He has killed his father and married his mother. Their incestuous union gives them two sons, Eteo-

---

2. Aristotle, *The Complete Works of Aristotle*, Revised Oxford Translation, ed. Jonathan Barnes, trans. Benjamin Jowett (Princeton, NJ: Princeton Uni Press, 1984), 4973 (1449b).

cles and Polyneices, and two daughters, Antigone and Ismene. Oedipus eventually discovers what he has done, blinds himself and lives out his life tended by Antigone. Eteocles and Polyneices agree to take turns ruling Thebes, but Eteocles changes his mind and refuses to step down when it is his brother's turn to rule. Polyneices raises an army and attacks Thebes, and during the ensuing battle the brothers kill each other.

Antigone begins after the battle and the double fratricide, which is the killing of one brother by another. Creon, whose name simply means "ruler," has taken the throne, and is desperate to restore order to Thebes following the bloody civil war. He orders the body of Eteocles to be buried with all the formal ritual for the dead. The body of Polyneices, however, is to remain where it fell to rot. This is an extreme thing to do in ancient Greek culture. It was a very important duty to make sure that members of one's own family received a proper burial; failing to do so was a matter of terrible shame and an offense to the gods.

Antigone Questions

What is Truth? The central matter concerning truth in *Antigone* is not easy to resolve; indeed, it is perhaps impossible. In Antigone's disagreement with Creon over his decree to leave her brother (and his nephew) unburied, she appeals to a higher law, the law of god. Are her claims about justice true? Is there a higher law than human law? She is so certain of the truth of her beliefs, and the justice of her actions, that she is willing to go to her death rather than refuse the call of her conscience. Antigone's appeal to a law higher than those of human beings initiates a tradition that has inspired many to disobey unjust human laws.

What is Justice? This is perhaps the central issue of the play and is intimately related to the question of the truth of Antigone's convictions about her duty, and of the existence of a higher law. The play raises important questions about law and justice. Is there a standard by which we can determine the justice of laws? How, if at all, is civil disobedience justified? Careful consideration of justice in *Antigone* may not reveal unambiguous answers for us today any more than it did for Greek audiences of the fifth century, but it can help us in the lifetime task of serious reflection.

What does it mean to be Human? This is another central question in *Antigone*, and in all Athenian Tragedy. The first choral ode in the play, traditionally called the "Ode to Man," offers Sophocles' answer to the question: "Numberless are the world's wonders, but none more wonderful than man. . . " The word that Fitz-gerald and Fitts translate here as "wonderful" has no equivalent in English. The Greek word *deinos* includes this sense of wonder but may also include clever-ness or even dreadfulness. Depending on the context, it might be translated as "awesome" or "awful. "[3] The ode may be read as a celebration of human powers and achievement, but also as a warning. It remains as relevant for us today as it was for Sophocles' original audience.

What is the Good Life? When are your convictions worth dying for? Antigone's certainty that her lawbreaking is justified continues to inspire while raising dif-ficult questions about what it means to live a good life. When is injustice so intolerable that acquiescence amounts to complicity? Antigone is lawless but obedient to what she sees as a higher law. . Her unbending devotion to duty compels her to give up her life. For Antigone, living with compromised princi-ples, or in violation of the laws of the gods, can never be a good life.

---

3. Paul Woodruff translates the line, "Many wonders, many terrors, / But none more wonderful than the human race / Or more dangerous." Sophocles, *Theban Plays*, trans. Peter Meineck and Paul Woodruff (Indianapolis: Hackett, 2003), 16. See also Sophocles, *Antigone*, trans. Ruby Blondell (Indianapolis, Hackett, 1998), 34, foot-note 2.

Antigone[1]

Sophocles (441 BCE)

CHARACTERS

ANTIGONE: daughter of Oedipus

ISMENE: daughter of Oedipus, sister of Antigone

CREON: king of Thebes

EURYDICE: wife of Creon

HAEMON: son of Creon and Euridice, engaged to Antigone

TEIRESIAS: an old blind prophet

BOY: a young lad guiding Teiresias

GUARD: a soldier serving Creon Messenger

CHORUS: Theban Elders

ATTENDANT

[In Thebes, directly in front of the royal palace, which stands in the background, its main doors facing the audience. Enter Antigone leading Ismene away from the palace.]

ANTIGONE

Now, dear Ismene, my own blood sister,
do you have any sense of all the troubles
Zeus keeps bringing on the two of us,
as long as we're alive? All that misery
which stems from Oedipus*? There's no suffering,   *their father
no shame, no ruin—not one dishonour—
which I have not seen in all the troubles
you and I go through. What's this they're saying now,
something our general has had proclaimed

1. Sophocles, *Antigone*, trans. Ian Johnston (Vancouver Island University, 2019). Retrieved from www. johnsto-niatexts. xhost. com/antigone. html. html. Permission graciously granted by author for this publication.

throughout the city? Do you know of it?   10
Have you heard? Or have you just missed the news?
Dishonours which better fit our enemies
are now being piled up on the ones we love.

ISMENE
I've had no word at all, Antigone,
nothing good or bad about our family,
not since we two lost both our brothers*,   *Eteocles and Polyneices
killed on the same day by a double blow.
And since the Argive* army, just last night,   *Greeks from Argos
has gone away, I don't know any more
if I've been lucky or face total ruin.

                                                             20

ANTIGONE
I know that. That's why I brought you here,
outside the gates, so only you can hear.

ISMENE
What is it? The way you look makes it seem
you're thinking of some dark and gloomy news.

ANTIGONE
Look—what's Creon doing with our two brothers?
He's honouring one with a full funeral
and treating the other one disgracefully!
Eteocles, they say, has had his burial
according to our customary rites,
to win him honour with the dead below.   30
But as for Polyneices, who perished
so miserably, an order has gone out
throughout the city—that's what people say.
He's to have no funeral or lament,
but to be left unburied and unwept,
a sweet treasure for the birds to look at,
for them to feed on to their heart's content.
That's what people say the noble Creon
has announced to you and me—I mean to me—

and now he's coming to proclaim the fact,   40
to state it clearly to those who have not heard.
For Creon this matter's really serious.
Anyone who acts against the order
will be stoned to death before the city.
Now you know, and you'll quickly demonstrate
whether you are nobly born, or else
a girl unworthy of her splendid ancestors.

ISMENE
O my poor sister, if that's what's happening,
what can I say that would be any help
to ease the situation or resolve it?   50

ANTIGONE
Think whether you will work with me in this
and act together.

ISMENE
                    In what kind of work?
What do you mean?

ANTIGONE
                    Will you help these hands
take up Polyneices' corpse and bury it?
ISMENE
What? You're going to bury Polyneices,
when that's been made a crime for all in Thebes?

ANTIGONE
Yes. I'll do my duty to my brother—
and yours as well, if you're not prepared to.
I won't be caught betraying him.

ISMENE
                    You're too rash.
Has Creon not expressly banned that act?   60

ANTIGONE
Yes. But he's no right to keep me from what's mine.

ISMENE
O dear. Think, Antigone. Consider
how our father died, hated and disgraced,
when those mistakes which his own search revealed
forced him to turn his hand against himself
and stab out both his eyes. Then that woman,
his mother and his wife*—her double role—   *Jocasta
destroyed her own life in a twisted noose.
Then there's our own two brothers, both butchered
in a single day—that ill-fated pair   70
with their own hands slaughtered one another
and brought about their common doom.
Now, the two of us are left here quite alone.
Think how we'll die far worse than all the rest,
if we defy the law and move against
the king's decree, against his royal power.
We must remember that by birth we're women,
and, as such, we shouldn't fight with men.
Since those who rule are much more powerful,
we must obey in this and in events   80
which bring us even harsher agonies.
So I'll ask those underground for pardon—
since I'm being compelled, I will obey
those in control. That's what I'm forced to do.
It makes no sense to try to do too much.

ANTIGONE
I wouldn't urge you to. No. Not even
if you were keen to act. Doing this with you
would bring me no joy. So be what you want.
I'll still bury him. It would be fine to die
while doing that. I'll lie there with him,   90
with a man I love, pure and innocent,
for all my crime. My honours for the dead
must last much longer than for those up here.

47

I'll lie down there forever. As for you,
well, if you wish, you can show contempt
for those laws the gods all hold in honour.

ISMENE
I'm not disrespecting them. But I can't act
against the state. That's not in my nature.

ANTIGONE
Let that be your excuse. I'm going now
to make a burial mound for my dear brother.   100

ISMENE
O poor Antigone, I'm so afraid for you.

ANTIGONE
Don't fear for me. Set your own fate in order.

ISMENE
Make sure you don't reveal to anyone
what you intend. Keep it closely hidden.
I'll do the same.

ANTIGONE
          No, no. Announce the fact—
if you don't let everybody know,
I'll despise your silence even more.

ISMENE
Your heart is hot to do cold deeds.

ANTIGONE
                    But I know
I'll please the ones I'm duty bound to please.

ISMENE
Yes, if you can. But you're after something   110
which you're incapable of carrying out.

ANTIGONE
Well, when my strength is gone, then I'll give up.

ISMENE
A vain attempt should not be made at all.

ANTIGONE
I'll hate you if you're going to talk that way.
And you'll rightly earn the loathing of the dead.
So leave me and my foolishness alone—
we'll get through this fearful thing. I won't suffer
anything as bad as a disgraceful death.

ISMENE
All right then, go, if that's what you think right.
But remember this—even though your mission   120
makes no sense, your friends do truly love you.

[*Exit Antigone away from the palace. Ismene watches her go and then turns slowly into the palace. Enter the Chorus of Theban elders.*]

CHORUS
O ray of sunlight,
most beautiful that ever shone
on Thebes, city of the seven gates,
you've appeared at last,
you glowing eye of golden day,
moving above the streams of Dirce, [2]
driving into headlong flight
the white-shield warrior from Argos,
who marched here fully armed,   130
now forced back by your sharper power.

2. Dirce is a river outside Thebes

CHORUS LEADER[3]
Against our land he marched,
sent here by the warring claims
of Polyneices, with piercing screams,
an eagle flying above our land,
covered wings as white as snow,
and hordes of warriors in arms,
helmets topped with horsehair crests.

CHORUS
Standing above our homes,
he ranged around our seven gates,   140
with threats to swallow us
and spears thirsting to kill.
Before his jaws had had their fill
and gorged themselves on Theban blood,
before Hephaistos' pine-torch flames
had seized our towers, our fortress crown,
he went back, driven in retreat.[4]
Behind him rings the din of war—
his enemy, the Theban dragon-snake,
too difficult for him to overcome.   150

CHORUS LEADER
Zeus hates an arrogant boasting tongue.
Seeing them march here in a mighty stream,
in all their clanging golden pride,
he hurled his fire and struck the man,
up there, on our battlements, as he began
to scream aloud his victory.

CHORUS
The man swung down, torch still in hand,
and smashed into unyielding earth—

3. This choral section re-tells the events of Polyneices attacking Thebes, which then results in the death of both brothers.

4. Hephaistos, divine son of Zeus and Hera, is the god of fire and the forge.

the one who not so long ago attacked,
who launched his furious, enraged assault,   160
to blast us, breathing raging storms.
But things turned out not as he'd hoped.
Great war god Ares assisted us—
he smashed them down and doomed them all
to a very different fate.

CHORUS LEADER
Seven captains at seven gates
matched against seven equal warriors
paid Zeus their full bronze tribute,
the god who turns the battle tide,
all but that pair of wretched men,   170
born of one father and one mother, too—
who set their conquering spears against each other
and then both shared a common death.

CHORUS
Now victory with her glorious name
has come, bringing joy to well-armed Thebes.
The battle's done—let's strive now to forget
with songs and dancing all night long,
with Bacchus leading us to make Thebes shake.[5]

[The palace doors are thrown open and guards appear at the doors.]

CHORUS LEADER
But here comes Creon, new king of our land,
son of Menoikeos. Thanks to the gods,   180
who've brought about our new good fortune.
What plan of action does he have in mind?
What's made him hold this special meeting,
with elders summoned by a general call?

[Enter Creon from the palace. He addresses the assembled elders.]

5. Bacchus, divine son of Zeus and the mortal Semele, is god of wine.

CREON

Men, after much tossing of our ship of state,
the gods have safely set things right again.
Of all the citizens I've summoned you,
because I know how well you showed respect
for the eternal power of the throne,
first with Laius and again with Oedipus,   190
once he restored our city. When he died,
you stood by his children, firm in loyalty.[6]
Now his sons have perished in a single day,
killing each other with their own two hands,
a double slaughter, stained with brother's blood.
And so I have the throne, all royal power,
for I'm the one most closely linked by blood
to those who have been killed. It's impossible
to really know a man, to know his soul,
his mind and will, before one witnesses   200
his skill in governing and making laws.
For me, a man who rules the entire state
and does not take the best advice there is,
but through fear keeps his mouth forever shut,
such a man is the very worst of men—
and always will be. And a man who thinks
more highly of a friend than of his country,
well, he means nothing to me. Let Zeus know,
the god who always watches everything,
I would not stay silent if I saw disaster   210
moving here against the citizens,
a threat to their security. For anyone
who acts against the state, its enemy,
I'd never make my friend. For I know well
our country is a ship which keeps us safe,
and only when it sails its proper course
do we make friends. These are the principles
I'll use in order to protect our state.

6. Laius was king of Thebes and father of Oedipus. Oedipus killed him (not knowing who he was) and became the next king of Thebes by saving the city from the devastation of the Sphinx. Oedipus is also dead, after wandering for many years.

That's why I've announced to all citizens
my orders for the sons of Oedipus—   220
Eteocles, who perished in the fight
to save our city, the best and bravest
of our spearmen, will have his burial,
with all those purifying rituals
which accompany the noblest corpses,
as they move below. As for his brother—
that Polyneices, who returned from exile,
eager to wipe out in all-consuming fire
his ancestral city and its native gods,
keen to seize upon his family's blood   230
and lead men into slavery—for him,
the proclamation in the state declares
he'll have no burial mound, no funeral rites,
and no lament. He'll be left unburied,
his body there for birds and dogs to eat,
a clear reminder of his shameful fate.
That's my decision. For I'll never act
to respect an evil man with honours
in preference to a man who's acted well.
Anyone who's well disposed towards our state,   240
alive or dead, that man I will respect.

CHORUS LEADER
Son of Menoikeos, if that's your will
for this city's friends and enemies,
it seems to me you now control all laws
concerning those who've died and us as well—
the ones who are still living.

CREON
                    See to it then,
and act as guardians of what's been proclaimed.

CHORUS
Give that task to younger men to deal with.

CREON
There are men assigned to oversee the corpse.

CHORUS LEADER
Then what remains that you would have us do?   250

CREON
Don't yield to those who contravene my orders.

CHORUS LEADER
No one is such a fool that he loves death.

CREON
Yes, that will be his full reward, indeed.
And yet men have often been destroyed
because they hoped to profit in some way.

[Enter a guard, coming towards the palace.]

GUARD
My lord, I can't say I've come out of breath
by running here, making my feet move fast.
Many times I stopped to think things over—
and then I'd turn around, retrace my steps.
My mind was saying many things to me,   260
"You fool, why go to where you know for sure
your punishment awaits?"—"And now, poor man,
why are you hesitating yet again?
If Creon finds this out from someone else,
how will you escape being hurt?" Such matters
kept my mind preoccupied. And so I went,
slowly and reluctantly, and thus made
a short road turn into a lengthy one.
But then the view that I should come to you
won out. If what I have to say is nothing,   270
I'll say it nonetheless. For I've come here
clinging to the hope that I'll not suffer
anything that's not part of my destiny.

54

CREON
What's happening that's made you so upset?

GUARD
I want to tell you first about myself.
I did not do it. And I didn't see
the one who did. So it would be unjust
if I should come to grief.

CREON
              You hedge* so much.   *Avoid telling the news directly
Clearly you have news of something ominous.

GUARD
Yes. Strange things that make me pause a lot.   280

CREON
Why not say it and then go—just leave.

GUARD
All right, I'll tell you. It's about the corpse.
Someone has buried it and disappeared,
after spreading thirsty dust onto the flesh
and undertaking all appropriate rites.

CREON
What are you saying? What man would dare this?

GUARD
I don't know. There was no sign of digging,
no marks of any pick axe or a mattock.
The ground was dry and hard and very smooth,
without a wheel track. Whoever did it   290
left no trace. When the first man on day watch
revealed it to us, we were all amazed.
The corpse was hidden, but not in a tomb.
It was lightly covered up with dirt,
as if someone wanted to avert a curse.

There was no trace of a wild animal
or dogs who'd come to rip the corpse apart.
Then the words flew round among us all,
with every guard accusing someone else.
We were about to fight, to come to blows—   300
no one was there to put a stop to it.
Every one of us was responsible,
but none of us was clearly in the wrong.
In our defence we pleaded ignorance.
Then we each stated we were quite prepared
to pick up red-hot iron, walk through flames,
or swear by all the gods that we'd not done it,
we'd no idea how the act was planned,
or how it had been carried out. At last,
when all our searching had proved useless,   310
one man spoke up, and his words forced us all
to drop our faces to the ground in fear.
We couldn't see things working out for us,
whether we agreed or disagreed with him.
He said we must report this act to you—
we must not hide it. And his view prevailed.
I was the unlucky man who won the prize,
the luck of the draw. That's why I'm now here,
not of my own free will or by your choice.
I know that—for no one likes a messenger   320
who comes bearing with him unwelcome news.

CHORUS LEADER
My lord, I've been wondering for some time now—
could this act not be something from the gods?

CREON
Stop now—before what you're about to say
enrages me completely and reveals
that you're not only old but stupid, too.
No one can tolerate what you've just said,
when you claim gods might care about this corpse.
Would they pay extraordinary honours

and bury as a man who'd served them well 330
someone who came to burn their offerings,
their pillared temples, to torch their lands
and scatter all its laws? Or do you see
gods paying respect to evil men? No, no.
For quite a while some people in the town
have secretly been muttering against me.
They don't agree with what I have decreed.
They shake their heads and have not kept their necks
under my yoke, as they are duty bound to do
if they were men who are content with me. 340
I well know that these guards were led astray—
such men urged them to carry out this act
for money. To foster evil actions,
to make them commonplace among all men,
nothing is as powerful as money.
It destroys cities, driving men from home.
Money trains and twists the minds in worthy men,
so they then undertake disgraceful acts.
Money teaches men to live as scoundrels,
familiar with every profane enterprise. 350
But those who carry out such acts for cash
sooner or later see how for their crimes
they pay the penalty. For if great Zeus
still has my respect, then understand this—
I swear to you on oath—unless you find
the one whose hands really buried him,
unless you bring him here before my eyes,
then death for you will never be enough.
No, not before you're hung up still alive
and you confess to this gross, violent act. 360
That way you'll understand in future days,
when there's a profit to be gained from theft,
you'll learn that it's not good to be in love
with every kind of monetary gain.
You'll know more men are ruined than are saved
when they earn profits from dishonest schemes.

GUARD
Do I have your permission to speak now,
or do I just turn around and go away?

CREON
But I find your voice so irritating—
don't you realize that?

GUARD
      Where does it hurt?   370
Is it in your ears or in your mind?

CREON
Why try to question where I feel my pain?

GUARD
The man who did it—he upsets your mind.
I offend your ears.

CREON
      My, my, it's clear to see
it's natural for you to chatter on.

GUARD
Perhaps. But I never did this.

CREON
      This and more—
you sold your life for silver.

GUARD
      How strange and sad
when the one who sorts this out gets it all wrong.

CREON
Well, enjoy your sophisticated views.
But if you don't reveal to me who did this,   380

you'll just confirm how much your treasonous gains
have made you suffer.

[Exit Creon back into the palace. The doors close behind him.]

GUARD

    Well, I hope he's found.
That would be best. But whether caught or not—
and that's something sheer chance will bring about—
you won't see me coming here again.
This time, against all hope and expectation,
I'm still unhurt. I owe the gods great thanks.

[Exit the Guard away from the palace.]

CHORUS[7]
There are many strange and wonderful things,
but nothing more strangely wonderful than man.
He moves across the white-capped ocean seas   390
blasted by winter storms, carving his way
under the surging waves engulfing him.
With his teams of horses he wears down
the unwearied and immortal earth,
the oldest of the gods, harassing her,
as year by year his ploughs move back and forth.

He snares the light-winged flocks of birds,
herds of wild beasts, creatures from deep seas,
trapped in the fine mesh of his hunting nets.
O resourceful man, whose skill can overcome   400
ferocious beasts roaming mountain heights.
He curbs the rough-haired horses with his bit
and tames the inexhaustible mountain bulls,
setting their savage necks beneath his yoke.

7. This is the famous "Ode to Man," where the chorus focuses on the wonders as well as the limitations as well
as potential dangers of being human.

He's taught himself speech and wind-swift thought,
trained his feelings for communal civic life,
learning to escape the icy shafts of frost,
volleys of pelting rain in winter storms,
the harsh life lived under the open sky.
That's man—so resourceful in all he does.   410
There's no event his skill cannot confront—
other than death—that alone he cannot shun,
although for many baffling sicknesses
he has discovered his own remedies.

The qualities of his inventive skills
bring arts beyond his dreams and lead him on,
sometimes to evil and sometimes to good.
If he treats his country's laws with due respect
and honours justice by swearing on the gods,
he wins high honours in his city.   420
But when he grows bold and turns to evil,
then he has no city. A man like that—
let him not share my home or know my mind.

[Enter the Guard, bringing Antigone with him. She is not resisting.]

CHORUS LEADER
What this? I fear some omen from the gods.
I can't deny what I see here so clearly—
that young girl there—it's Antigone.
O you poor girl, daughter of Oedipus,
child of a such a father, so unfortunate,
what's going on? Surely they've not brought you here
because you've disobeyed the royal laws,   430
because they've caught you acting foolishly?

GUARD
This here's the one who carried out the act.
We caught her as she was burying the corpse.
Where's Creon?

[The palace doors open. Enter Creon with attendants.]

CHORUS LEADER
       He's coming from the house—
and just in time.

CREON
       Why have I come "just in time"?
What's happening? What is it?

GUARD
          My lord,
human beings should never take an oath
there's something they'll not do—for later thoughts
contradict what they first meant. I'd have sworn
I'd not soon venture here again. Back then,   440
the threats you made brought me a lot of grief.
But there's no joy as great as what we pray for
against all hope. And so I have come back,
breaking that oath I swore. I bring this girl,
captured while she was honouring the grave.
This time we did not draw lots. No. This time
I was the lucky man, not someone else.
And now, my lord, take her for questioning.
Convict her. Do as you wish. As for me,
by rights I'm free and clear of all this trouble.   450

CREON
This girl here—how did you catch her? And where?

GUARD
She was burying that man. Now you know
all there is to know.

CREON
         Do you understand
just what you're saying? Are your words the truth?

GUARD
We saw this girl giving that dead man's corpse
full burial rites—an act you'd made illegal.
Is what I say simple and clear enough?

CREON
How did you see her, catch her in the act?

GUARD
It happened this way. When we got there,
after hearing those awful threats from you,
we swept off all the dust covering the corpse,
so the damp body was completely bare.
Then we sat down on rising ground upwind,
to escape the body's putrid rotting stench.
We traded insults just to stay awake,
in case someone was careless on the job.
That's how we spent the time right up 'til noon,
when the sun's bright circle in the sky
had moved half way and it was burning hot.
Then suddenly a swirling windstorm came,   470
whipping clouds of dust up from the ground,
filling the plain—some heaven-sent trouble.
In that level place the dirt storm damaged
all the forest growth, and the air around
was filled with dust for miles. We shut our mouths
and just endured this scourge sent from the gods.
A long time passed. The storm came to an end.
That's when we saw the girl. She was shrieking—
a distressing painful cry, just like a bird
who's seen an empty nest, its fledglings gone.   480
That's how she was when she saw the naked corpse.
She screamed out a lament, and then she swore,
calling evil curses down upon the ones
who'd done this. Then right away her hands
threw on the thirsty dust. She lifted up
a finely made bronze jug and then three times
poured out her tributes to the dead.

When we saw that, we rushed up right away
and grabbed her. She was not afraid at all.
We charged her with her previous offence   490
as well as this one. She just kept standing there,
denying nothing. That made me happy—
though it was painful, too. For it's a joy
escaping troubles which affect oneself,
but painful to bring evil on one's friends.
But all that is of less concern to me
than my own safety.

CREON
        You there—you with your face
bent down towards the ground, what do you say?
Do you deny you did this or admit it?

ANTIGONE
I admit I did it. I won't deny that.   500

CREON [to the Guard]
You're dismissed—go where you want. You're free—
no serious charges made against you.

[Exit the Guard. Creon turns to interrogate Antigone.]

Tell me briefly—not in some lengthy speech—
were you aware there was a proclamation
forbidding what you did?

ANTIGONE
        I'd heard of it.
How could I not? It was public knowledge.

CREON
And yet you dared to break those very laws?

ANTIGONE
Yes. Zeus did not announce those laws to me.

63

And Justice living with the gods below
sent no such laws for men. I did not think   510
anything which you proclaimed strong enough
to let a mortal override the gods
and their unwritten and unchanging laws.
They're not just for today or yesterday,
but exist forever, and no one knows
where they first appeared. So I did not mean
to let a fear of any human will
lead to my punishment among the gods.
I know all too well I'm going to die—
how could I not? —it makes no difference   520
what you decree. And if I have to die
before my time, well, I count that a gain.
When someone has to live the way I do,
surrounded by so many evil things,
how can she fail to find a benefit
in death? And so for me meeting this fate
won't bring any pain. But if I'd allowed
my own mother's dead son to just lie there,
an unburied corpse, then I'd feel distress.
What's going on here does not hurt me at all.   530
If you think what I'm doing now is stupid,
perhaps I'm being charged with foolishness
by someone who's a fool.

CHORUS LEADER
        It's clear enough
the spirit in this girl is passionate—
her father was the same. She has no sense
of compromise in times of trouble.

CREON [to the Chorus Leader]
But you should know the most obdurate* wills   *stubborn
are those most prone to break. The strongest iron
tempered in the fire to make it really hard—
that's the kind you see most often shatter.   540
I'm well aware the most tempestuous* horses   *wild or stormy

64

are tamed by one small bit. Pride has no place
in anyone who is his neighbour's slave.
This girl here was already very insolent*   *arrogant
in contravening* laws we had proclaimed.   *violating
Here she again displays her proud contempt—
having done the act, she now boasts of it.
She laughs at what she's done. Well, in this case,
if she gets her way and goes unpunished,
then she's the man here, not me. No. She may be   550
my sister's child, closer to me by blood
than anyone belonging to my house
who worships Zeus Herkeios in my home,
but she'll not escape my harshest punishment—
her sister, too, whom I accuse as well. [8]
She had an equal part in all their plans
to do this burial. Go summon her here.
I saw her just now inside the palace,
her mind out of control, some kind of fit.

[Exit attendants into the palace to fetch Ismene.]

When people hatch their mischief in the dark   560
their minds often convict them in advance,*   *i. e. they have a guilty conscience
betraying their treachery. How I despise
a person caught committing evil acts
who then desires to glorify the crime.

ANTIGONE
Take me and kill me—what more do you want?

CREON
Me? Nothing. With that I have everything.

ANTIGONE
Then why delay? There's nothing in your words
that I enjoy—may that always be the case!

8. Zeus Herkeios refers to Zeus of the Courtyard, a patron god of worship within the home.

And what I say displeases you as much.
But where could I gain greater glory   570
than setting my own brother in his grave?
All those here would confirm this pleases them
if their lips weren't sealed by fear—being king,
which offers all sorts of various benefits,
means you can talk and act just as you wish.

CREON
In all of Thebes, you're the only one
who looks at things that way.

ANTIGONE
                        They share my views,
but they keep their mouths shut just for you.

CREON
These views of yours—so different from the rest—
don't they bring you any sense of shame?   580

ANTIGONE
No—there's nothing shameful in honouring
my mother's children.

CREON
                        You had a brother
killed fighting for the other side.

ANTIGONE
Yes—from the same mother and father, too.

CREON
Why then give tributes which insult his name?

ANTIGONE
But his dead corpse won't back up what you say.

CREON
Yes, he will, if you give equal honours
to a wicked man.

ANTIGONE
But the one who died
was not some slave—it was his own brother.

CREON
Who was destroying this land—the other one   590
went to his death defending it.

ANTIGONE
That may be,
but Hades still desires equal rites for both.[9]

CREON
A good man does not wish what we give him
to be the same an evil man receives.

ANTIGONE
Who knows? In the world below perhaps
such actions are no crime.

CREON
An enemy
can never be a friend, not even in death.

ANTIGONE
But my nature is to love. I cannot hate.

CREON
Then go down to the dead. If you must love,
love them. No woman's going to govern me—   600
no, no—not while I'm still alive.

9. Hades, a brother of Zeus, is god of the underworld, lord of the dead.

[Enter two attendants from the house bringing Ismene to Creon.]

CHORUS LEADER
Ismene's coming. There—right by the door.
She's crying. How she must love her sister!
From her forehead a cloud casts its shadow
down across her darkly flushing face—
and drops its rain onto her lovely cheeks.

CREON
You there—you snake lurking in my house,
sucking out my life's blood so secretly.
I'd no idea I was nurturing two pests,
who aimed to rise against my throne. Come here.   610
Tell me this—do you admit you played your part
in this burial, or will you swear an oath
you had no knowledge of it?

ISMENE
           I did it—
I admit it, and she will back me up.
So I bear the guilt as well.

ANTIGONE
           No, no—
justice will not allow you to say that.
You didn't want to. I did not work with you.

ISMENE
But now you're in trouble, I'm not ashamed
of suffering, too, as your companion.

ANTIGONE
Hades and the dead can say who did it—   620
I don't love a friend whose love is only words.

ISMENE
You're my sister. Don't dishonour me.
Let me respect the dead and die with you.

ANTIGONE
Don't try to share my death or make a claim
to actions which you did not do. I'll die—
and that will be enough.

ISMENE
                    But if you're gone,
what is there in life for me to love?

ANTIGONE
Ask Creon. He's the one you care about.

ISMENE
Why hurt me like this? It doesn't help you.

ANTIGONE
If I am mocking you, it pains me, too.   630

ISMENE
Even now is there some way I can help?

ANTIGONE
Save yourself. I won't envy your escape.

ISMENE
I feel so wretched leaving you to die.

ANTIGONE
But you chose life—it was my choice to die.

ISMENE
But not before I'd said those words just now.

ANTIGONE
Some people may approve of how you think—
others will believe my judgment's good.

ISMENE
But the mistake's the same for both of us.

ANTIGONE
Be brave. You're alive. But my spirit died
some time ago so I might help the dead   640

CREON
I'd say one of these girls has just revealed
how mad she is—the other's been that way
since she was born.

ISMENE
                My lord, whatever good sense
people have by birth no longer stays with them
once their lives go wrong—it abandons them.

CREON
In your case, that's true, once you made your choice
to act in evil ways with wicked people.

ISMENE
How could I live alone, without her here?

CREON
Don't speak of her being here. Her life is over.

ISMENE
You're going to kill your own son's bride?   650

CREON
Why not? There are other fields for him to plough.

ISMENE
No one will make him a more loving wife
than she will.

CREON
       I have no desire my son
should have an evil wife.

ANTIGONE
       Dearest Haemon,
how your father wrongs you.

CREON
       I've had enough of this—
you and your marriage.

ISMENE
       You really want that?
You're going to take her from him?

CREON
       No, not me.
Hades is the one who'll stop the marriage.

CHORUS LEADER
So she must die—that seems decided on.

CREON
Yes—for you and me the matter's closed.   660

[Creon turns to address his attendants.]

No more delay. You slaves, take them inside.
From this point on they must act like women
and have no liberty to wander off.
Even bold men run when they see Hades
coming close to them to snatch their lives.

[The attendants take Antigone and Ismene into the palace, leaving Creon and the Chorus on stage.]

CHORUS[10]
Those who live without tasting evil
have happy lives—for when the gods
shake a house to its foundations,
then inevitable disasters strike,
falling upon whole families,   670
just as a surging ocean swell
running before cruel Thracian winds
across the dark trench of the sea
churns up the deep black sand
and crashes headlong on the cliffs,
which scream in pain against the wind.

I see this house's age-old sorrows,
the house of Labdakos's children,
sorrows falling on the sorrows of the dead,
one generation bringing no relief   680
to generations after it—some god
strikes at them—on and on without an end.
For now the light which has been shining
over the last roots of Oedipus's house
is being cut down with a bloody knife
belonging to the gods below—
for foolish talk and frenzy in the soul.[11]

O Zeus, what human trespasses
can check your power? Even Sleep,
who casts his nets on everything,   690
cannot master that—nor can the months,

10. This choral ode discusses the relationship between humans and the gods, particularly when the gods become angered and curse an entire family line as they did with Antigone's family, the House of Labdakos.

11. Labdakos is the father of Laius and hence grandfather of Oedipus and great-grandfather of Antigone and Ismene.

the tireless months the gods control.
A sovereign who cannot grow old,
you hold Olympus as your own,
in all its glittering magnificence.[12]
From now on into all future time,
as in the past, your law holds firm.
It never enters lives of human beings
in its full force without disaster.

Hope ranging far and wide brings comfort   700
to many men—but then hope can deceive,
delusions born of volatile desire.
It comes upon the man who's ignorant
until his foot is seared in burning fire.
Someone's wisdom has revealed to us
this famous saying—sometimes the gods
lure a man's mind forward to disaster,
and he thinks evil's something good.
But then he lives only the briefest time
free of catastrophe.

[The palace doors open.]
CHORUS LEADER
      Here comes Haemon,   710
your only living son. Is he grieving
the fate of Antigone, his bride,
bitter that his marriage hopes are gone?

CREON
We'll soon find out—more accurately
than any prophet here could indicate.

[Enter Haemon from the palace.]

My son, have you heard the sentence that's been passed
upon your bride? And have you now come here

---

12. Olympus is a mountain in northern Greece where, according to tradition, the major gods live.

angry at your father? Or are you loyal to me,
on my side no matter what I do?

HAEMON
Father, I'm yours. For me your judgments   720
and the ways you act on them are good—
I shall follow them. I'll not consider
any marriage a greater benefit
than your fine leadership.

CREON
            Indeed, my son,
that's how your heart should always be resolved,
to stand behind your father's judgment
on every issue. That's what men pray for—
obedient children growing up at home
who will pay back their father's enemies,
evil to them for evil done to him,   730
while honouring his friends as much as he does.
A man who fathers useless children—
what can one say of him except he's bred
troubles for himself, and much to laugh at
for those who fight against him? So, my son,
don't ever throw good sense aside for pleasure,
for some woman's sake. You understand
how such embraces can turn freezing cold
when an evil woman shares your life at home.
What greater wound is there than a false friend?   740
So spit this girl out—she's your enemy.
Let her marry someone else in Hades.
Since I caught her clearly disobeying,
the only culprit in the entire city,
I won't perjure myself before the state*.   *contradict my own oath/law
No—I'll kill her. And so let her appeal
to Zeus, the god of blood relationships.
If I foster any lack of full respect
in my own family, I surely do the same
with those who are not linked to me by blood.   750

74

The man who acts well with his household
will be found a just man in the city.
I'd trust such a man to govern wisely
or to be content with someone ruling him.
And in the thick of battle at his post
he'll stand firm beside his fellow soldier,
a loyal, brave man. But anyone who's proud
and violates our laws or thinks he'll tell
our leaders what to do, a man like that
wins no praise from me. No. We must obey   760
whatever man the city puts in charge,
no matter what the issue—great or small,
just or unjust. For there's no greater evil
than a lack of leadership. That destroys
whole cities, turns households into ruins,
and in war makes soldiers break and run away.
When men succeed, what keeps their lives secure
in almost every case is their obedience.
That's why they must support those in control
and never let some woman beat us down.   770
If we must fall from power, let that come
at some man's hand—at least, we won't be called
inferior to any woman.

CHORUS LEADER
Unless we're being deceived by our old age,
what you've just said seems reasonable to us.

HAEMON
Father, the gods instill good sense in men—
the greatest of all the things which we possess.
I could not find your words somehow not right—
I hope that's something I never learn to do.
But other words might be good, as well.   780
Because of who you are, you can't perceive
all the things men say or do—or their complaints.
Your gaze makes citizens afraid—they can't
say anything you would not like to hear.

But in the darkness I can hear them talk—
the city is upset about the girl.
They say of all women here she least deserves
the worst of deaths for her most glorious act.
When in the slaughter her own brother died,
she did not just leave him there unburied,   790
to be ripped apart by carrion dogs or birds.
Surely she deserves some golden honour?
That's the dark secret rumour people speak.
For me, father, nothing is more valuable
than your well being. For any children,
what could be a greater honour to them
than their father's thriving reputation?
A father feels the same about his sons.
So don't let your mind dwell on just one thought,
that what you say is right and nothing else.   800
A man who thinks that only he is wise,
that he can speak and think like no one else,
when such men are exposed, then all can see
their emptiness inside. For any man,
even if he's wise, there's nothing shameful
in learning many things, staying flexible.
You notice how in winter floods the trees
which bend before the storm preserve their twigs.
The ones who stand against it are destroyed,
root and branch. In the same way, those sailors   810
who keep their sails stretched tight, never easing off,
make their ship capsize—and from that point on
sail with their rowing benches all submerged.
So end your anger. Permit yourself to change.
For if I, as a younger man, may state
my views, I'd say it would be for the best
if men by nature understood all things—
if not, and that is usually the case,
when men speak well, it good to learn from them.

CHORUS LEADER
My lord, if what he's said is relevant,   820

76

it seems appropriate to learn from him,
and you too, Haemon, listen to the king.
The things which you both said were excellent.

CREON
And men my age—are we then going to school
to learn what's wise from men as young as him?

HAEMON
There's nothing wrong in that. And if I'm young,
don't think about my age—look at what I do.

CREON
And what you do—does that include this,
honouring those who act against our laws?

HAEMON
I would not encourage anyone   830
to show respect to evil men.

CREON
                    And her—
is she not suffering from the same disease?

HAEMON
The people here in Thebes all say the same—
they deny she is.

CREON
                    So the city now
will instruct me how I am to govern?

HAEMON
Now you're talking like someone far too young.
Don't you see that?

CREON
                    Am I to rule this land
at someone else's whim or by myself?

HAEMON

A city which belongs to just one man
is no true city.

CREON

      According to our laws,   840
does not the ruler own the city?

HAEMON

By yourself you'd make an excellent king
but in a desert.

CREON

      It seems as if this boy
is fighting on the woman's side.

HAEMON

         That's true—
if you're the woman. I'm concerned for you.

CREON

You're the worst there is—you set your judgment up
against your father.

HAEMON

       No, not when I see
you making a mistake and being unjust.

CREON

Is it a mistake to honour my own rule?

HAEMON

You're not honouring that by trampling on   850
the gods' prerogatives*.   *exclusive privilege

CREON
>   You foul creature—
you're worse than any woman.

HAEMON
>   You'll not catch me
giving way to some disgrace.

CREON
>   But your words
all speak on her behalf.

HAEMON
>   And yours and mine—
and for the gods below.

CREON
>   You woman's slave—
don't try to win me over.

HAEMON
>   What do you want—
to speak and never hear someone reply?

CREON
You'll never marry her while she's alive.

HAEMON
Then she'll die—and in her death kill someone else.

CREON
Are you so insolent you threaten me?   860

HAEMON
Where's the threat in challenging a bad decree?

CREON
You'll regret parading what you think like this—
you—a person with an empty brain!

HAEMON
If you were not my father, I might say
you were not thinking straight.

CREON
                    Would you, indeed?
Well, then, by Olympus, I'll have you know
you'll be sorry for demeaning me
with all these insults.

[Creon turns to his attendants.]

                    Go bring her out—
that hateful creature, so she can die right here,
with him present, before her bridegroom's eyes.   870

HAEMON
No. Don't ever hope for that. She'll not die
with me just standing there. And as for you—
your eyes will never see my face again.
So let your rage charge on among your friends
who want to stand by you in this.

[Exit Haemon, running back into the palace.]

CHORUS LEADER
My lord, Haemon left in such a hurry.
He's angry—in a young man at his age
the mind turns bitter when he's feeling hurt.

CREON
Let him dream up or carry out great deeds
beyond the power of man, he'll not save these girls—   880
their fate is sealed.

CHORUS LEADER
Are you going to kill them both?

CREON
No—not the one whose hands are clean. You're right.

CHORUS LEADER
How do you plan to kill Antigone?

CREON
I'll take her on a path no people use,
and hide her in a cavern in the rocks,
while still alive. I'll set out provisions,
as much as piety requires, to make sure
the city is not totally corrupted. [13]
Then she can speak her prayers to Hades,
the only god she worships, for success   890
avoiding death—or else, at least, she'll learn,
although too late, how it's a waste of time
to work to honour those whom Hades holds.

CHORUS [14]
O Eros, the conqueror in every fight,
Eros, who squanders all men's wealth,
who sleeps at night on girls' soft cheeks,
and roams across the ocean seas
and through the shepherd's hut—
no immortal god escapes from you,
nor any man, who lives but for a day. [15]   900
And the one whom you possess goes mad.
Even in good men you twist their minds,
perverting them to their own ruin.

---

13. The killing of a family member could bring on divine punishment in the form of a pollution involving the entire city (as in the case of Oedipus). Creon is, one assumes, taking refuge in the notion that he will not be executing Antigone directly.

14. This choral ode discusses the power of desire, particularly sexual desire. After Haemon's argument with Creon, the chorus is beginning to take pity on both him and, as you'll see below, Antigone.

15. Eros is the young god of erotic sexual passion.

You provoke these men to family strife.
The bride's desire seen glittering in her eyes—
that conquers everything, its power
enthroned beside eternal laws, for there
the goddess Aphrodite works her will,
whose ways are irresistible. [16]

[Antigone enters from the palace with attendants who are taking her away to her execution.]

CHORAL LEADER
When I look at her I forget my place.   910
I lose restraint and can't hold back my tears—
Antigone going to her bridal room
where all are laid to rest in death.

ANTIGONE
Look at me, my native citizens,
as I go on my final journey,
as I gaze upon the sunlight one last time,
which I'll never see again—for Hades,
who brings all people to their final sleep,
leads me on, while I'm still living,
down to the shores of Acheron. [17]   920
I've not yet had my bridal chant,
nor has any wedding song been sung—
for my marriage is to Acheron.

CHORUS
Surely you carry fame with you and praise,
as you move to the deep home of the dead.
You were not stricken by lethal disease
or paid your wages with a sword.
No. You were in charge of your own fate.
So of all living human beings, you alone
make your way down to Hades still alive.   930

16. Aphrodite is the goddess of sexual desire.

17. Acheron is one of the major rivers of the underworld.

ANTIGONE

I've heard about a guest of ours,
daughter of Tantalus, from Phrygia—
she went to an excruciating death
in Sipylus, right on the mountain peak.
The stone there, just like clinging ivy,
wore her down, and now, so people say,
the snow and rain never leave her there,
as she laments. Below her weeping eyes
her neck is wet with tears. God brings me
to a final rest which most resembles hers.   940

CHORUS

But Niobe was a goddess, born divine—
and we are human beings, a race which dies.
But still, it's a fine thing for a woman,
once she's dead, to have it said she shared,
in life and death, the fate of demi-gods. [18]

ANTIGONE

O you are mocking me! Why me—
by our fathers' gods—why do you all,
my own city and the richest men of Thebes,
insult me now right to my face,
without waiting for my death?   950
Well at least I have Dirce's springs,
the holy grounds of Thebes,
a city full of splendid chariots,
to witness how no friends lament for me
as I move on—you see the laws
which lead me to my rock-bound prison,
a tomb made just for me. Alas!
In my wretchedness I have no home,

---

18. The last two speeches refer to Niobe, daughter of Tantalus (a son of Zeus). Niobe had seven sons and seven daughters and boasted that she had more children than the goddess Leto. As punishment Artemis and Apollo, Leto's two children, destroyed all Niobe's children. Niobe turned to stone in grief and was reportedly visible on Mount Sipylus (in Asia Minor). The Chorus's claim that Niobe was a goddess or semi-divine is odd here, since her story is almost always a tale of human presumption and divine punishment for human arrogance.

not with human beings or corpses,
not with the living or the dead.   960

CHORUS

You pushed your daring to the limit, my child,
and tripped against Justice's high altar—
perhaps your agonies are paying back
some compensation for your father.[19]

ANTIGONE

Now there you touch on my most painful thought—
my father's destiny—always on my mind,
along with that whole fate which sticks to us,
the splendid house of Labdakos—the curse
arising from a mother's marriage bed,
when she had sex with her own son, my father.   970
From what kind of parents was I born,
their wretched daughter? I go to them,
unmarried and accursed, an outcast.
Alas, too, for my brother Polyneices,
who made a fatal marriage and then died—
and with that death killed me while still alive.[20]

CHORUS

To be piously devout shows reverence,
but powerful men, who in their persons
incorporate authority, cannot bear
anyone to break their rules. Hence, you die   980
because of your own selfish will.

ANTIGONE

Without lament, without a friend,
and with no marriage song, I'm being led

19. The Chorus here is offering the traditional suggestion that present afflictions can arise from a family curse originating in previous generations (in Antigone's case, from Oedipus).

20. Polyneices married the daughter of Adrastus, an action which enabled him to acquire the army to attack Thebes.

in this miserable state, along my final road.
So wretched that I no longer have the right
to look upon the sun, that sacred eye.
But my fate prompts no tears, and no friend mourns.

CREON

Don't you know that no one faced with death
would ever stop the singing and the groans,
if that would help? Take her and shut her up,   990
as I have ordered, in her tomb's embrace.
And get it done as quickly as you can.
Then leave her there alone, all by herself—
she can sort out whether she wants suicide
or remains alive, buried in a place like that.
As far as she's concerned, we bear no guilt.
But she's lost her place living here with us.[21]

ANTIGONE

O my tomb and bridal chamber—
my eternal hollow dwelling place,
where I go to join my people. Most of them   1000
have perished—Persephone has welcomed them
among the dead.[22] I'm the last one, dying here
the most evil death by far, as I move down
before the time allotted for my life is done.
But I go nourishing the vital hope
my father will be pleased to see me come,
and you, too, my mother, will welcome me,
as well as you, my own dear brother.
When you died, with my own hands I washed you.
I arranged your corpse and at the grave mound   1010
poured out libations. But now, Polyneices,
this is my reward for covering your corpse.

21. Creon's logic seems to suggest that because he is not executing Antigone directly and is leaving her a choice between committing suicide and slowly starving to death in the cave, he has no moral responsibility for what happens.

22. Persephone is the wife of Hades and thus goddess of the underworld.

However, for wise people I was right
to honour you. I'd never have done it
for children of my own, not as their mother,
nor for a dead husband lying in decay—
no, not in defiance of the citizens.
What law do I appeal to, claiming this?
If my husband died, there'd be another one,
and if I were to lose a child of mine   1020
I'd have another with some other man.
But since my father and my mother, too,
are hidden away in Hades' house,
I'll never have another living brother.
That was the law I used to honour you.
But Creon thought that I was in the wrong
and acting recklessly for you, my brother.
Now he seizes me by force and leads me here—
no wedding and no bridal song, no share
in married life or nurturing children.   1030
Instead I go in sorrow to my grave,
without my friends, to die while still alive.
What holy justice have I violated?
In my wretchedness, why should I still look
up to the gods? Which one can I invoke
to bring me help, when for my reverence
they charge me with impiety*? Well then,   *irreverence
if this is something fine among the gods,
I'll come to recognize that I've done wrong.
But if these people here are being unjust   1040
may they endure no greater punishment
than the injustices they're doing to me.

CHORUS LEADER
The same storm blasts continue to attack
the mind in this young girl.

CREON
          Then those escorting her
will be sorry they're so slow.

ANTIGONE

        Alas, then,
those words mean death is very near at hand.

CREON

I won't encourage you or cheer you up,
by saying the sentence won't be carried out.

ANTIGONE

O city of my fathers
in this land of Thebes—   1050
and my ancestral gods,
I am being led away.
No more delaying for me.
Look on me, you lords of Thebes,
the last survivor of your royal house,
see what I have to undergo,
the kind of men who do this to me,
for paying reverence to true piety.

[Antigone is led away under escort.]

CHORUS[23]

In her brass-bound room fair Danaë as well
endured her separation from the heaven's light,   1060
a prisoner hidden in a chamber like a tomb,
although she, too, came from a noble line.[24]
And she, my child, had in her care
the liquid streaming golden seed of Zeus.
But the power of fate is full of mystery.
There's no evading it, no, not with wealth,
or war, or walls, or black sea-beaten ships.

---

23. This choral ode describes the fate of a number of noble family lines who were betrayed by the gods.

24. Danaë was daughter of Acrisus, King of Argos. Because of a prophecy that he would be killed by a son born to Danaë, Acrisus imprisoned her. But Zeus made love to her in the form of a golden shower, and she gave birth to Perseus, who, once grown, killed Acrisus accidentally.

And the hot-tempered child of Dryas,
king of the Edonians, was put in prison,
closed up in the rocks by Dionysus,   1070
for his angry mocking of the god.[25]
There the dreadful flower of his rage
slowly withered, and he came to know
the god who in his frenzy he had mocked
with his own tongue. For he had tried
to hold in check women in that frenzy
inspired by the god, the Bacchanalian fire.
More than that—he'd made the Muses angry,
challenging the gods who love the flute.[26]

Beside the black rocks where the twin seas meet,   1080
by Thracian Salmydessos at the Bosphorus,
close to the place where Ares dwells,
the war god witnessed the unholy wounds
which blinded the two sons of Phineus,
inflicted by his savage wife—the sightless holes
cried out for someone to avenge those blows
made with her sharpened comb in blood-stained hands.[27]

In their misery they wept, lamenting
their wretched suffering, sons of a mother
whose marriage had gone wrong. And yet,   1090
she was an offspring of an ancient family,
the race of Erechtheus, raised far away,
in caves surrounded by her father's winds,
Boreas' child, a girl who raced with horses
across steep hills—child of the gods.

25. These lines refer to Lycurgus son of Dryas, a Thracian king. He attacked the god Dionysus and was punished with blinding or with being torn apart.

26. The anger of the Muses at a Thracian who boasted of his flute playing is not normally a part of the Lycurgus story but refers to another Thracian, Thamyras.

27. The black rocks were a famous hazard to shipping. They moved together to smash any ship moving between them. The Bosphorus is the strait between the Black Sea and the Propontis (near the Hellespont). This verse and the next refer to the Thracian king Phineas, whose second wife blinded her two step sons (from Phineas's first wife Cleopatra) by stabbing out their eyes.

But she, too, my child, suffered much
from the immortal Fates.[28]

[Enter Teiresias, led by a young boy.]

TEIRESIAS
Lords of Thebes, we two have walked a common path,
one person's vision serving both of us.
The blind require a guide to find their way.   1100

CREON
What news do you have, old Teiresias?

TEIRESIAS
I'll tell you—and you obey the prophet.

CREON
I've not rejected your advice before.

TEIRESIAS
That's the reason why you've steered the city
on its proper course.

CREON
          From my experience
I can confirm the help you give.

TEIRESIAS
            Then know this—
your luck is once more on Fate's razor edge.

CREON
What? What you've just said makes me nervous.

28. Cleopatra was the grand-daughter of Erechtheus, king of Athens. Boreas, father of Erechtheus, was god of the North Wind.

TEIRESIAS

You'll know—once you hear the tokens of my art.
As I was sitting in my ancient place   1110
receiving omens from the flights of birds
who all come there where I can hear them,
I note among those birds an unknown cry—
evil, unintelligible, angry screaming.
I knew that they were tearing at each other
with murderous claws. The noisy wings
revealed that all too well. I was afraid.
So right away up on the blazing altar
I set up burnt offerings. But Hephaestus
failed to shine out from the sacrifice—   1120
dark slime poured out onto the embers,
oozing from the thighs, which smoked and spat,
bile was sprayed high up into the air,
and the melting thighs lost all the fat
which they'd been wrapped in. The rites had failed—
there was no prophecy revealed in them.
I learned that from this boy, who is my guide,
as I guide other men.[29] Our state is sick—
your policies have done this. In the city
our altars and our hearths have been defiled,   1130
all of them, with rotting flesh brought there
by birds and dogs from Oedipus's son,
who lies there miserably dead. The gods
no longer will accept our sacrifice,
our prayers, our thigh bones burned in fire.
No bird will shriek out a clear sign to us,
for they have gorged themselves on fat and blood
from a man who's dead. Consider this, my son.
All men make mistakes—that's not uncommon.
But when they do, they're no longer foolish   1140
or subject to bad luck if they try to fix
the evil into which they've fallen,

---

29. Teiresias's offering failed to catch fire. His interpretation is that it has been rejected by the gods, a very unfavourable omen.

once they give up their intransigence*.   *stubbornness
Men who put their stubbornness on show
invite accusations of stupidity.
Make concessions to* the dead—don't ever stab   *accommodations for
a man who's just been killed. What's the glory
in killing a dead person one more time?
I've been concerned for you. It's good advice.
Learning can be pleasant when a man speaks well,   1150
especially when he seeks your benefit.

CREON
Old man, you're all like archers shooting at me!
For you all I've now become your target—
even prophets have been aiming at me.
I've long been bought and sold as merchandise
among that tribe. Well, go make your profits.
If it's what you want, then trade with Sardis
for their golden-silver alloy—or for gold
from India, but you'll never hide that corpse
in any grave. Even if Zeus's eagles   1160
should choose to seize his festering* body   *rotting
and take it up, right to the throne of Zeus,
not even then would I, in trembling fear
of some defilement, permit that corpse
a burial. For I know well that no man
has the power to pollute the gods.
But, old Teiresias, among human beings
the wisest suffer a disgraceful fall
when, to promote themselves, they use fine words
to spread around abusive insults.   1170

TEIRESIAS
Alas, does any man know or think about . . .

CREON [interrupting]
Think what? What sort of pithy* common thought   *clever
are you about to utter?

91

TEIRESIAS *[ignoring the interruption]*
    . . . how good advice
is valuable—worth more than all possessions.

CREON
I think that's true, as much as foolishness
is what harms us most.

TEIRESIAS
     Yet that's the sickness
now infecting you.

CREON
    I have no desire
to denigrate* a prophet when I speak.   *belittle

TEIRESIAS
But that's what you are doing, when you claim
my oracles are false.

CREON
    The tribes of prophets—   1180
all of them—are fond of money.

TEIRESIAS
     And kings?
Their tribe loves to benefit dishonestly.

CREON
You know you're speaking of the man who rules you.

TEIRESIAS
I know—thanks to me you saved the city
and now are in control.[30]

---

30. This is the second reference to the fact that at some point earlier Teiresias has given important political help to Creon. It is not at all clear what this refers to.

CREON
        You're a wise prophet,
but you love doing wrong.

TEIRESIAS
        You will force me
to speak of secrets locked inside my heart.

CREON
Do it—just don't speak to benefit yourself.

TEIRESIAS
I do not think that I'll be doing that—
not as far as you're concerned.

CREON
        You can be sure   1190
you won't change my mind and enrich yourself.

TEIRESIAS
Then understand this well—you will not see
the sun race through its cycle many times
before you lose a child of your own loins,
a corpse in payment for these corpses.
You've thrown down to those below someone
from up above—in your arrogance
you've moved a living soul into a grave,
leaving here a body owned by gods below—
unburied, dispossessed, unsanctified*.   *not made sacred/holy   1200
That's no concern of yours or gods above.
In this you violate the ones below.
And so destroying avengers wait for you,
Furies of Hades and the gods, who'll see
you caught up in this very wickedness.
Now see if I speak as someone who's been bribed.
It won't be long before in your own house
the men and women all cry out in sorrow,
and cities rise in hate against you—all those

whose mangled soldiers have had burial rites   1210
from dogs, wild animals, or flying birds
who carry the unholy stench back home,
to every city hearth. [31] Like an archer,
I shoot these arrows now into your heart
because you have provoked me. I'm angry—
so my aim is good. You'll not escape their pain.
Boy, lead us home so he can vent his rage
on younger men and keep a quieter tongue
and a more temperate mind than he has now.

[Exit Teiresias, led by the young boy.]

CHORUS LEADER
My lord, my lord, such dreadful prophecies—   1220
and now he's gone. Since my hair changed colour
from black to white, I know here in the city
he's never uttered a false prophecy.

CREON
I know that, too—and it disturbs my mind.
It's dreadful to give way, but to resist
and let destruction hammer down my spirit—
that's a fearful option, too.

CHORUS LEADER
                  Son of Menoikeos,
you need to listen to some good advice.

CREON
Tell me what to do. Speak up. I'll do it.

CHORUS LEADER
Go and release the girl from her rock tomb.   1230
Then prepare a grave for that unburied corpse.

31. Teiresias here is apparently accusing Creon of refusing burial to the dead allied soldiers Polyneices brought with him from other cities.

CREON

This is your advice? You think I should concede?

CHORUS LEADER

Yes, my lord, as fast as possible.
Swift footed injuries sent from the gods
hack down those who act imprudently.

CREON

Alas—it's difficult. But I'll give up.
I'll not do what I'd set my heart upon.
It's not right to fight against necessity.

CHORUS LEADER

Go now and get this done. Don't give the work
to other men to do.

CREON

     I'll go just as I am.   1240
Come, you servants, each and every one of you.
Come on. Bring axes with you. Go there quickly—
up to the higher ground. I've changed my mind.
Since I'm the one who tied her up, I'll go
and set her free myself. Now I'm afraid.
Until one dies the best thing well may be
to follow our established laws.

[Creon and his attendants hurry off stage.]

CHORUS

O you with many names,
you glory of that Theban bride,
and child of thundering Zeus,   1250
you who cherish famous Italy,
and rule the welcoming valley lands
of Eleusianian Deo—
O Bacchus—you who dwell
in the bacchants' mother city Thebes,

beside Ismenus' flowing streams,
on land sown with the teeth
of that fierce dragon.[32]

Above the double mountain peaks,
the torches flashing through the murky smoke   1260
have seen you where Corcyian nymphs
move on as they worship you
by the Kastalian stream.
And from the ivy-covered slopes
of Nysa's hills, from the green shore
so rich in vines, you come to us,
visiting our Theban ways,
while deathless voices all cry out
in honour of your name, "Evoë. "[33]

You honour Thebes, our city,   1270
above all others, you and your mother
blasted by that lightning strike.[34]
And now when all our people here
are captive to a foul disease,
on your healing feet you come
across the moaning strait
or over the Parnassian hill.

You who lead the dance,
among the fire-breathing stars,
who guard the voices in the night,   1280
child born of Zeus, O my lord,
appear with your attendant Thyiads,

32. In these lines the Chorus celebrates Dionysus, the god born in Thebes to Semele, daughter of king Cadmus. The bacchants are those who worship Dionysus. Eleusis, a region on the coast near Athens, was famous for the its Eleusinian Mysteries, a secret ritual of worship. Deo is a reference to the goddess Demeter, who was worshipped at Eleusis. The Theban race sprang up from dragon's teeth sown in a field by Cadmus, founder of the city.

33. *Evoë* is a cry of celebration made by worshippers of Dionysus.

34. Semele, Dionysus's human mother, was destroyed by Zeus lightning bolt, because of the jealousy of Hera, Zeus's wife.

who dance in frenzy all night long,
for you their patron, Iacchus.[35]

[Enter a Messenger.]

MESSENGER
All you here who live beside the home
of Amphion and Cadmus—in human life
there's no set place which I would praise or blame.[36]
The lucky and unlucky rise or fall
by chance day after day—and how these things
are fixed for men no one can prophesy.   1290
For Creon, in my view, was once a man
we all looked up to. For he saved the state,
this land of Cadmus, from its enemies.
He took control and reigned as its sole king—
and prospered with the birth of noble children.
Now all is gone. For when a man has lost
what gives him pleasure, I don't include him
among the living—he's a breathing corpse.
Pile up a massive fortune in your home,
if that's what you want—live like a king.   1300
If there's no pleasure in it, I'd not give
to any man a vapour's shadow for it,
not compared to human joy.

CHORUS LEADER
Have you come with news of some fresh trouble
in our house of kings?

MESSENGER
                 They are dead—
and those alive bear the responsibility
for those who've died.

35. Thyiads were worshippers of Dionysus, and Iacchus was a divinity associated with Dionysus.

36. Amphion was legendary king of Thebes, husband of Niobe.

CHORUS LEADER
      Who did the killing?
Who's lying dead? Tell us.

MESSENGER
      Haemon has been killed.
No stranger shed his blood.

CHORUS LEADER
      At his father's hand?
Or did he kill himself?

MESSENGER
      By his own hand—
angry at his father for the murder.   1310

CHORUS LEADER
Teiresias, how your words have proven true!

MESSENGER
That's how things stand. Consider what comes next.

CHORUS LEADER
I see Creon's wife, poor Eurydice—
she's coming from the house—either by chance,
or else she's heard there's news about her son.

[Enter Eurydice from the palace with some attendants.]

EURYDICE
Citizens of Thebes, I heard you talking,
as I was walking out, going off to pray,
to ask for help from goddess Pallas.
While I was unfastening the gate,
I heard someone speaking of bad news   1320
about my family. I was terrified.
I collapsed, fainting back into the arms

of my attendants. So tell the news again—
I'll listen. I'm no stranger to misfortune.

MESSENGER
Dear lady, I'll speak of what I saw,
omitting not one detail of the truth.
Why should I ease your mind with a report
which turns out later to be incorrect?
The truth is always best. I went to the plain,
accompanying your husband as his guide.   1330
Polyneices' corpse, still unlamented,
was lying there, the greatest distance off,
torn apart by dogs. We prayed to Pluto
and to Hecate, goddess of the road,
for their good will and to restrain their rage.
We gave the corpse a ritual wash, and burned
what was left of it on fresh-cut branches.
We piled up a high tomb of his native earth.
Then we moved to the young girl's rocky cave,
the hollow cavern of that bride of death.   1340
From far away one man heard a voice
coming from the chamber where we'd put her
without a funeral—a piercing cry.
He went to tell our master Creon,
who, as he approached the place, heard the sound,
an unintelligible scream of sorrow.
He groaned and then spoke out these bitter words,
"Has misery made me a prophet now?
And am I travelling along a road
that takes me to the worst of all disasters?   1350
I've just heard the voice of my own son.
You servants, go ahead—get up there fast.
Remove the stones piled in the entrance way,
then stand beside the tomb and look in there
to see if that was Haemon's voice I heard,
or if the gods have been deceiving me."
Following what our desperate master asked,

we looked. In the furthest corner of the tomb
we saw Antigone hanging by the neck,
held up in a noose—fine woven linen.   1360
Haemon had his arms around her waist—
he was embracing her and crying out
in sorrow for the loss of his own bride,
now among the dead, his father's work,
and for his horrifying marriage bed.
Creon saw him, let out a fearful groan,
then went inside and called out anxiously,
"You unhappy boy, what have you done?
What are you thinking? Have you lost your mind?
Come out, my child—I'm begging you—please come."   1370
But the boy just stared at him with savage eyes,
spat in his face and, without saying a word,
drew his two-edged sword. Creon moved away,
so the boy's blow failed to strike his father.
Angry at himself, the ill-fated lad
right then and there leaned into his own sword,
driving half the blade between his ribs.
While still conscious he embraced the girl
in his weak arms, and, as he breathed his last,
he coughed up streams of blood on her fair cheek.   1380
Now he lies there, corpse on corpse, his marriage
has been fulfilled in chambers of the dead.
The unfortunate boy has shown all men
how, of all the evils which afflict mankind,
the most disastrous one is thoughtlessness.

[Eurydice turns and slowly returns into the palace.]

CHORUS LEADER
What do you make of that? The queen's gone back.
She left without a word, good or bad.

MESSENGER
I'm surprised myself. It's about her son—
she heard that terrible report. I hope

she's gone because she doesn't think it right   1390
to mourn for him in public. In the home,
surrounded by her servants, she'll arrange
a period of mourning for the house.
She's discreet and has experience—
she won't make mistakes.

CHORUS LEADER
            I'm not sure of that.
to me her staying silent was extreme—
it seems to point to something ominous,
just like a vain excess of grief.

MESSENGER
            I'll go in.
We'll find out if she's hiding something secret,
deep within her passionate heart. You're right—   1400
excessive silence can be dangerous.

[The Messenger goes up the stairs into the palace. Enter Creon from the side, with atten-
dants. Creon is holding the body of Haemon.]

CHORUS LEADER
Here comes the king in person—carrying
in his arms, if it's right to speak of this,
a clear reminder that this evil comes
not from some stranger, but his own mistakes.

CREON
Aaiii—mistakes made by a foolish mind,
cruel mistakes that bring on death.
You see us here, all in one family—
the killer and the killed.
O the profanity of what I planned!   1410
Alas, my son, you died so young—
a death before your time.
Aaiii ... aaiii ... you're dead ... gone—
not your own foolishness but mine.

CHORUS LEADER
Alas, it seems you've learned to see what's right—
but far too late.

CREON
          Aaiiii . . . I've learned it in my pain.
Some god clutching a great weight struck my head,
then hurled me onto pathways in the wilderness,
throwing down and casting underfoot
what brought me joy.

          Sad . . . so sad . . .   1420
the wretched agony of human life.

[The Messenger reappears from the palace.]

MESSENGER
My lord, you come like one who stores up evil,
what you hold in your arms and what you'll see
before too long inside the house.

CREON
          What's that?
Is there something still more evil than all this?

MESSENGER
Your wife is dead—blood mother of that corpse—
killed with a sword—her wounds are new, poor lady.

CREON
Aaiiii . . . . a gathering place for death . . .
no sacrifice can bring this to an end.
Why are you destroying me? You there—   1430
you bringer of this dreadful news, this agony,
what are you saying now? Aaiii . . .
You kill a man then kill him once again.
What are you saying, boy? What news?

A slaughter heaped on slaughter—
my wife, alas . . . she's dead?

MESSENGER *[opening the palace doors, revealing the body of Eurydice]*
Look here. No longer is she hidden in the house.

CREON
Alas, how miserable I feel—to look upon
this second horror. What remains for me,
what's Fate still got in store? I've just held   1440
my own son in my arms, and now I see
right here in front of me another corpse.
Alas for this suffering mother.
Alas, my son . . .

MESSENGER
Stabbed with a sharp sword at the altar,
she let her darkening eyesight fail,
once she had cried out in sorrow
for the glorious fate of Megareos,
who died some time ago, and then again
for Haemon, and then, with her last breath,   1450
she called out evil things against you,
the killer of your sons. [37]

CREON
Aaaii . . . My fear now makes me tremble.
Why won't someone now strike out at me,
pierce my heart with a two-edged sword?
How miserable I am . . . aaiii . . .
how full of misery and pain . . .

37. Megareos was Haemon's brother, who, we are to understand on the basis of this reference, died nobly some time before the play begins. It is not clear how Creon might have been responsible for his death. In another version of the story, Creon has a son Menoeceos, who kills himself in order to save the city.

MESSENGER
By this woman who lies dead you stand charged
with the deaths of both your sons.

CREON
                    What about her?
How did she die so violently?

MESSENGER
                    She killed herself,   1460
with her own hands she stabbed her belly,
once she heard her son's unhappy fate.

CREON
Alas for me ... the guilt for all of this is mine—
it can never be removed from me or passed
to any other mortal man. I, and I alone ...
I murdered you ... I speak the truth.
Servants—hurry and lead me off,
get me away from here, for now
what I am in life is nothing.

CHORUS LEADER
What you advise is good—if good can come   1470
with all these evils. When we face such things
the less we say the better.

CREON
Let that day come, O let it come,
the fairest of all destinies for me,
the one which brings on my last day.
O let it come, so that I never see
another dawn.

CHORUS LEADER
That's something for the times ahead.
Now we need to deal with what confronts us here.

What's yet to come is the concern of those   1480
whose task it is to deal with it.

CREON
                    In that prayer
I spoke of everything I long for.

CHORUS
                        Pray for nothing.
There's no release for mortal human beings,
not from events which destiny has set.

CREON
Then take this foolish man away from here.
I killed you, my son, without intending to,
and you, as well, my wife. How useless I am now.
I don't know where to look or find support.
Everything I touch goes wrong, and on my head
fate climbs up with its overwhelming load.   1490

[The Attendants help Creon move up the stairs into the palace, taking Haemon's body with them.]

CHORUS
The most important part of true success
is wisdom—not to act impiously
towards the gods, for boasts of arrogant men
bring on great blows of punishment—
so in old age men can discover wisdom.

Antigone. Questions for Discussion

1. Compare and contrast Ismene and Antigone. Identify specific passages to support your answer.

2. Antigone and Creon both refuse to back down or seek compromise. What do they share in common? Where and how is their thinking different? Does the text make us sympathetic to one or both of them? Why or why not?

3. What is the importance of gender in the play? Identify specific passages that support your answer.

4. What seems to be Creon's "fatal flaw" or "tragic flaw"? You might also consider whether Antigone may also possess a "fatal" or "tragic" flaw.

5. Antigone appeals to God's law as a higher standard to judge the laws of human beings. Do you believe there is a higher law (whether or not of divine origin)? Why or why not? If not, how do you determine whether a law is just or not?

6. The "Ode to Man" (the first ode in the play) celebrates human power over nature. How does our present situation, where human beings have become the dominate force for climate change, affect your reading of the ode?

7. Although *Antigone* is an ancient text, there are certainly modern, if not quite so immediately tragic, applications. What modern controversies over different definitions or forms of justice seem particularly relevant in light of your reading of the play?

Introduction to Plato's Allegory of the Cave

Plato was born in Athens around 428 BCE. He was born to a wealthy aristocratic family, and as a young man came under the influence of the famed philosopher Socrates (c. 470–c. 399 BCE). At the age of 70, Socrates was unjustly charged with impiety and corrupting the youth, and executed by the deeply corrupt democratic regime in Athens. Having witnessed the depravity of the Athenian democracy, Plato rejected politics as a path to political reform. As Eric Voegelin says, Plato "understood...that a reform cannot be achieved by a well-intentioned leader who recruits his followers from the very people whose moral confusion is the source of disorder."[1] Instead he turned with hope to the youth. With the financial support of his friend Dion, Plato founded the first university in a grove of olive trees known as the "academy," a site sacred to Athena, the goddess of wisdom. Plato's Academy remained the premier center for learning in the ancient world long after his death at the age of eighty in 347 BCE, and his influence on Western civilization continues to this day.

In his philosophical work Plato never speaks in his own voice. His writings are all in dialogue form; that is, they read a bit like little plays that feature Socrates as the main speaker in conversation with others. The present selection is taken from a much larger dialogue, *The Republic*, in which Plato explores the nature and value of justice for both the individual and the community. In this brief story he offers a parable that manages to explain nearly his whole philosophical vision. But the allegory also works in many different ways, and on many different levels. The powerful metaphors of light and darkness, ascent and descent, the figures of the sun, the cave, fire and shadows, and the themes of conversion, transformation, education, imprisonment and liberation, appearance and reality, ignorance and knowledge, make this rich parable as relevant and compelling to our age as it was in the classical age of ancient Greece.

At the most basic level the allegory of the cave is about the education of the philosopher. It captures his ascent from the darkness to the light, from appearance to reality, from the way things seem to be to the way things are. It is also about the return of the philosopher to those still imprisoned by mere falsehood and lies, and

---

1. Eric Voegelin, *Order and History*, vol. 3, *Plato and Aristotle* (Baton Rouge: Louisiana University Press, 1957), 5.

his death at the hands of the comfortably ignorant. This parable is also intended to explain Plato's metaphysics, or theory of reality. Very briefly, the inside of the cave represents the world of the senses—this world—the one we can see with our eyes. The fire in the cave represents the sun, and the shadows cast on the wall of the cave represent the objects of our senses (what we see). The cave allegory also helps us understand Plato's epistemology (theory of knowledge), and his ethics (theory of the good life). Indeed, he answers in this one parable the four big questions. Let's try to tease them out.

Allegory of the Cave Questions

What is Truth? Unlike the sophists, itinerant professors of rhetoric who taught that moral truth was relative to culture, Plato argued that all truth was objective and knowable. Merely believing something to be true was simply not enough for Plato. The only beliefs that counted as real knowledge were those that were true, and that you could justify with good reasons. For Plato, you can't know something by accident. If you can't justify your belief, even if it's true, then you don't *know it*. His model for knowledge was the science of mathematics, especially geometry.

To understand this, let's consider a thought experiment Plato uses in another dialogue, *The Meno*. There Socrates asks an uneducated youth to draw a square in the sand and asks him how to construct a square twice the size of the original. Of course, not having studied geometry, the youth has no idea. Through a series of questions, however, Socrates leads the youth to the solution, which is to take the diagonal of the square and use it as the side of another square. The resulting square will be exactly twice the area of the original (see figure ##). Plato took this kind of knowledge to be the paradigm of all genuine knowledge. It is a belief that is both true and justified.

But what do we really "know" when we know this truth in geometry? What is the object of our knowledge? It would make sense to say that we now know squares. But it can't be about the square objects we see around us, since they're not perfect squares, after all. In fact, we cannot draw a perfect square. The ones we draw, see around us in square things, e. g. , floor tiles, etc. , are not perfect squares either. In fact, for Plato, we can never *see* a perfect square with our eyes, but can only *think* a perfect square with our intellect. The square that the truths of geometry are true *of* is the *universal* idea of the square, or "square-ness," so to speak.

So, Plato reasons that besides the imperfect world of particular things that we have contact with through our senses, there is another perfect world of universals that we have contact with through the intellect. The objects, for example, of our knowledge of the truths of geometry are in this other unseen world we can *think of in our minds* but can't see in front of us. The objects in this parallel world Plato calls forms, or ideas. He argues that they are the most real, since they are eternal and unchanging, and knowable. The objects of the world of the senses, however, are fleeting and temporary—they come into existence and pass away. The objects of the world are *becoming* rather than *being*. Finally, he argues that the objects we *see* are imperfect copies of the perfect ideas we *think*. The squares we can see, or draw in the sand, are imperfect copies of the universal perfect idea of the square we can only think.

The cave allegory is about these two worlds. An allegory is a story, or some other work of art, that is intended to reveal a meaning beyond what it is literally said or shown. The cave interior represents the world of particular objects we can see. Outside the cave represents the world of the forms, or ideas, the world that this one is based on. The prisoner who escapes is the philosopher, the lover of wisdom, whose education is likened to being dragged up a steep ascent into the light of reality by a friend and mentor. Once out of the cave, after much difficulty, the liberated prisoner can see the sun, the source of all that is. The sun is the symbol for what Plato simply calls "The Good," the source of all things that are real to the degree that they are real. For Plato, some things are more real than others.

What is Justice? As mentioned above, *The Republic*, from which the cave allegory is taken, is about the nature and value of justice for the individual and the community (*polis*). There are many things we might describe as just. We can talk about just laws, just judgements, just people, and so on. These are all very different kinds of things. What is it, then, that all just things have in common? What *makes them just*? For Plato the ideal form of justice was a universal idea. Just as there are many imperfect squares we can see, and these are imperfect copies of the real universal idea of "squareness," so too with justice and just things. Justice in our everyday world is always an imperfect copy of the real thing, which is only something we can "see" with the eye of the intellect. The philosopher, then, in her or his ascent to the world of ideas, has knowledge of justice, has seen the perfect idea of justice with her or his intellect, and so can recognize it in this world, as well as its opposite, injustice. Furthermore, it is the love of and allegiance to the form of the Good, represented by the figure of the sun, that empowers the philosopher to know the right, and do the good. Knowledge of the ideal form of justice orders the soul, and makes a person just. It is transformative. This knowledge is why Plato argues that only philosophers can safely be trusted with political power, and that only philosophers should rule.

What does it mean to be Human? For Plato the human being was caught between two worlds. The human being has a mortal body and an immortal soul. The body is clearly in the world of the senses, the world of becoming, and is perishing. The soul has contact, through reason and the intellect, with the world of ideal forms. Plato also taught that the soul had three parts: reason, spirit and appetite. Appetite included our bodily desires, and if uncontrolled by the spirit (or properly ordered emotions), the soul was corrupted and not all that it could be. A just soul is one where reason rules the lower parts, and is in a kind of harmony, like a finely tuned musical instrument. Most people, Plato thought, had disordered souls, and more or less blindly followed their appetites while disregarding the dictates of reason. Only the philosopher, who had been outside the cave, had converted, or turned around to see The Good (symbolized by the sun in the story). Only they could truly know the beauty of a just soul. Most people took far more care of their body, such as by avoiding disease, than they did of their soul. The knowledge of The Good, which comes from the philosopher's escape from the cave, is transformative and heals her soul. This knowledge of The Good gives her an understanding of what is genuinely most important in life and profoundly influences he choices she makes at every turn.

What is the Good Life? By now you can probably guess Plato's answer to this question. The philosophical life is the best life, the only life really worthy of a human being. The word "philosophy" comes from two Greek words, *philein* (to love) and *sophia* (wisdom); it means the love of wisdom, or knowledge for its own sake. The best life for Plato is also the highest expression of human nature; it is a well-ordered life guided by the love of and allegiance to the transformative experience of The Good beyond the cave.

Plato's Allegory of the Cave[1]

Translated from the Greek by Benjamin Jowett
Translation modified by Phillip W. Schoenberg[2]

PART I

Socrates Asks Glaucon to imagine the scene of the story.
Make sure you can picture the details, too.

SOCRATES: And now let me show in an image how far our nature is educated or uneducated. Imagine human beings living in a underground cave, which has its opening towards the light. They have been here from their childhood, and have their legs and necks chained so that they cannot move, and can only see in front of themselves because they are prevented by the chains from turning round their heads. Above and behind them a fire is blazing at a distance, and between the fire and the prisoners there is a raised path; and you will see, if you look, a low wall built along the path, like the screen which marionette players have in front of them, over which they show the puppets.

GLAUCON: I see.

SOCRATES: Further, imagine people walking along the wall carrying all sorts of vessels, and statues and figures of animals made of wood and stone and various materials, which appear over the wall? Some of them are talking, others silent.

---

1. *The Republic of Plato.* Trans. Benjamin Jowett. 3d ed. The Clarendon Press, Oxford, 1888, pp. xcviii-xcix (Stephanus numbering: 514a to 517e).

2. Benjamin Jowett (1817–1893) was one of the most outstanding Hellenists of his age, and his English language translations of Plato are a treasure. His usage, however, can sometimes pose an unnecessary challenge to undergraduates coming to Plato for the first time in the twenty-first century. For this reason, I have made some relatively minor changes to Jowett's diction, word choice and (rarely) sentence structure. In a few cases I have consulted the Greek to be sure my changes remained faithful to Plato. I have also recast this portion of the dialogue with names of the speakers in bold and removed the indications of this in the text (e. g. , 'he replied,' or 'I said').

GLAUCON: A strange parable, and they are strange prisoners.

SOCRATES: They are like us. They see only their own shadows, or the shadows of one another, which the fire casts on the opposite wall of the cave?

GLAUCON: That's right. How could they see anything but the shadows if they were never allowed to move their heads?

SOCRATES: And what about the objects which are being carried, wouldn't they only see the shadows of those objects, too?

GLAUCON: Yes.

SOCRATES: And if they were able to converse with one another, would they not suppose that they were naming what was actually before them?

GLAUCON: Very true.

PART 2
Plato explains the prisoners' problem. They think the shadows on the cave wall are real things, but they're only shadows of real things.

SOCRATES: And suppose further that the prison had an echo which came from the other side, would they not be sure to think, when one of the 'puppeteers' spoke, that the voice which they heard came from the passing shadow?

GLAUCON: No question.

SOCRATES: To them, the truth would be literally nothing but the shadows of the images.

GLAUCON: That is certain.

PART 3
At first the prisoners refuse to accept freedom. Even when they're released
they refuse to believe that the shadows are not the real things.

SOCRATES: And now look again, and see what will naturally happen if the prisoners are released and shown their error. At first, when any of them is liberated and compelled suddenly to stand up and turn his neck round and walk and look towards the light, he will feel pain. The glare will hurt him, and he will be unable to see the realities that in his former state he had seen the shadows. Then imagine someone saying to him, that what he saw before was an illusion, but that now, when he is approaching nearer to being and his eye is turned towards more real existence, he has a clearer vision. What would he say? Imagine further that his teacher is pointing to the objects as they pass and requiring him to name them. Won't he be confused? Will he not think that the shadows which he formerly saw are truer than the objects which are now shown to him?

GLAUCON: Far truer.

SOCRATES: And if he is compelled to look straight at the light of the fire, will he not have a pain in his eyes which will make him turn away to take refuge in the objects of vision which he can see, and which he will still think are clearer than the things which are now being shown to him?

GLAUCON: True.

PART 4
They have to be dragged out of the cave, and it's so bright outside,
they can't see anything at first, and it hurts.

SOCRATES: And suppose once more that he is reluctantly dragged up a steep and rugged ascent, and held fast until he is forced into the presence of the sun itself, is he not likely to be pained and irritated? When he approaches the light his eyes will be dazzled, and he will not be able to see anything at all of what are now called realities.

GLAUCON: Not right away.

SOCRATES: He will need to get accustomed to the sight of the upper world. And first he will see the shadows best, next the reflections of people and other objects in the water, and then the objects themselves. Then he will gaze upon the light of the moon and the stars and the spangled heaven. And he will see the sky and the stars by night better than the sun or the light of the sun by day?

GLAUCON: Certainly.

PART 5
Finally, they see the sun, which is the source of all light, that by which the eye can see (don't try this at home).

SOCRATES: Last of all he will be able to see the sun, and not mere reflections of it in the water, but he will see it in his own proper place, and not in another. And he will contemplate it as he is.

GLAUCON: Certainly.

SOCRATES: He will then proceed to argue that this is what gives the season of the year, and is the guardian of all that is in the visible world, and in a certain way the cause of everything which he and his friends have ever seen?

GLAUCON: Clearly, he would first see the sun and then reason about it.

PART 6
They feel sorry for their old friends, still in prison in the cave.

SOCRATES: And when he remembered his old habitation, and the 'wisdom' of the cave and his fellow prisoners, don't you think he would consider himself happy, but pity them?

GLAUCON: Certainly, he would.

SOCRATES: And if they were in the habit of conferring honors among themselves on those who were quickest to observe the passing shadows and to remark which of them went before, and which followed after, and which were together, and who were therefore best able to draw conclusions as to the future, do you think that he would care for such honors and glories, or envy others who received them? Would he not say with Homer, 'Better to be the poor servant of a poor master,' and to endure anything, rather than think as they do and live after the way they do?

GLAUCON: Yes, I think that he would rather suffer anything than believe falsehoods and live in this miserable way.

PART 7
But back in the darkness of the cave, once again they can't see.
Now their eyes need to adjust to the darkness. Their old friends can see better in
the cave than those who have been liberated.

SOCRATES: Imagine once more, someone like that coming suddenly out of the sunshine to be replaced in his old situation. Wouldn't it be hard for his eyes to see in the darkness?

GLAUCON: To be sure.

SOCRATES: And if there were a contest, and he had to compete in measuring the shadows with the prisoners who had never left the cave, while his sight was still weak, and before his eyes had adjusted to the darkness (and this would take a long time), would he not be thought ridiculous? People would say that up he went and down he came without his eyes, and that it was better not even to think of leaving the cave. And if anyone tried to free someone else, and lead him up to the light, let them only catch the offender, and they would put him to death.

GLAUCON: No question.

PART 8
Socrates Explains the Cave.

SOCRATES: This entire allegory, you may now understand, Glaucon, according to what was said earlier. The prison-house is the world of sight, the light of the fire is the sun, and you will be correct, if you interpret the journey upwards to be the ascent of the soul into the intellectual world according to the way I understand it, which, at your desire, I have expressed—whether rightly or wrongly, God only knows. But, whether true or false, my opinion is that in the world of knowledge the idea of good appears last of all, and is seen only with an effort; and, when seen, is also inferred to be the universal author of all things that are beautiful and right, parent of light and of the lord of light in this visible world, and the immediate source of reason and truth in the intellectual world. And that this is the power upon which he who would act rationally either in public or private life must have his eye fixed.

GLAUCON: I agree, as far as I am able to understand you.

SOCRATES: Moreover, you shouldn't be surprised that those who have made it that far up are unwilling to descend to human affairs, for their souls are always running back to the upper world where they desire to live, a very natural desire, if our allegory may be trusted.

GLAUCON: Yes, very natural.

Allegory of the Cave. Questions for Discussion

1. Have you had a transformative experience that you think the cave could adequately represent? Are all the elements of the parable in your case, too, or only some? Are there crucial aspects missing?

2. The cave is also about transcendence, about experiences that lie outside of the material world. What do you think about the concept of a world beyond this world that anchors our knowledge, and supports our reality? Would intellectual contact with such a world be transformative, as the allegory of the cave suggests?

3. The cave allegory presupposes Plato's two-world metaphysics, or theory of reality. The interior of the cave represents the natural world, and the exterior of the cave represents the real world. How does this square with your own world view, and the modern scientific world view?

4. The cave is a metaphor for education as transformation. Can you identify aspects of your own educational experience that correlate with the various elements in the cave allegory? Do you expect transformation from your college experience? Is the difficulty worth it? Why?

5. Have you changed your mind on important matters? Was it easy for people in your life to accept this, or did they feel threatened by changes in your worldview? How might the cave allegory help think through such experiences?

The Middle Ages
through the Renaissance

The Middle Ages through the Renaissance: Overview
0–17th Century CE

Shifting Religious Tides

Starting with Judaism in around 2000 BCE, religion begins to shift from a belief in many gods (polytheism) to a belief in a single, all powerful, all-knowing deity (monotheism). In most ancient traditions, polytheism was firmly based in animism and many gods were strongly associated with nature. The Greek gods are a great example. Today, polytheistic religions, including Hinduism, still thrive across the globe.

Formal monotheistic religions all stem from Judaism and are called "Abrahamic" religions: Judaism, Christianity, and Islam.

As Christianity began to take hold in what is now the Middle East and spread across the globe, we see the development of what is now Catholicism. St. Augustine, a converted Christian from Northern Africa, was one of the early Christian leaders who influenced the development of the Catholic church and Catholic doctrine. He set the stage for the Medieval Christian world.

The Middle Ages (also called the Medieval Period): c. 500–1400 CE

Life in these times was very difficult. There were great conflicts and external invasion threats across Europe, and as a result, people needed protection in order to survive if not actually to thrive. Additionally, much of the population lived under a relatively constant threat of poverty and starvation.

As a result, feudalism, a hierarchical class system, was created to provide protections in exchange for work/payment. At the top of feudal systems was the king, and underneath him were church officials and the noble class, wealthy and powerful landowners (lords) who lived on manors that received his protection. Just below the nobility was a warrior class of knights. The people the lords protected were peasants, called vassals or serfs, who worked the land that they did not own and were subject to high taxes.

King

Church Officials   Nobles

Knights

Peasants and Serfs

This class system is part of a larger hierarchy that arose within the Catholic Church, called the Great Chain of Being that ranks all things, starting with God at the top and ending with rocks and inanimate objects at the bottom:

God

The Angels

Demons

Humans: Man

Woman

Animals

Plants

Stones

Within this system, there were sub-classifications as well. For humans, men were considered higher than women, and wealthy powerful lords were ranked lower than kings but higher than knights and vassals.

During this challenging time, the Catholic Church gained incredible power, placing itself at the highest pinnacle of human life, where priests had the power to access God's wisdom and translate it for the rest of the population. There were power challenges between kings and the highest leaders of the Church.

At this time, the Church had developed a strong hierarchy itself, from the Pope down to the monks who lived in seclusion from the outside world. Monasteries held virtually all of Western Civilization's written texts in their libraries, and the early monks were the producers of most of the world's written texts.

While the Catholic Church dominated Europe at this time, the Church considered Islam to be a major threat. During the four Crusades from the 11th–13th centuries, European soldiers as well as peasants traveled to the Holy Lands to fight against the rising Islamic and Jewish powers and to reclaim Jerusalem as a sacred Christian site, though Jerusalem is the sacred city for all Abrahamic religions. While the Crusaders briefly regained control over Jerusalem, they were ultimately defeated, leaving the Holy Land in Muslim control.

Additionally, given the poor living conditions and the overabundance of rats, the bubonic plague spread throughout Europe in 1347 and killed about one-third of the population. This dramatic population shift necessitated major changes in social and economic systems, effectively ending feudalism and creating more opportunities for the rise of the merchant class, which set the stage for a middle class.

The Renaissance: 1300–1600 CE

The word renaissance comes from French and means "re-birth," and this revival occurs on many different levels. In particular, it is a re-birth of the classics (particularly the Greek but also Roman) and of classical knowledge as well as a re-birth of the arts. In addition, the European Renaissance period represents the time when the focus shifts from God to humans and to humanism, culminating in the rise of the belief in the importance of the individual.

The Italian poet Dante Alighieri is often considered to be right at the border of the end of the Middle Ages and the beginning of the Renaissance. The worldview of his epic, *The Divine Comedy*, represents the medieval mindset and emphasis on God's plan for the universe and for each individual within it. However, he also included elements of humanism and of the artistic and philosophical trends that would become elements of the Renaissance, including his decision to write in Italian rather than Latin, his critique of the corruption of the Catholic Church, and his inclusion of the Greek and Roman classics and their authors in his work.

The Renaissance began in Italy and then spread to other countries. It included numerous visual artists, with Leonardo da Vinci and Michelangelo perhaps the most famous of the many writers, architects and artists that changed the ways we think about art and perspective to this day.

Renaissance ideas and inspiration spread quickly, particularly with the help of the invention of the Gutenberg printing press around 1452. While the Chinese had been using a printing system for over 600 years, in Europe most texts were still handwritten or hand-copied by monks and were mainly preserved in specialized libraries that the general public could not access. Additionally, since most of the population was not literate, priests and other officials transmitted knowledge orally. The printing press provided access to written texts that would have been previously unavailable, and over time it promoted greater levels of literacy in the general public. Additionally, it spread information and new ideas more quickly across broader geographical regions.

In England, the Renaissance took place from the early 15th to early 16th century. By this time, the Protestant Reformation had occurred and England had become a Protestant country under the rule of Queen Elizabeth 1. While the Italian movement was dominated more by visual artists, the Elizabethan Age is most famous for the works of a poet and playwright, William Shakespeare, whose works reveal much to us even today about the complex psychology of the human condition.

Introduction to St. Augustine and *The Confessions*
(354–430 CE)

St. Augustine of Hippo

You may never have heard of St. Augustine, who is one of the earliest leaders in Christianity, but there are elements of his life and his beliefs that are embedded in the Catholic tradition as well as American culture more generally.

Augustine was born and raised in North Africa, and while his mother was Christian, his father was not, and in fact his father was more aligned with Roman values like getting ahead in life by making money. Augustine himself was not baptized into the church at a young age, and he lived a worldly life, choosing not to marry but still having sexual affairs with women. He wasn't satisfied with this life, though, and went through a long process of conversion to Christianity at age 33, which in those times would have been considered middle age.

Within Catholic history, St. Augustine is known for a number of important ideas and innovations:

First, Augustine's early studies were in the Greek philosophers, especially Plato. While others in the early church considered Plato's work to be a precursor of Christianity, St. Augustine gets most of the credit for the introduction of Neoplatonism (New Platonism) that re-envisions Plato's ideas, particularly his Theory of Forms and the Allegory of the Cave, in a Christian light.

Part of this re-casting of Plato included the idea of two "worlds." The ideal world is the City of God, where God and the heavenly beings live in perfect harmony, and the "earthly" world, the City of Man, is an imperfect and corrupt reflection where humans try their best to live but can never live in the true light of God until they die and are saved by Jesus Christ.

Consider the Allegory of the Cave: the cave is ignorance (from a Christian perspective, ignorance of God), and the sun is God. Enlightenment isn't just general philosophical enlightenment but in this case acceptance of God into one's heart. For St. Augustine, all humans must possess free will in order to actively choose God (or turn from the darkness towards the light). Simultaneously, St. Augustine believed that some humans were predestined to be saved, and this is where one of the paradoxes of Christianity starts to take shape: how can predestination (i. e. fate) and free will co-exist?

In St. Augustine's conception of humanity, humans are inherently sinful, and St. Augustine himself created the idea of original sin that is fundamental to nearly all Christian faiths. He believed that humans were born with the inherited sin of Adam and Eve's eating from the Tree of the Knowledge of Good and Evil (i. e. the apple, which was probably something more like a fig), which is described in the Book of Genesis. No matter how hard humans try, and even after the sacrament of baptism, which cleanses the soul of original sin, they continue to commit sins and must continually confess, repent, and be forgiven. Only when the faithful (and penitent) die and leave their mortal bodies can the soul be fully cleansed and be prepared to enter the City of God.

This controversy over whether we are born naturally corrupt and will always lean towards evil or born good and are corrupted somewhere down the line on Earth is a debate that will likely rage on as long as humans exist. In some ways, we are more like the Romans, who believed that through self-help we could reach our fullest potential and that Rome could achieve a perfectly just state. We are constantly striving to overcome challenges, to become "better" people. However, St. Augustine's beliefs that we inherit flaws and challenges and that we have work to do on this earth to counter and defeat those challenges are embedded in our culture in fascinating ways.

The Confessions

The Confessions is Augustine's autobiographical account of his early life, conversion to Christianity, and his study and meditations on Christianity following his conversion.

If you are a religious or spiritual person, just about all religious "conversion" or "awakening" stories follow a similar pattern to St. Augustine's work. Even modern books about enlightenments or awakenings, whether spiritual or not, follow a number of Augustine's ideas.

In the first three books, Augustine retells the story of his infancy through puberty and his early leanings toward sin, first small vices that closely approximated shoplifting or other small thefts of items, and then larger sins, particularly those surrounding lust and sexual intercourse outside of marriage. At the end of Book 3, Augustine learns of Manichaeism, a blend of several different religions where dual forces of good and evil are equally balanced in the world and the forces of evil are totally separate from and the opposite of the good. Manichaean beliefs countered the Christian doctrine that God is *omniscient* (all-knowing or all-seeing), *omnipotent* (all-powerful), and *omnipresent* (all-present), so therefore all good and evil must come from God. In Books 4 and 5, Augustine describes his nine years of following the Manichean tradition before leaning back towards the Christian faith of his mother. Books 6 through 9 describe Augustine's efforts to learn all he can and to seek enlightenment, which arrives in Book 8. His final acceptance of Christ in his baptism occurs in Book 9, as well as a review of his conversion experience. Books 10–13 provide an extended analysis of God's efforts to save humankind through Augustine's interpretation of the biblical Book of Genesis.

We will be studying two books: Book 2, where he describes a childhood episode in which he stole something just for the thrill of the sin, and Book 8, which documents his final conversion experience.

The Confessions Questions

What is Truth? In *The Confessions,* St. Augustine actively searches for the Truth. He studies different philosophies and religions, seeking answers to his questions about truth and his purpose in life. He also repeatedly strays far from the truth, led by his earthly desires, even though he knows that he will not find the truth in such pleasures of the body. For Christians, *The Confessions* is a guidebook to searching for and finding truth. For those who are not Christian, how does Augustine's search help us to think about our own lives in terms of purpose and finding truths and/or an absolute Truth? How do we learn to recognize illusions or temptations that cause us to stray from what we know to be truths?

What is Justice? St. Augustine criticized the Roman belief that perfect justice can be attained on earth. For the Romans, outward signs of wealth and power reflected inner virtues and therefore contributed to the creation of a perfectly just society. Augustine believed that true justice could only be found in the ideal City of God, never in the City of Man. Do you believe that we as humans can create a truly just society or are we destined to fall victim to corruption, greed, and domination of the powerful over the weak? What, in the end, is "good enough" for the City of Man, which is the world as we know it?

What does it mean to be Human? For St. Augustine, humans are inherently flawed and cannot reach perfection on our own, but humans are capable of becoming so much more with God's grace. In St. Augustine's eyes, we are divided between our reason and our will, and more often than not our will overcomes our reason, not because we don't know what is "right" but because we choose to avoid or ignore it. As you read Book Two in particular, consider how Augustine focuses on his crime and even more so on his motives. Why do you think all humans at some point in life seek the thrill of sin or wickedness or just plain naughty behavior?

What is the Good Life? St. Augustine asks us to question our desires for earthly pleasures and understand how we are driven and controlled by those desires. We certainly observe plenty of extreme examples where individuals find themselves addicted to food, substances like alcohol and/or drugs, or sex. However, even those of us who don't have those extreme tendencies can benefit from thinking about the balance between following our desires and controlling them for the sake of ourselves and/or others. What is St. Augustine's balance? Is that ours, or is there a different balance that suits us better?

From *Augustine: Confessions* (397–400 CE)
Trans. Albert C. Outler[1]

BOOK TWO

He concentrates here on his sixteenth year, a year of idleness, lust, and adolescent mischief. The memory of stealing some pears prompts a deep probing of the motives and aims of sinful acts. "I became to myself a wasteland."

CHAPTER I

1. I wish now to review in memory my past wickedness and the carnal* corruptions of my soul—not because I still love them, but that I may love thee, O my God. For love of thy love I do this, recalling in the bitterness of self-examination my wicked ways, that thou mayest grow sweet to me, thou sweetness without deception! Thou sweetness happy and assured! Thus thou mayest gather me up out of those fragments in which I was torn to pieces, while I turned away from thee, O Unity, and lost myself among "the many." For as I became a youth, I longed to be satisfied with worldly things, and I dared to grow wild in a succession of various and shadowy loves. My form* wasted away, and I became corrupt in thy eyes, yet I was still pleasing to my own eyes—and eager to please the eyes of men.

*sexual, bodily

*body

CHAPTER II

2. But what was it that delighted me save* to love and to be loved? Still I did not keep the moderate way of the love of mind to mind— the bright path of friendship. Instead, the mists of passion steamed

*except

1. *Augustine: Confessions*, trans. Albert C. Outler (1955). Retrieved from https://www. ling. upenn. edu/courses/ hum100/augustinconf. pdf. This text is in the Public Domain. Limited footnotes citing biblical sources are utilized from the Outler translation. Book overviews are slightly amended for language and all side annotations are additions made by the editor of this text.

up out of the puddly concupiscence* of the flesh, and the hot   *desire
imagination of puberty, and they so obscured* and overcast my   *made dim
heart that I was unable to distinguish pure affection from unholy
desire. Both boiled confusedly within me, and dragged my unstable youth down over the cliffs of unchaste* desires and plunged   *impure
me into a gulf of infamy*. Thy anger had come upon me, and I   *evil
knew it not. I had been deafened by the clanking of the chains of
my mortality, the punishment for my soul's pride, and I wandered
farther from thee, and thou didst permit me to do so. I was tossed
to and fro, and wasted, and poured out, and I boiled over in my
fornications*—and yet thou didst hold thy peace, O my tardy Joy!   *sex
Thou didst still hold thy peace, and I wandered still farther from
thee into more and yet more barren fields of sorrow, in proud de-
jection* and restless lassitude. *   *low spirit *fatigue

3. If only there had been someone to regulate my disorder and
turn to my profit the fleeting* beauties of the things around me,   *passing
and to fix a bound* to their sweetness, so that the tides of my   *boundary
youth might have spent themselves upon the shore of marriage!
Then they might have been tranquilized and satisfied with having
children, as thy law prescribes, O Lord—O thou who dost form
the offspring of our death and art able also with a tender hand to
blunt the thorns which were excluded from thy paradise![2] For thy
omnipotence* is not far from us even when we are far from thee.   *all powerfulness
Now, on the other hand, I might have given more vigilant heed* to   *alertness
the voice from the clouds: "Nevertheless, such shall have trouble
in the flesh, but I spare you,"[3] and, "It is good for a man not to
touch a woman,"[4] and, "He that is unmarried cares for the things
that belong to the Lord, how he may please the Lord; but he that
is married cares for the things that are of the world, how he may
please his wife."[5] I should have listened more attentively to these
words, and, thus having been "made a eunuch* for the Kingdom   *castrated man

2. See Genesis 3:18.

3. 1 Corinthains 7:28.

4. 1 Corinthians 7:1.

5. 1 Corinthians 7:32, 33.

of Heaven's sake,"[6] I would have with greater happiness expected thy embraces.

4. But, fool that I was, I foamed in my wickedness as the sea and, forsaking* thee, followed the rushing of my own tide, and burst out of all thy bounds. But I did not escape thy scourges*. For what mortal can do so? Thou were always by me, mercifully angry and flavoring all my unlawful pleasures with bitter discontent, in order that I might seek pleasures free from discontent. But where could I find such pleasure save in thee, O Lord—save in thee, who dost teach us by sorrow, who wounds us to heal us, and dost kill us that we may not die apart from thee. Where was I, and how far was I exiled from the delights of thy house, in that sixteenth year of the age of my flesh, when the madness of lust held full sway in me— that madness which grants indulgence* to human shamelessness, even though it is forbidden by thy laws—and I gave myself entirely to it? Meanwhile, my family took no care to save me from ruin by marriage, for their sole care was that I should learn how to make a powerful speech and become a persuasive orator.

*giving up
*punishment

*favor

CHAPTER III

5. Now, in that year my studies were interrupted. I had come back from Madaura, a neighboring city where I had gone to study grammar and rhetoric; and the money for a further term at Carthage was being got together for me. This project was more a matter of my father's ambition than of his means, for he was only a poor citizen of Tagaste.

To whom am I narrating all this? Not to thee, O my God, but to my own kind in thy presence—to that small part of the human race who may chance to come upon these writings. And to what end? That I and all who read them may understand what depths there are from which we are to cry unto thee. For what is more surely heard in thy ear than a confessing heart and a faithful life?

6. See Matthew 19:12.

Who did not extol* and praise my father, because he went quite   *glorify
beyond his means to supply his son with the necessary expenses
for a far journey in the interest of his education? For many far
richer citizens did not do so much for their children. Still, this
same father troubled himself not at all as to how I was progressing
toward thee nor how chaste* I was, just so long as I was skillful in   *pure
speaking—no matter how barren I was to thy tillage*, O God, who   *cultivation
art the one true and good Lord of my heart, which is thy field. [7]

6. During that sixteenth year of my age, I lived with my parents,
having a holiday from school for a time—this idleness* imposed   *laziness
upon me by my parents' straitened* finances. The thornbushes of   *limited
lust grew rank about my head, and there was no hand to root them
out. Indeed, when my father saw me one day at the baths and perceived that I was becoming a man, and was showing the signs of
adolescence, he joyfully told my mother about it as if already looking forward to grandchildren, rejoicing in that sort of inebriation*   *drunkenness
in which the world so often forgets thee, its Creator, and falls in
love with thy creature instead of thee—the inebriation of that invisible wine of a perverted* will which turns and bows down to in-   *corrupted
famy.* But in my mother's breast thou had already begun to build   *evil reputation
thy temple and the foundation of thy holy habitation—whereas
my father was only a catechumen*, and that but recently. She was,   *convert
therefore, startled with a holy fear and trembling: for though I
had not yet been baptized, she feared those crooked ways in which
they walk who turn their backs to thee and not their faces.

7. Woe is me! Do I dare affirm that thou didst hold thy peace, O
my God, while I wandered farther away from thee? Didst thou
really then hold thy peace? Then whose words were they but thine
which by my mother, thy faithful handmaid, thou didst pour into
my ears? None of them, however, sank into my heart to make
me do anything. She deplored* and, as I remember, warned me   *regretted
privately with great solicitude*, "not to commit fornication*; but   *anxiety *sexual
above all things never to defile another man's wife." These ap-   intercourse
peared to me but womanish counsels, which I would have blushed

7. See 1 Corinthians 3:9.

to obey. Yet they were from thee, and I knew it not. I thought that thou were silent and that it was only she who spoke. Yet it was through her that thou didst not keep silence toward me; and in rejecting her counsel I was rejecting thee— I, her son, "the son of thy handmaid, thy servant. "[8] But I did not realize this, and rushed on headlong with such blindness that, among my friends, I was ashamed to be less shameless than they, when I heard them boasting of their disgraceful exploits—yes, and glorying all the more the worse their baseness was. What is worse, I took pleasure in such exploits, not for the pleasure's sake only but mostly for praise. What is worthy of vituperation* except vice* itself? Yet I made myself out worse than I was, in order that I might not go lacking for praise. And when in anything I had not sinned as the worst ones in the group, I would still say that I had done what I had not done, in order not to appear contemptible* because I was more innocent than they; and not to drop in their esteem* because I was more chaste*.

*condemnation
*wickedness

*pitiful
*regard
*innocent

8. Behold with what companions I walked the streets of Babylon*! I rolled in its mire* and lolled about on it, as if on a bed of spices and precious ointments. And, drawing me more closely to the very center of that city, my invisible enemy trod me down and seduced me, for I was easy to seduce. My mother had already fled out of the midst of Babylon and was progressing, albeit slowly, toward its outskirts. For in counseling me to chastity*, she did not bear in mind what her husband had told her about me. And although she knew that my passions were destructive even then and dangerous for the future, she did not think they should be restrained by the bonds of conjugal affection*—if, indeed, they could not be cut away to the quick. She took no heed of this, for she was afraid lest a wife should prove a hindrance and a burden to my hopes. These were not her hopes of the world to come, which my mother had in thee, but the hope of learning, which both my parents were too anxious that I should acquire—my father, because he had little or no thought of thee, and only vain thoughts for me; my mother, because she thought that the usual course of study would not only

*city of sin
*mud

*sexual abstinence

*marriage

8. Psalms 116:16.

130

be no hindrance* but actually a furtherance toward my eventual *obstacle
return to thee. This much I conjecture*, recalling as well as I can *guess
the temperaments* of my parents. Meantime, the reins of disci- *personalities
pline were slackened on me, so that without the restraint of due
severity, I might play at whatsoever I fancied, even to the point of
dissoluteness*. And in all this there was that mist which shut out *lack of restraint
from my sight the brightness of thy truth, O my God; and my
iniquity* bulged out, as it were, with fatness!⁹ *wickedness

CHAPTER IV

9. Theft is punished by thy law, O Lord, and by the law written
in men's hearts, which not even ingrained wickedness can erase.
For what thief will tolerate another thief stealing from him? Even
a rich thief will not tolerate a poor thief who is driven to theft by
want*. Yet I had a desire to commit robbery, and did so, compelled *need
to it by neither hunger nor poverty, but through a contempt* for *scorn
welldoing and a strong impulse to iniquity*. For I pilfered* some- *evil *stole
thing which I already had in sufficient measure, and of much better quality. I did not desire to enjoy what I stole, but only the theft
and the sin itself.

There was a pear tree close to our own vineyard, heavily laden* *loaded
with fruit, which was not tempting either for its color or for its flavor. Late one night—having prolonged* our games in the streets *extended
until then, as our bad habit was—a group of young scoundrels,
and I among them, went to shake and rob this tree. We carried
off a huge load of pears, not to eat ourselves, but to dump out to
the hogs, after barely tasting some of them ourselves. Doing this
pleased us all the more because it was forbidden. Such was my
heart, O God, such was my heart—which thou didst pity even
in that bottomless pit. Behold, now let my heart confess to thee
what it was seeking there, when I was being gratuitously wanton*, *extravagant
having no inducement* to evil but the evil itself. It was foul, and I *persuasion
loved it. I loved my own undoing. I loved my error—not that for
which I erred but the error itself. A depraved* soul, falling away *corrupt
from security in thee to destruction in itself, seeking nothing from
the shameful deed but shame itself.

9. See Psalms 73:7.

CHAPTER V

10. Now there is a comeliness* in all beautiful bodies, and in gold   *beauty
and silver and all things. The sense of touch has its own power
to please and the other senses find their proper objects in physical sensation. Worldly honor also has its own glory, and so do
the powers to command and to overcome: and from these there
springs up the desire for revenge. Yet, in seeking these pleasures,
we must not depart from thee, O Lord, nor deviate* from thy   *depart
law. The life which we live here has its own peculiar attractive-
ness because it has a certain measure of comeliness of its own and
a harmony with all these inferior* values. The bond of human   *lesser
friendship has a sweetness of its own, binding many souls together
as one. Yet because of these values, sin is committed, because we
have an inordinate* preference for these goods of a lower order   *excessive
and neglect the better and the higher good—neglecting thee, O
our Lord God, and thy truth and thy law. For these inferior values have their delights, but not at all equal to my God, who hath
made them all. For in him do the righteous* delight and he is the   *moral
sweetness of the upright in heart.

11. When, therefore, we inquire why a crime was committed, we do
not accept the explanation unless it appears that there was the desire to obtain some of those values which we designate inferior, or
else a fear of losing them. For truly they are beautiful and comely,
though in comparison with the superior and celestial* goods they   *heavenly
are abject* and contemptible. A man has murdered another man—   *hopeless
what was his motive? Either he desired his wife or his property
or else he would steal to support himself; or else he was afraid
of losing something to him; or else, having been injured, he was
burning to be revenged. Would a man commit murder without a
motive, taking delight simply in the act of murder? Who would
believe such a thing? Even for that savage and brutal man [Cat-
iline], of whom it was said that he was gratuitously* wicked and   *excessively
cruel, there is still a motive assigned to his deeds. "Lest through
idleness*," he says, "hand or heart should grow inactive."[10] And to   *laziness
what purpose? Why, even this: that, having once got possession

10. Cicero, *De Cataline*, 16.

of the city through his practice of his wicked ways, he might gain
honors, empire, and wealth, and thus be exempt* from the fear of   *free
the laws and from financial difficulties in supplying the needs of
his family—and from the consciousness of his own wickedness.
So it seems that even Catiline himself loved not his own villainies,
but something else, and it was this that gave him the motive for
his crimes.

CHAPTER VI

12. What was it in you, O theft of mine, that I, poor wretch, doted*   *worshipped
on—you deed of darkness—in that sixteenth year of my age?
Beautiful you were not, for you were a theft. But are you anything
at all, so that I could analyze the case with you? Those pears that
we stole were fair to the sight because they were thy creation, O
Beauty beyond compare, O Creator of all, O thou good God—
God the highest good and my true good. Those pears were truly
pleasant to the sight, but it was not for them that my miserable
soul lusted, for I had an abundance of better pears. I stole those
simply that I might steal, for, having stolen them, I threw them   *reward
away. My sole gratification* in them was my own sin, which I was
pleased to enjoy; for, if any one of these pears entered my mouth,
the only good flavor it had was my sin in eating it. And now, O
Lord my God, I ask what it was in that theft of mine that caused
me such delight; for behold it had no beauty of its own—certainly
not the sort of beauty that exists in justice and wisdom, nor such as
is in the mind, memory senses, and the animal life of man; nor yet
the kind that is the glory and beauty of the stars in their courses;
nor the beauty of the earth, or the sea—teeming with spawning
life, replacing in birth that which dies and decays. Indeed, it did
not have that false and shadowy beauty which attends the decep-
tions of vice*.   *wickedness

13. For thus we see pride wearing the mask of high-spiritedness,
although only thou, O God, art high above all. Ambition seeks
honor and glory, whereas only thou shouldst be honored above
all, and glorified forever. The powerful man seeks to be feared,
because of his cruelty; but who ought really to be feared but God
only? What can be forced away or withdrawn out of his power—

when or where or whither. or by whom? The enticements* of the *temptations
wanton* claim the name of love; and yet nothing is more enticing* *pampered *alluring
than thy love, nor is anything loved more healthfully than thy
truth, bright and beautiful above all. Curiosity prompts a desire
for knowledge, whereas it is only thou who knowest all things supremely. Indeed, ignorance and foolishness themselves go masked
under the names of simplicity and innocence; yet there is no being
that has true simplicity like thine, and none is innocent as thou
art. Thus it is that by a sinner's own deeds he is himself harmed.
Human sloth* pretends to long for rest, but what sure rest is there *laziness
save in the Lord? Luxury would fain* be called plenty and abun- *willingly
dance; but thou art the fullness and unfailing abundance of un-
fading joy. Prodigality* presents a show of liberality*; but thou art *wastefulness *generosity
the most lavish* giver of all good things. Covetousness* desires *generous *envious
to possess much; but thou art already the possessor of all things.   greed
Envy contends that its aim is for excellence; but what is so excel-
lent as thou? Anger seeks revenge; but who avenges more justly
than thou? Fear recoils at the unfamiliar and the sudden changes
which threaten things beloved, and is wary for its own security;
but what can happen that is unfamiliar or sudden to thee? Or
who can deprive thee of what thou lovest? Where, really, is there
unshaken security save with thee? Grief languishes* for things lost *weakens
in which desire had taken delight, because it wills to have nothing
taken from it, just as nothing can be taken from thee.

14. Thus the soul commits fornication* when she is turned from *sexual intercourse
thee, and seeks apart from thee what she cannot find pure and un-
tainted until she returns to thee. All things thus imitate thee—but
pervertedly*—when they separate themselves far from thee and *corruptedly
raise themselves up against thee. But, even in this act of perverse
imitation, they acknowledge thee to be the Creator of all nature,
and recognize that there is no place whither they can altogether
separate themselves from thee. What was it, then, that I loved in
that theft? And wherein was I imitating my Lord, even in a corrupted and perverted way? Did I wish, if only by gesture, to rebel
against thy law, even though I had no power to do so actually—so
that, even as a captive, I / might produce a sort of counterfeit* *imitation/fake
liberty, by doing with impunity* deeds that were forbidden, in *freedom

a deluded* sense of omnipotence*? Behold this servant of thine, *deceived *all
fleeing from his Lord and following a shadow! O rottenness! O powerfulness
monstrousness of life and abyss* of death! Could I find pleasure *gaping hole
only in what was unlawful, and only because it was unlawful?

CHAPTER VII

15. "What shall I render unto the Lord"[11] for the fact that while
my memory recalls these things my soul no longer fears them? I
will love thee, O Lord, and thank thee, and confess to thy name,
because thou hast put away from me such wicked and evil deeds.
To thy grace I attribute* it and to thy mercy, that thou hast melted *credit
away my sin as if it were ice. To thy grace also I attribute whatsoever of evil I did not commit—for what might I not have done,
loving sin as I did, just for the sake of sinning? Yea, all the sins
that I confess now to have been forgiven me, both those which I
committed willfully and those which, by thy providence*, I did not *divine guidance
commit. What man is there who, when reflecting upon his own
infirmity*, dares to ascribe* his chastity and innocence to his own *disability *credit
powers, so that he should love thee less—as if he were in less need
of thy mercy in which thou forgivest the transgressions* of those *sins
that return to thee? As for that man who, when called by thee,
obeyed thy voice and shunned* those things which he here reads *rejected
of me as I recall and confess them of myself, let him not despise
me—for I, who was sick, have been healed by the same Physician* *God
by whose aid it was that he did not fall sick, or rather was less sick
than I. And for this let him love thee just as much—indeed, all
the more—since he sees me restored from such a great weakness
of sin by the selfsame Saviour by whom he sees himself preserved
from such a weakness.

CHAPTER VIII

16. What profit did I, a wretched one, receive from those things
which, when I remember them now, cause me shame—above all,
from that theft, which I loved only for the theft's sake? And, as
the theft itself was nothing, I was all the more wretched in that I
loved it so. Yet by myself alone I would not have done it—I still

11. Psalms 116:12.

recall how I felt about this then—I could not have done it alone. I loved it then because of the companionship of my accomplices* with whom I did it. I did not, therefore, love the theft alone—yet, indeed, it was only the theft that I loved, for the companionship was nothing. What is this paradox*? Who is it that can explain it to me but God, who illumines* my heart and searches out the dark corners thereof? What is it that has prompted my mind to inquire about it, to discuss and to reflect upon all this? For had I at that time loved the pears that I stole and wished to enjoy them, I might have done so alone, if I could have been satisfied with the mere act of theft by which my pleasure was served.

*partners in crime

*contradiction
*enlightens

CHAPTER IX

17. By what passion, then, was I animated*? It was undoubtedly depraved* and a great misfortune for me to feel it. But still, what was it? "Who can understand his errors?"[12]

*full of life
*corrupt

We laughed because our hearts were tickled at the thought of deceiving the owners, who had no idea of what we were doing and would have strenuously* objected. Yet, again, why did I find such delight in doing this which I would not have done alone? Is it that no one readily laughs alone? No one does so readily; but still sometimes, when men are by themselves and no one else is about, a fit of laughter will overcome them when something very droll* presents itself to their sense or mind. Yet alone I would not have done it—alone I could not have done it at all.

*aggressively

*humorous

Behold, my God, the lively review of my soul's career is laid bare before thee. I would not have committed that theft alone. My pleasure in it was not what I stole but, rather, the act of stealing. Nor would I have enjoyed doing it alone—indeed I would not have done it! O friendship all unfriendly! You strange seducer of the soul, who hungers for mischief from impulses of mirth* and wantonness*, who craves another's loss without any desire for one's own profit or revenge—so that, when they say, "Let's go, let's do it," we are ashamed not to be shameless.

*cheerfulness
*lewdness

12. Psalms 19:12.

CHAPTER X

18. Who can unravel such a twisted and tangled knottiness? It is unclean. I hate to reflect upon it. I hate to look on it. But I do long for thee, O Righteousness and Innocence, so beautiful and comely to all virtuous eyes—I long for thee with an insatiable satiety*.   *unable to be satisfied
With thee is perfect rest, and life unchanging. He who enters into thee enters into the joy of his Lord,[13] and shall have no fear and shall achieve excellence in the Excellent. I fell away from thee, O my God, and in my youth I wandered too far from thee, my true support. And I became to myself a wasteland.

BOOK EIGHT

Conversion to Christ. Augustine is deeply impressed by his friend Simplicianus' story of the conversion to Christ of the famous orator and philosopher, Marius Victorinus. He is stirred to imitate him, but finds himself still imprisoned by his inability to control his sexual desires and his preoccupation with worldly affairs. He is then visited by a court official, Ponticianus, who tells him and his friend Alypius the stories of the conversion of Anthony and also of two imperial "secret service agents." These stories throw him into a violent turmoil, in which his divided will struggles against himself. He almost succeeds in making the decision for controlling his sexual appetites, but is still held back. Finally, a child's song, overheard by chance, sends him to the Bible; a text from St. Paul resolves the crisis; the conversion is a fact. Alypius also makes his decision, and the two inform his rejoicing mother, Monica.

CHAPTER I

1. O my God, let me remember with gratitude and confess to thee thy mercies toward me. Let my bones be bathed in thy love, and let them say: "Lord, who is like unto thee?[14] Thou hast broken my bonds in sunder*, I will offer unto thee the sacrifice of thanksgiv-   *two
ing."[15] And how thou didst break them I will declare, and all who

13. See Matthew 25:21.

14. Psalms 35:10.

15. See Psalms 116: 16, 17.

worship thee shall say, when they hear these things: "Blessed be the Lord in heaven and earth, great and wonderful is his name."[16]

Thy words had stuck fast in my breast, and I was hedged* round about by thee on every side. Of thy eternal life I was now certain, although I had seen it "through a glass darkly."[17] And I had been relieved of all doubt that there is an incorruptible* substance and that it is the source of every other substance. Nor did I any longer crave greater certainty about thee, but rather greater steadfastness* in thee. But as for my temporal* life, everything was uncertain, and my heart had to be purged of the old leaven*. "The Way"—the Saviour himself—pleased me well, but as yet I was reluctant to pass through the strait* gate. ,

*surrounded

*not corruptible

*loyalty
*earthly
*yeast

*narrow, strict

And thou didst put it into my mind, and it seemed good in my own sight, to go to Simplicianus, who appeared to me a faithful servant of thine, and thy grace shone forth in him. I had also been told that from his youth up he had lived in entire devotion to thee. He was already an old man, and because of his great age, which he had passed in such a zealous discipleship* in thy way, he appeared to me likely to have gained much wisdom—and, indeed, he had. From all his experience, I desired him to tell me—setting before him all my agitations*—which would be the most fitting. way for one who felt as I did to walk in thy way.

*enthusiasticfollower

*anxieties

2. For I saw the Church full; and one man was going this way and another that. Still, I could not be satisfied with the life I was living in the world. Now, indeed, my passions had ceased to excite me as of old with hopes of honor and wealth, and it was a grievous* burden to go on in such servitude*. For, compared with thy sweetness and the beauty of thy house—which I loved—those things delighted me no longer. But I was still tightly bound by the love of women; nor did the apostle*, forbid me to marry, although he exhorted* me to something better, wishing earnestly that all men were as he himself was.

*serious
*slavery

*disciple, follower
*urged

16. See Psalms 8:1.

17. 1 Corinthians 13:12.

But I was weak and chose the easier way, and for this single reason my whole life was one of inner turbulence and listless* indecision, because from so many influences I was compelled—even though unwilling—to agree to a married life which bound me hand and foot. I had heard from the mouth of Truth that "there are eunuchs* who have made themselves eunuchs for the Kingdom of Heaven's sake"[18] but, said he, "He that is able to receive it, let him receive it." Of a certainty, all men are vain* who do not have the knowledge of God, or have not been able, from the good things that are seen, to find him who is good. But I was no longer fettered* in that vanity*. I had surmounted* it, and from the united testimony* of thy whole creation had found thee, our Creator, and thy Word—God with thee, and together with thee and the Holy Spirit, one God—by whom thou hast created all things. There is still another sort of wicked men, who "when they knew God, they glorified him not as God, neither were thankful."[19] Into this also I had fallen, but thy right hand held me up and bore* me away, and thou didst place me where I might recover. For thou hast said to men, "Behold the fear of the Lord, this is wisdom,"[20] and, "Be not wise in your own eyes,"[21] because "they that profess themselves to be wise become fools."[22] But I had now found the goodly pearl; and I ought to have sold all that I had and bought it—yet I hesitated.

*lacking energy

*castrated male

*prideful

*imprisoned *pride
*overcome *proof

*carried

CHAPTER II

3. I went, therefore, to Simplicianus, the spiritual father of Ambrose (then a bishop), whom Ambrose truly loved as a father. I recounted* to him all the mazes of my wanderings, but when I mentioned to him that I had read certain books of the Platonists which Victorinus—formerly professor of rhetoric at Rome, who died a Christian, as I had been told—had translated into Latin, Simplicianus congratulated me that I had not fallen upon the

*told

18. Matthew 19:12.

19. Romans 1:21.

20. Job 28:28.

21. Proverbs 3:7.

22. Romans 1:22.

writings of other philosophers, which were full of fallacies* and   *errors
deceit, "after the beggarly* elements of this world,"²³ whereas in   *poverty-stricken
the Platonists, at every turn, the pathway led to belief in God and
his Word.

Then, to encourage me to copy the humility* of Christ, which   *humbleness
is hidden from the wise and revealed to babes, he told me about
Victorinus himself, whom he had known intimately at Rome. And
I cannot refrain from* repeating what he told me about him. For it   *stop
contains a glorious proof of thy grace, which ought to be confessed
to thee: how that old man, most learned, most skilled in all the
liberal arts; who had read, criticized, and explained so many of the
writings of the philosophers; the teacher of so many noble sena-
tors; one who, as a mark of his distinguished service in office had
both merited* and obtained a statue in the Roman Forum—which   *earned
men of this world esteem* a great honor—this man who, up to an   *valued highly
advanced age, had been a worshiper of idols, a communicant in the
sacrilegious* rites to which almost all the nobility of Rome were   *against religious
wedded; and who had inspired the people with the love of Osiris
and "The dog Anubis, and a medley crew Of monster gods who
'gainst Neptune stand in arms 'Gainst Venus and Minerva, steel-
clad Mars,"²⁴ whom Rome once conquered, and now worshiped;
all of which old Victorinus had with thundering eloquence* de-   *persuasiveness
fended for so many years—despite all this, he did not blush to
become a child of thy Christ, a babe at thy font, bowing his neck
to the yoke of humility and submitting his forehead to the igno-
miny* of the cross.   *humiliation

4. O Lord, Lord, "who didst bow the heavens and didst descend,
who didst touch the mountains and they smoked,"²⁵ by what
means didst thou find thy way into that breast? He used to read
the Holy Scriptures, as Simplicianus said, and thought out and
studied all the Christian writings most studiously*. He said to   *seriously
Simplicianus—not openly but secretly as a friend—"You must

23. Colossians 2:8.

24. Virgil, *Aeneid*, VIII, 698.

25. Psalms 144:5.

know that I am a Christian." To which Simplicianus replied, "I shall not believe it, nor shall I count you among the Christians, until I see you in the Church of Christ." Victorinus then asked, with mild mockery, "Is it then the walls that make Christians?" Thus he often would affirm* that he was already a Christian, and as often Simplicianus made the same answer; and just as often his jest* about the walls was repeated. He was fearful of offending his friends, proud demon worshipers, from the height of whose Babylonian dignity, as from the tops of the cedars of Lebanon which the Lord had not yet broken down, he feared that a storm of enmity* would descend upon him. But he steadily gained strength from reading and inquiry*, and came to fear lest he should be denied by Christ before the holy angels if he now was afraid to confess him before men. Thus he came to appear to himself guilty of a great fault, in being ashamed of the sacraments of the humility* of thy Word, when he was not ashamed of the sacrilegious rites* of those proud demons, whose pride he had imitated and whose rites he had shared. From this he became bold-faced against vanity* and shamefaced toward the truth. Thus, suddenly and unexpectedly, he said to Simplicianus—as he himself told me—"Let us go to the church; I wish to become a Christian." Simplicianus went with him, scarcely able to contain himself for joy. He was admitted to the first sacraments* of instruction, and not long afterward gave in his name that he might receive the baptism of regeneration*. At this Rome marveled and the Church rejoiced. The proud saw and were enraged; they gnashed their teeth and melted away! But the Lord God was thy servant's hope and he paid no attention to their vanity and lying madness*.

*confirm

*joke

*hatred

*research

*humbleness
*rituals
-
*pride

*Christian rituals
*spiritual renewal

*insanity

5. Finally, when the hour arrived for him to make a public profession of his faith—which at Rome those who are about to enter into thy grace make from a platform in the full sight of the faithful people, in a set form of words learned by heart—the presbyters* offered Victorinus the chance to make his profession more privately, for this was the custom for some who were likely to be afraid through bashfulness*. But Victorinus chose rather to profess his salvation in the presence of the holy congregation. For there was no salvation in the rhetoric* which he taught: yet he had

*priests

*shyness

*persuasive speaking

professed that openly. Why, then, should he shrink* from naming thy Word before the sheep of thy flock, when he had not shrunk* from uttering his own words before the mad multitude*?

*fearfully avoid
*fearfully avoided
*insane crowd

So, then, when he ascended the platform to make his profession, everyone, as they recognized him, whispered his name one to the other, in tones of jubilation*. Who was there among them that did not know him? And a low murmur ran through the mouths of all the rejoicing multitude*: "Victorinus! Victorinus!" There was a sudden burst of exaltation* at the sight of him, and suddenly they were hushed that they might hear him. He pronounced the true faith with an excellent boldness, and all desired to take him to their very heart—indeed, by their love and joy they did take him to their heart. And they received him with loving and joyful hands.

*joy

*happy crowd
*celebration

CHAPTER III

6. O good God, what happens in a man to make him rejoice more at the salvation of a soul that has been despaired of* and then de-livered from greater danger than over one who has never lost hope, or never been in such imminent* danger? For thou also, O most merciful Father, "dost rejoice more over one that repents* than over ninety and nine just persons that need no repentance*."[26] And we listen with much delight whenever we hear how the lost sheep is brought home again on the shepherd's shoulders while the angels rejoice; or when the piece of money is restored to its place in the treasury* and the neighbors rejoice with the woman who found it.[27] And the joy of the solemn* festival of thy house constrains us to tears when it is read in thy house: about the younger son who "was dead and is alive again, was lost and is found." For it is thou who rejoices both in us and in thy angels, who are holy through holy love. For thou art ever the same because thou knowest un-changeably all things which remain neither the same nor forever. 7. What, then, happens in the soul when it takes more delight at finding or having restored to it the things it loves than if it had always possessed them? Indeed, many other things bear witness

*hopeless

*threatening

*regrets

*secure place
*serious

26. Luke 15:4.

27. See Luke, Ch. 15.

that this is so—all things are full of witnesses, crying out, "So it is. "The commander triumphs in victory; yet he could not have conquered if he had not fought; and the greater the peril of the battle, the more the joy of the triumph. The storm tosses the voyagers, threatens shipwreck, and everyone turns pale in the presence of death. Then the sky and sea grow calm, and they rejoice as much as they had feared. A loved one is sick and his pulse indicates danger; all who desire his safety are themselves sick at heart; he recovers, though not able as yet to walk with his former strength; and there is more joy now than there was before when he walked sound and strong. Indeed, the very pleasures of human life—not only those which rush upon us unexpectedly and involuntarily*, *without choice but also those which are voluntary* and planned—men obtain by *by choice difficulties. There is no pleasure in caring and drinking unless the pains of hunger and thirst have preceded. Drunkards even eat certain salt meats in order to create a painful thirst— and when the drink allays this, it causes pleasure. It is also the custom that the affianced* bride should not be immediately given in marriage so *engaged that the husband may not esteem her any less, whom as his betrothed* he longed for. *fiancee

8. This can be seen in the case of base* and dishonorable pleasure. *low But it is also apparent in pleasures that are permitted and lawful: in the sincerity of honest friendship; and in him who was dead and lived again, who had been lost and was found. The greater joy is everywhere preceded by the greater pain. What does this mean, O Lord my God, when thou art an everlasting joy to thyself, and some creatures about thee are ever rejoicing in thee? What does it mean that this portion of creation thus ebbs and flows, alternately in want and satiety*? Is this their mode & of being and is this all *need & fullness thou hast allotted to them: that, from the highest heaven to the lowest earth, from the beginning of the world to the end, from the angels to the worm, from the first movement to the last, thou wast assigning to all their proper places and their proper seasons—to all the kinds of good things and to all thy just works? Alas, how high thou art in the highest and how deep in the deepest! Thou never departest from us, and yet only with difficulty do we return to thee.

CHAPTER IV

9. Go on, O Lord, and act: stir us up and call us back; inflame* *excite
us and draw us to thee; stir us up and grow sweet to us; let us
now love thee, let us run to thee. Are there not many men who,
out of a deeper pit of darkness than that of Victorinus, return to
thee—who draw near to thee and are illuminated by that light
which gives those who receive it power from thee to become thy
sons? But if they are less well-known, even those who know them
rejoice* less for them. For when many rejoice together the joy of *celebrate
each one is fuller, in that they warm one another, catch fire from
each other; moreover, those who are well-known influence many
toward salvation and take the lead with many to follow them.
Therefore, even those who took the way before them rejoice over
them greatly, because they do not rejoice over them alone. But it
ought never to be that in thy tabernacle* the persons of the rich *place of worship
should be welcome before the poor, or the nobly born before the
rest—since "thou hast rather chosen the weak things of the world
to confound* the strong; and hast chosen the base things of the *confuse
world and things that are despised, and the things that are not, in
order to bring to nought* the things that are."[28] It was even "the *nothing
least of the apostles*" by whose tongue thou didst sound forth *Jesus' disciples
these words. And when Paulus the proconsul* had his pride over- *governor
come by the onslaught of the apostle and he was made to pass
under the easy yoke* of thy Christ and became an officer of the *servitude
great King, he also desired to be called Paul instead of Saul, his
former name, in testimony to such a great victory. For the enemy is
more overcome in one on whom he has a greater hold, and whom
he has hold of more completely. But the proud he controls more
readily through their concern about their rank and, through them,
he controls more by means of their influence. The more, therefore,
the world prized the heart of Victorinus (which the devil had held
in an impregnable stronghold*) and the tongue of Victorinus (that *bulletproof fort
sharp, strong weapon with which the devil had slain so many), all
the more exultingly* should Thy sons rejoice because our King *enthusiastically
hath bound* the strong man, and they saw his vessels* taken from *tied up *Victorinus'
heart and tongue

28. 1 Corinthians 1:27.

him and cleansed, and made fit for 'thy honor and "profitable to the Lord for every good work. "[29]

CHAPTER V

10. Now when this man of thine, Simplicianus, told me the story of Victorinus, I was eager to imitate him. Indeed, this was Simplicianus' purpose in telling it to me. But when he went on to tell how, in the reign of the Emperor Julian*, there was a law passed by which Christians were forbidden to teach literature and .. rhetoric; and how Victorinus, in ready obedience to the law, chose to abandon his "school of words" rather than thy Word, by which thou makest eloquent the tongues of the dumb—he appeared to me not so much brave as happy, because he had found a reason for giving his time wholly to thee. For this was what I was longing to do; but as yet I was bound by the iron chain of my own will. The enemy held fast my will, and had made of it a chain, and had bound me tight with it. For out of the perverse will came lust, and the service of lust ended in habit, and habit, not resisted, became necessity. By these links, as it were, forged together—which is why I called it "a chain"—a hard bondage held me in slavery. But that new will which had begun to spring up in me freely to worship thee and to enjoy thee, O my God, the only certain Joy, was not able as yet to overcome my former willfulness, made strong by long indulgence*. Thus my two wills—the old and the new, the carnal* and the spiritual—were in conflict within me; and by their discord they tore my soul apart.

*Roman Emperor (361–363) A.D.

*sympathy

*bodily

11. Thus I came to understand from my own experience what I had read, how "the flesh lusts against the Spirit, and the Spirit against the flesh. "[30] I truly lusted both ways, yet more in that which I approved in myself than in that which I disapproved in myself. For in the latter it was not now really I that was involved, because here I was rather an unwilling sufferer than a willing actor. And yet it was through me that habit had become an armed enemy against

29. 2 Timothy 2:21.

30. Galatians 5:17.

me, because I had willingly come to be what I unwillingly found myself to be.

Who, then, can with any justice speak against it, when just punishment follows the sinner? I had now no longer my accustomed* excuse that, as yet, I hesitated to forsake* the world and serve thee because my perception of the truth was uncertain. For now it was certain. But, still bound to the earth, I refused to be thy soldier; and was as much afraid of being freed from all entanglements* as we ought to fear to be entangled*.

*usual

*give up

*

traps

*trapped

12. Thus with the baggage* of the world I was sweetly burdened, as one in Slumber*, and my musings* on thee were like the efforts of those who desire to awake, but who are still overpowered with drowsiness and fall back into deep slumber. And as no one wishes to sleep forever (for all men rightly count waking better)—yet a man will usually defer* shaking off his drowsiness when there is a heavy lethargy* in his limbs; and he is glad to sleep on even when his reason disapproves, and the hour for rising has struck—so was I assured that it was much better for me to give myself up to thy love than to go on yielding* myself to my own lust. Thy love satisfied and vanquished* me; my lust pleased and fettered* me. I had no answer to thy calling to me, "Awake, you who sleep, and arise from the dead, and Christ shall give you light."[31] On all sides, thou didst show me that thy words are true, and I, convicted* by the truth, had nothing at all to reply but the drawling and drowsy words: "Presently; see, presently. Leave me alone a little while." But "presently, presently," had no present; and my "leave me alone a little while" went on for a long while. In vain* did I "delight in thy law in the inner man" while "another law in my members* warred against the law of my mind and brought me into captivity* to the law of sin which is in my members." For the law of sin is the tyranny* of habit, by which the mind is drawn and held, even against its will. Yet it deserves to be so held because it so willingly falls into the habit. "O wretched man that I am! Who shall deliver

*burdens

*sleep *thoughts

*put off

*sluggishness

*giving into

*MISSING

*chained

*proven guilty

*hopelessly

*body parts

*prison

*oppression

31. Ephesians 5:14.

me from the body of this death" but thy grace alone, through Jesus Christ our Lord? [32]

CHAPTER VI

13. And now I will tell and confess unto thy name, O Lord, my helper and my redeemer, how thou didst deliver me from the chain of sexual desire by which I was so tightly held, and from the slavery of worldly business. With increasing anxiety I was going about my usual affairs, and daily sighing to thee. I attended thy church as frequently as my business, under the burden of which I groaned, left me free to do so. Alypius was with me, disengaged* at last from *free his legal post, after a third term as assessor*, and now waiting for *judge's assistant private clients to whom he might sell his legal ' advice as I sold the power of speaking (as if it could be supplied by teaching). But Nebridius had consented*, for the sake of our friendship, to teach *agreed under Verecundus—a citizen of Milan and professor of grammar, and a very intimate friend of us all— who ardently* desired, and by *passionately right of friendship demanded from us, the faithful aid he greatly needed. Nebridius was not drawn to this by any desire of gain— for he could have made much more out of his learning had he been so inclined—but as he was a most sweet and kindly friend, he was unwilling, out of respect for the duties of friendship, to slight* our *carelessly perform request. But in this he acted very discreetly*, taking care not to *carefully become known to those persons who had great reputations in the world. Thus he avoided all distractions of mind, and reserved as many hours as possible to pursue or read or listen to discussions about wisdom.

14. On a certain day, then, when Nebridius was away—for some reason I cannot remember—there came to visit Alypius and me at our house one Ponticianus, a fellow countryman of ours from Africa, who held high office in the emperor's court. What he wanted with us I do not know; but we sat down to talk together, and it chanced that he noticed a book on a game table before us. He took it up, opened it, and, contrary to his expectation, found it to be the apostle Paul, for he imagined that it was one of my wea-

32. Romans 7:22–25.

risome rhetoric textbooks. At this, he looked up me with a smile and expressed his delight and wonder that he had so unexpectedly found this book and only this one, lying before my eyes; for he was indeed a Christian and a faithful one at that, and often he prostrated* himself before thee, our God, in the church in constant daily prayer. When I had told him that I had given much attention to these writings, a conversation followed in which he spoke of Anthony, the Egyptian monk, whose name was in high repute* among thy servants, although up to that time not familiar to me. When he learned this, he lingered* on the topic, giving us an account of this eminent* man, and marveling at our ignorance. We in turn were amazed to hear of thy wonderful works so fully manifested* in recent times—almost in our own—occurring in the true faith and the Catholic Church. We all wondered—we, that these things were so great, and he, that we had never heard of them.

*knelt in submission

*well respected

*stayed

*respected

*made visible

15. From this, his conversation turned to the multitudes* in the monasteries and their manners so fragrant to thee, and to the teeming* solitudes of the wilderness, of which we knew nothing at all. There was even a monastery at Milan, outside the city's walls, full of good brothers under the fostering* care of Ambrose—and we were ignorant of it. He went on with his story, and we listened intently and in silence. He then told us how, on a certain afternoon, at Trier, when the emperor was occupied watching the gladiatorial* games, he and three comrades went' out for a walk in the gardens close to the city walls. There, as they chanced to walk two by two, one strolled away with him, while the other two went on by themselves. As they rambled*, these first two came upon a certain cottage where lived some of thy servants, some of the "poor in spirit" ("of such is the Kingdom of Heaven"), where they found the book in which was written the life of Anthony! One of them began to read it, to marvel and to be inflamed* by it. While reading, he meditated on embracing* just such a life, giving up his worldly employment to seek thee alone. These two belonged to the group of officials called "secret service agents." Then, suddenly being overwhelmed with a holy love and a sober shame and as if in anger with himself, he fixed his eyes on his friend,

*many people

*abundant

*parent-like

*gladiators'

*walked

*excited
*taking up

exclaiming: "Tell me, I beg you, what goal are we seeking in all these toils of ours? What is it that we desire? What is our motive in public service? Can our hopes in the court rise higher than to be 'friends of the emperor'? But how frail*, how beset with peril*, *fragile *dangerous is that pride! Through what dangers must we climb to a greater danger? And when shall we succeed? But if I chose to become a friend of God, see, I can become one now." Thus he spoke, and in the pangs of the travail* of the new life he turned his eyes again *hardships onto the page and continued reading; he was inwardly changed, as thou didst see, and the world dropped away from his mind, as soon became plain to others. For as he read with a heart like a stormy sea, more than once he groaned. Finally he saw the better course, and resolved on it. Then, having become thy servant, he said to his friend: "Now I have broken loose from those hopes we had, and I am determined to serve God; and I enter into that service from this hour in this place. If you are reluctant to imitate me, do not oppose me." The other replied that he would continue bound in his friendship, to share in so great a service for so great a prize. So both became thine, and began to "build a tower", counting the cost—namely, of forsaking* all that they had and following thee[33]. *giving up Shortly after, Ponticianus and his companion, who had walked with him in the other part of the garden, came in search of them to the same place, and having found them reminded them to return, as the day was declining*. But the first two, making known *evening to Ponticianus their resolution* and purpose, and how a resolve *decision had sprung up and become confirmed in them, entreated* them *asked not to take it ill if they refused to join themselves with them. But Ponticianus and his friend, although not changed from their former course, did nevertheless (as he told us) bewail* themselves *feel sorrow and congratulated their friends on their godliness, recommending themselves to their prayers. And with hearts inclining again toward earthly things, they returned to the palace. But the other two, setting their affections on heavenly things, remained in the cottage. Both of them had affianced* brides who, when they heard *engaged of this, likewise dedicated their virginity to thee.

33. See Luke 14:28–33.

CHAPTER VII

16. Such was the story Ponticianus told. But while he was speaking, thou, O Lord, turned me toward myself, taking me from behind my back, where I had put myself while unwilling to exercise self-scrutiny*. And now thou didst set me face to - face with myself, that I might see how ugly I was, and how crooked and sordid*, bespotted and ulcerous. And I looked and I loathed* myself; but whither to fly from myself I could not discover. And if I sought to turn my gaze away from myself, he would continue his narrative, and thou wouldst oppose me to myself and thrust me before my own eyes that I might discover my iniquity* and hate it. I had known it, but acted as though I knew it not—I winked* at it and forgot it.

*self-examination
*filthy
*hated

*sin
*ignored

17. But now, the more ardently* I loved those whose wholesome affections I heard reported—that they had given themselves up wholly to thee to be cured—the more did I abhor* myself when compared with them. For many of my years—perhaps twelve— had passed away since my nineteenth, when, upon the reading of Cicero's Hortensius, I was roused* to a desire for wisdom. And here I was, still postponing the abandonment of this world's happiness to devote myself to the search. For not just the finding alone, but also the bare search for it, ought to have been preferred above the treasures and kingdoms of this world; better than all bodily pleasures, though they were to be had for the taking. But, wretched* youth that I was—supremely wretched even in the very outset of my youth—I had entreated chastity* of thee and had prayed, "Grant me chastity and continence*, but not yet. " For I was afraid lest*-thou shouldst hear me too soon, and too soon cure me of my disease of lust which I desired to have satisfied rather than extinguished. And I had wandered through perverse ways of godless superstition—not really sure of it, either, but preferring it to the other, which I did not seek in piety*, but opposed in malice*.

*passionately

*hate

*awakened

*miserable
*sexual purity
*self-restraint
*for fear that

*faith
*hatefulness

18. And I had thought that I delayed from day to day in rejecting those worldly hopes and following thee alone because there did not appear anything certain by which I could direct my course. And now the day had arrived in which I was laid bare to my-

self and my conscience was to chide* me: "Where are you, O my   *scold
tongue? You said indeed that you were not willing to cast off the
baggage* of vanity for uncertain truth. But behold now it is cer-   *burden
tain, and still that burden oppresses you. At the same time those
who have not worn themselves out with searching for it as you
have, nor spent ten years and more in thinking about it, have had
their shoulders unburdened and have received wings to fly away.
"Thus was I inwardly confused, and mightily confounded* with   *confused
a horrible shame, while Ponticianus went ahead speaking such
things. And when he had finished his story and the business he
came for, he went his way. And then what did I not say to myself,
within myself? With what scourges* of rebuke* did I not lash my   *punishment *disapproval
soul to make it follow me, as I was struggling to go after thee?
Yet it drew back. It refused. It would not make an effort. All its
arguments were exhausted and confuted*. Yet it resisted in sullen*   *refuted *gloomy
disquiet, fearing the cutting off of that habit by which it was being
wasted to death, as if that were death itself.

CHAPTER VIII

19. Then, as this vehement* quarrel, which I waged with my soul   *forceful
in the chamber of my heart, was raging inside my inner dwelling,
agitated* both in mind and countenance*, I seized upon Alyp-   *disturbed *expression
ius and exclaimed: "What is the matter with us? What is this?
What did you hear? The uninstructed start up and take heaven,
and we—with all our learning but so little heart—see where we
wallow* in flesh and blood! Because others have gone before us,   *roll around
are we ashamed to follow, and not rather ashamed at our not following?" I scarcely knew what I said, and in my excitement I flung
away from him, while he gazed at me in silent astonishment. For I
did not sound like myself: my face, eyes, color, tone expressed my
meaning more clearly than my words.

There was a little garden belonging to our lodging, of which we
had the use— as of the whole house—for the master, our landlord,
did not live there. The tempest* in my breast hurried me out into   *storm
this garden, where no one might interrupt the fiery struggle in
which I was engaged with myself, until it came to the outcome
that thou knewest though I did not. But I was mad for health,

and dying for life; knowing what evil thing I was, but not knowing what good thing I was so shortly to become.

I fled into the garden, with Alypius following step by step; for I had no secret in which he did not share, and how could he leave me in such distress? We sat down, as far from the house as possible. I was greatly disturbed in spirit, angry at myself with a turbulent indignation* because I had not entered thy will and covenant*, O my God, while all my bones cried out to me to enter, extolling* it to the skies. The way therein is not by ships or chariots or feet— indeed it was not as far as I had come from the house to the place where we were seated. For to go along that road and indeed to reach the goal is nothing else but the will to go. But it must be a strong and single will, not staggering and swaying about this way and that—a changeable, twisting, fluctuating* will, wrestling with itself while one part falls as another rises.

*outrage   *sacred promise
*praising
*changing

20. Finally, in the very fever of my indecision, I made many motions with my body; like men do when they will to act but cannot, either because they do not have the limbs or because their limbs are bound or weakened by disease, or incapacitated* in some other way. Thus if I tore my hair, struck my forehead, or, entwining my fingers, clasped my knee, these I did because I willed it. But I might have willed it and still not have done it, if the nerves had not obeyed my will. Many things then I did, in which the will and power to do were not the same. Yet I did not do that one thing which seemed to me infinitely more desirable, which before long I should have power to will because shortly when I willed, I would will with a single will. For in this, the power of willing is the power of doing; and as yet I could not do it. Thus my body more readily obeyed the slightest wish of the soul in moving its limbs at the order of my mind than my soul obeyed itself to accomplish in the will alone its great resolve.

*disabled

CHAPTER IX

21. How can there be such a strange anomaly*? And why is it? Let thy mercy shine on me, that I may inquire and find an answer, amid the dark labyrinth* of human punishment and in the dark-

*abnormality

*maze

est contritions* of the sons of Adam. Whence such an anomaly?   *repentances
And why should it be? The mind commands the body, and the
body obeys. The mind commands itself and is resisted. The mind
commands the hand to be moved and there is such readiness that
the command is scarcely distinguished from the obedience in act.
Yet the mind is mind, and the hand is body. The mind commands
the mind to will, and yet though it be itself it does not obey itself.
Whence this strange anomaly and why should it be? I repeat: The
will commands itself to will, and could not give the command unless it wills; yet what is commanded is not done. But actually the
will does not will entirely; therefore it does not command entirely.
For as far as it wills, it commands. And as far as it does not will, the
thing commanded is not done. For the will commands that there
be an act of will—not another, but itself. But it does not command
entirely. Therefore, what is commanded does not happen; for if
the will were whole and entire, it would not even command it to
be, because it would already be. It is, therefore, no strange anomaly
partly to will and partly to be unwilling. This is actually an infir-   *disability
mity* of mind, which cannot wholly rise, while pressed down by
habit, even though it is supported by the truth. And so there are
two wills, because one of them is not whole, and what is present
in this one is lacking in the other.

CHAPTER X

22. Let them perish from thy presence, O God, as vain* talkers,   *prideful
and deceivers of the soul perish, who, when they observe that there
are two wills in the act of deliberation*, go on to affirm* that there   *study *confirm
are two kinds of minds in us: one good, the other evil. They are
indeed themselves evil when they hold these evil opinions—and
they shall become good only when they come to hold the truth
and consent to the truth that thy apostle may say to them: "You
were formerly in darkness, but now are you in the light in the
Lord. "[34] But they desired to be light, not "in the Lord," but in
themselves. They conceived the nature of the soul to be the same
as what God is, and thus have become a thicker darkness than they
were; for in their dread arrogance* they have gone farther away   *self-importance

34. Ephesians 5:8.

from thee, from thee "the true Light, that - lights every man that comes into the world." Mark what you say and blush for shame; draw near to him and be enlightened, and your faces shall not be ashamed. [35] While I was deliberating* whether I would serve the Lord my God now, as I had long purposed to do, it was I who willed and it was also I who was unwilling. In either case, it was I. I neither willed with my whole will nor was I wholly unwilling. And so I was at war with myself and torn apart by myself. And this strife was against my will; yet it did not show the presence of another mind, but the punishment of my own. Thus it was no more I who did it, but the sin that dwelt* in me—the punishment of a sin freely committed by Adam, and I was a son of Adam.

*thinking

*lived

23. For if there are as many opposing natures as there are opposing wills, there will not be two but many more. If any man is trying to decide whether he should go to their conventicle* or to the theater, the Manicheans at once cry out, "See, here are two natures—one good, drawing this way, another bad, drawing back that way; for how else can you explain this indecision between conflicting wills?" But I reply that both impulses are bad—that which draws to them and that which draws back to the theater. But they do not believe that the will which draws to them can be anything but good. Suppose, then, that one of us should try to decide, and through the conflict of his two wills should waver* whether he should go to the theater or to our Church. Would not those also waver about the answer here? For either they must confess, which they are unwilling to do, that the will that leads to our church is as good as that which carries their own adherents* and those captivated* by their mysteries; or else they must imagine that there are two evil natures and two evil minds in one man, both at war with each other, and then it will not be true what they say, that there is one good and another bad. Else they must be converted to the truth, and no longer deny that when anyone deliberates there is one soul fluctuating between conflicting wills.

*meeting

*hesitate

*followers
*enthralled

35. See Psalms 34:5.

24. Let them no longer maintain that when they perceive two wills to be Contending* with each other in the same man the contest is between two opposing minds, of two opposing substances, from two opposing principles, the one good and the other bad. Thus, O true God, thou dost reprove* and confute* and convict them. For both wills may be bad: as when a man tries to decide whether he should kill a man by poison or by the sword; whether he should take possession of this field or that one belonging to someone else, when he cannot get both; whether he should squander* his money to buy pleasure or hold onto his money through the motive of covetousness*; whether he should go to the circus or to the theater, if both are open on the same day; or, whether he should take a third course, open at the same time, and rob another man's house; or, a fourth option, whether he should commit adultery*, if he has the opportunity—all these things concurring in the same space of time and all being equally longed for, although impossible to do at one time. For the mind is pulled four ways by four antagonistic* wills—or even more, in view of the vast range of human desires—but even the Manicheans do not affirm that there are these many different substances. The same principle applies as in the action of good wills. For I ask them, "Is it a good thing to have delight in reading the apostle, or is it a good thing to delight in a sober psalm*, or is it a good thing to discourse* on the gospel?" To each of these, they will answer, "It is good." But what, then, if all delight us equally and all at the same time? Do not different wills distract* the mind when a man is trying to decide what he should choose? Yet they are all good, and are at variance* with each other until one is chosen. When this is done the whole united will may go forward on a single track instead of remaining as it was before, divided in many ways. So also, when eternity attracts us from above, and the pleasure of earthly delight pulls us down from below, the soul does not will either the one or the other with all its force, but still it is the same soul that does not will this or that with a united will, and is therefore pulled apart with grievous perplexities*, because for truth's sake it prefers this, but for custom's sake it does not lay that aside.

*Opposing

*scold *prove wrong

*waste

*envy

*sex outside of marriage

*opposing

*sacred song *talk

*lose focus

*opposed

*confusion

CHAPTER XI

25. Thus I was sick and tormented, reproaching* myself more bitterly than ever, rolling and writhing* in my chain till it should be utterly broken. By now I was held but slightly, but still was held. And thou, O Lord, didst press upon me in my inmost heart with a severe mercy, redoubling* the lashes* of fear and shame; lest I should again give way and that same slender remaining tie not be broken off, but recover strength and enchain* me yet more securely.

*scolding

*wriggling in pain

*doubling *whippings

*chain

I kept saying to myself, "See, let it be done now; let it be done now." And as I said this I all but came to a firm decision. I all but did it—yet I did not quite. Still I did not fall back to my old condition, but stood aside for a moment and drew breath. And I tried again, and lacked only a very little of reaching the resolve— and then somewhat less, and then all but touched and grasped it. Yet I still did not quite reach or touch or grasp the goal, because I hesitated to die to death and to live to life. And the worse way, to which I was habituated*, was stronger in me than the better, which I had not tried. And up to the very moment in which I was to become another man, the nearer the moment approached, the greater horror did it strike in me. But it did not strike me back, nor turn me aside, but held me in suspense.

*accustomed to

26. It was, in fact, my old mistresses, trifles of trifles* and vanities of vanities*, who still enthralled* me. They tugged at my fleshly garments and softly whispered: "Are you going to part with us? And from that moment will we never be with you any more? And from that moment will not this and that be forbidden you forever? "What were they suggesting to me in those words "this or that"? What is it they suggested, O my God? Let thy mercy guard the soul of thy servant from the vileness* and the shame they did suggest! And now I scarcely heard them, for they were not openly showing themselves and opposing me face to face; but muttering, as it were, behind my back; and furtively* plucking at me as I was leaving, trying to make me look back at them. Still they delayed me, so that I hesitated to break loose and shake myself free of them and leap over to the place to which I was being called—for

*trivial things

*egoisms *hypnotized

*foulness

*sneakily

unruly habit kept saying to me, "Do you think you can live without them?"

27. But now it said this very faintly; for in the direction I had set my face, and yet toward which I still trembled to go, the chaste* dignity of continence* appeared to - me—cheerful but not wanton*, modestly alluring* me to come and doubt nothing, * extending her holy hands, full of a multitude of good examples—to receive and embrace me. There were there so many young men and maidens, a multitude of youth and every age, grave widows and ancient virgins; and continence* herself in - their midst: not barren, but a fruitful mother of children—her joys—by thee, O Lord, her husband. And she smiled on me with a challenging smile as if to say: "Can you not do what these young men and maidens can? Or can any of them do it of themselves, and not rather in the Lord their God? The Lord their God gave me to them. Why do you stand in your own strength, and so stand not? Cast* yourself on him; fear not. He will not flinch* and you will not fall. Cast yourself on him without fear, for he will receive and heal you. " And I blushed violently, for I still heard the muttering of those "trifles" and hung suspended. Again she seemed to speak: "Stop your ears against those unclean members of yours, that they may be mortified*. They tell you of delights, but not according to the law of the Lord thy God." This struggle raging in my heart was nothing but the contest of self against self. And Alypius kept close beside me, and awaited in silence the outcome of my extraordinary agitation*.

*pure
*self-restraint
*lustful *attracting

*self-restraint

*Throw
*shrink back

*ashamed

*turmoil

CHAPTER XII

28. Now when deep reflection had drawn up out of the secret depths of my soul all my misery and had heaped it up before the sight of my heart, there arose a mighty storm, accompanied by a mighty rain of tears. That I might give way fully to my tears and lamentations*, I stole away from Alypius, for it seemed to me that solitude was more appropriate for the business of weeping. I went far enough away that I could feel that even his presence was no restraint* upon me. This was the way I felt at the time, and he realized it. I suppose I had said something before I started up and he noticed that the sound of my voice was choked with weep-

*wailings

*restriction

ing. And so he stayed alone, where we had been sitting together, greatly astonished*. I flung myself down under a fig tree—how I know not—and gave free course to my tears. The streams of my eyes gushed out an acceptable sacrifice to thee. And, not indeed in these words, but to this effect, I cried to thee: "And thou, O Lord, how long? How long, O Lord? Wilt thou be angry forever? Oh, remember not against us our former iniquities*."[36] For I felt that I was still enthralled by them. I sent up these sorrowful cries: "How long, how long? Tomorrow and tomorrow? Why not now? Why not this very hour make an end to my uncleanness?"

*surprised

*sins

29. I was saying these things and weeping in the most bitter contrition* of my heart, when suddenly I heard the voice of a boy or a girl I know not which—coming from the neighboring house, chanting over and over again, "Pick it up, read it; pick it up, read it." Immediately I ceased weeping and began most earnestly to think whether it was usual for children in some kind of game to sing such a song, but I could not remember ever having heard the like. So, damming the torrent* of my tears, I got to my feet, for I could not but think that this was a divine command to open the Bible and read the first passage I should light upon. For I had heard how Anthony, accidentally coming into church while the gospel was being read, received the admonition* as if what was read had been addressed to him: "Go and sell what you have and give it to the poor, and you shall have treasure in heaven; and come and follow me."[37] By such an oracle* he was forthwith converted to thee. So I quickly returned to the bench where Alypius was sitting, for there I had put down the apostle's book when I had left there. I snatched it up, opened it, and in silence read the paragraph on which my eyes first fell: "Not in rioting and drunkenness, not in chambering and wantonness*, not in strife and envying, but put on the Lord Jesus Christ, and make no provision for the flesh to fulfill the lusts thereof."[38] I wanted to read no further, nor did I need to. For instantly, as the sentence ended, there was infused

*repentance

*flood

*advice

*prophecy

*lust

36. See Psalms 6:3, 79:8.

37. Matthew 19:21.

38. Romans 13:13.

in my heart something like the light of full certainty and all the gloom of doubt vanished away.

30. Closing the book, then, and putting my finger or something else for a mark I began—now with a tranquil countenance*—to tell it all to Alypius. And he in turn disclosed to me what had been going on in himself, of which I knew nothing. He asked to see what I had read. I showed him, and he looked on even further than I had read. I had not known what followed. But indeed it was this, "Him that is weak in the faith, receive."[39] This he applied to himself, and told me so. By these words of warning he was strengthened, and by exercising his good resolution and purpose—all very much in keeping with his character, in which, in these respects, he was always far different from and better than I—he joined me in full commitment without any restless hesitation.

*peaceful expression

Then we went in to my mother, and told her what happened, to her great joy. We explained to her how it had occurred—and she leaped for joy triumphant; and she blessed thee, who art "able to do exceedingly abundantly above all that we ask or think."[40] For she saw that thou hadst granted her far more than she had ever asked for in all her pitiful and doleful lamentations*. For thou didst so convert me to thee that I sought neither a wife nor any other of this world's hopes, but set my feet on that rule of faith which so many years before thou hadst showed her in her dream about me. And so thou didst turn her grief into gladness more plentiful than she had ventured to desire, and dearer and purer than the desire she used to cherish of having grandchildren of my flesh.
cherish of having grandchildren of my flesh.

*sad wailings

39. Romans 14:1.

40. Ephesians 3:20.

The Confessions. Questions for Discussion

1. Why do you think Augustine chose to title his autobiography *Confessions*? What is he confessing? To whom is he confessing? What seems to be the primary purpose of his autobiography?

2. Augustine inserts quite a few quotes from the bible into his autobiography. What effect does this have on his story? Why do you think he found them so important to include?

3. What role does friendship play in Augustine's account of his spiritual journey—both in Book Two and in Book Eight? What does Augustine think are the dangers as well as the possibilities of friendship?

Book Two

4. Why is he so upset that he stole a few pears? How do you interpret the symbolism of the stolen fruit? Why might he have chosen this particular story to tell us, rather than another "small" sin?

5. Consider a time when you "sinned" or did something that you knew was wrong just because you knew it was wrong. What did you do? Why did you do it, even though you knew you shouldn't? Did you feel guilty? Why or why not? Did you confess (whether or not you were caught in the act)? Why or why not?

Book Eight

6. This book starts off with two different stories of conversion that Augustine hears as he tries to find enlightenment in Christianity—first his friend Simpliciano's story of the conversion of Marius Victorinus, and second the court official Ponticianus's story of the conversion of St. Anthony. How do these two different conversion stories help prepare for his own conversion in different ways? Why do you think they were necessary, either in Augustine's life and/or in this autobiographical account of his conversion?

7. Consider the various elements of Augustine's moment of conversion: he's alone in a garden under a tree, he hears a child's song directing him to open his book and read it, he follows the directions, randomly opening the page and reading the first lines he sees, and suddenly here is the enlightenment he's been seeking. Consider the various ways that these elements might work symbolically. We see some similar elements from Book II and then we'll also find elements in our study of Dante Alighieri's *Divine Comedy*.

Introduction to Dante Alighieri and
The Divine Comedy

Dante Alighieri

Dante Alighieri was a Medieval Italian poet (1265–1321). Although he originally wrote love poetry, Dante's most famous work is *La Divina Commedia*, the first Christian epic poem. When we use the phrase "the fifth circle of hell," we are referring to Dante's vision of the cosmos.

In this epic, Dante included many aspects of his personal life, including politics (he was exiled after his political rivals took control over his native Florence), love (he had a lifelong unrequited love for Beatrice Portinari, who plays a large inspirational role as a character in the poem), and his Christian faith.

If you're familiar with the Greek epics *The Iliad* and *The Odyssey*, *The Divine Comedy* follows this tradition with a number of its features. It's a very long narrative poem; it attempts to explain the world and the culture of Italy; it follows a poetic form, rhythm, and conventions that are similar though not identical to Greek epic; and our main character, Dante, follows the hero's journey through the afterlife and back to earth again with the help of two primary mentors, Virgil (a Roman epic poet) and Dante's beloved Beatrice (who died before Dante wrote the epic).

Unlike Greek epics, Dante's poem focuses on a Christian worldview and explains how three of the most important events of Christianity (Christ's crucifixion, death, and resurrection) show us how readers should and can live a Christian life and effectively prepare our souls for the afterlife. In this sense, this epic is also an allegory, though a much longer one than Plato's *Allegory of the Cave*.

The epic is divided into 3 canticles (volumes). Within each canticle, the poem is separated into cantos (chapters). Dante makes himself the hero of his own journey, following the path of Jesus over the weekend of Easter, beginning on Good Friday, the day that Christians observe as Jesus Christ's crucifixion. Dante follows Christ's descent into Hell (*Inferno*), ascent of Mt. Purgatory (*Purgatorio*), and finally ascension to Heaven (*Paradiso*) on Easter Sunday. Along the way, Dante travels through and interacts with characters in the different circles (levels) that correspond to specific sins in Hell/Purgatory and virtues in Paradise. Dante the character returns to earth after his travels—the ultimate hero's journey for a mortal man, although in Christianity you'd have to recognize Jesus and not Dante as the ultimate of all heroes.

It's important to note that Dante did not "actually" make this journey. This poem is not a religious text that represents the Catholic Church, although it does follow Medieval Catholic doctrine. This is a work of allegory in which Dante finds himself "lost" in the dark woods in the middle part of his life and works on this long journey to rediscover his life's purpose and meaning. Dante the poet means for us to follow his character's journey and learn with him along the way. It is on many levels a work of fiction, but it shines a light on many truths, whether or not you are Christian or even religious at all.

Divine Justice

In Catholicism, Hell is the place where people who have not begged God for forgiveness are condemned and punished for eternity after their death. Since they have actively turned away from God, they cannot be forgiven but they also cannot take responsibility for their sins. They cannot see the error of their ways. Thus, there is no way for them to earn or receive God's forgiveness after death. Purgatory, typically represented as a mountain, is a place for those who have died with sins on their souls but who repented (sometimes at the last minute!), and so in purgatory they "pay" for their sins in order to be worthy of heaven someday, which might involve a very, very long wait. Unlike Hell, the souls in Purgatory understand the nature of their sins and the ways that their punishments will help them become worthy of salvation in heaven. In both the *Inferno* and *Purgatorio*, the punishment for sins perfectly (often ironically) fits the crime; Dante called this system of justice *contrapasso*. Paradise, or heaven, is the ultimate reward, where worthy souls reside along with the angels. In medieval times, this was portrayed as a set of perfect spheres where those beings closest to God are the "highest" forms in the cosmos.

The Inferno (Hell)

The Inferno is by far the most popular of the three canticles of *The Divine Comedy*. Not only does it come first in the epic, but it's also filled with wit, sarcasm, and ironic examples of divine justice for those who fell away from Christ's path—or who never made it onto the path in the first place.

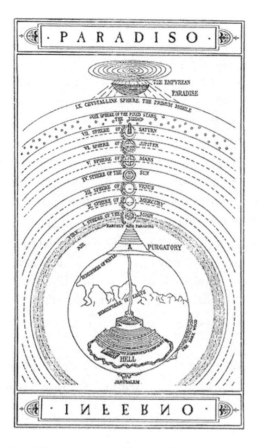

http://christianpoetryshifted. weebly. com/up-
loads/1/9/5/9/19598335/2752378. jpg? 378

The epic begins with Dante finding himself lost in the woods, where he encounters dangerous creatures and the gates of Hell. Virgil, the epic poet of ancient
Rome, has been sent to be his guide (or mentor) in his journey through Hell and
Purgatory. Clearly, this has been planned out in advance—Dante has been blessed
with this opportunity to travel Christ's route with guides to help him along the way.

As Dante and Virgil descend into Hell, they travel down the levels that correspond, though not exactly, to the seven deadly sins. Although all of the sins are
unforgivable, there are worse sins than others, so the sins and punishments become
more severe at each level (circle). In each circle, they encounter creatures and characters from the stories of ancient mythology and history into Dante's own time.
When he learns the stories and the punishments of these characters, Dante begins
not only to recognize his own weaknesses and sins but also begins to prepare his
own soul for its ultimate salvation.

UPPER HELL

1st Circle: *Limbo*	Limbo is nowhere land. It's not on Earth, or in Heaven, or in Hell. It's where the non-believers who preceded Christianity go. It lacks the greatness of Heaven, but it's more like the ancient Greeks' idea of the afterlife in the Elysian Fields.
2nd Circle: *Lust*	This is the first circle of punishment in Hell. The sin of lust is considered the "lightest" of sins, but it's still punishable by damnation because the sinner has taken the "right love"—love for God—and granted it to another, or others. It's also a sin of "excess" of sexual desire, of allowing sensual pleasure to overcome reason.
3rd Circle: *Gluttony*	Gluttony is another form of excess, like sexual desire, but in this case it's almost always exclusively reserved for the excessive bodily pleasure of consuming—food, drink, drugs, alcohol. Like lust, it's also a sin of excess, of allowing sensual pleasure to overcome reason.
4th Circle: *Greed*	Greed is the excessive desire to accumulate things.
5th Circle: *Anger*	Anger is called "wrath" in the seven deadly sins. We've all experienced anger that's healthy, but wrath leads us to other sins.

LOWER HELL

6th Circle: *Heresy*	Heresy is defined as "belief or opinion contrary to orthodox religious (especially Christian) doctrine." Heretics are those who have acted against the Catholic Church and therefore against God. Not only that; they also lead others astray. Dante puts corrupt church members, including historical church leaders as well as those in his own time, in this circle.
7th Circle: *Violence*	This far down in Hell, violence is pretty extreme. This circle is subdivided into three different subcircles: Violence committed by murderers and thugs Violence against self (suicide in the Catholic Church was a crime against God, who dictates a person's lifespan) Blasphemers (violent speech against God) and Sodomites (homosexuality was considered violence against God's commandments)

8th Circle: *Fraud*	Fraud is the act of trying to deceive someone, to pretend that you are someone other than who you actually are (as created by God). Dante subdivides this circle into 10 subcircles (called ditches) based on the many different types of fraud

       Seducers

       Flatterers

       Simonists (people who bought and sold sacred objects and positions) (Corruption of the church)

       Diviners, Astrologers and Magicians

       Barrators (lawyers who abuse the law by filing suits all the time for their own profit—i. e. Ambulance chasers)

       Hypocrites

       Thieves

       Fraudulent Counselors (leading other people astray)

       Sowers of Scandal and Schism (those who create or spread scandals and promote divisions among people)

       Falsifiers (counterfeiters, liars, etc.)

9th Circle: *Treachery*	Treachery is the act of betraying someone. In this case, most of the characters that appear here have betrayed their leader.

       Traitors against kin

       Traitors against country

       Traitors against God

       The worst crime possible was Lucifer's betrayal of God by raising an army and trying to overthrow him, so God cast Lucifer out of heaven and his fall to the center of the earth created the pit of Hell that Dante has been traveling all the way through the Inferno.

The Divine Comedy: The Inferno Questions

What is Truth? While it is not "true" that Dante Alighieri the poet descended into Hell, ascended through Purgatory and Heaven only to end up back in Italy to write his epic poem, the *Divine Comedy* operates on a number of assumptions about Truth. Consider the largest of Truths that are assumed and discussed in the cantos we read, and how the smallest of truths in terms of facts and the motives of one's actions are portrayed.

What is Justice? Both the *Inferno* and *Purgatorio* establish a global view of Divine Justice, God's justice as determined by the traditions and holy texts of the Catholic Church. The idea of *contrapasso*, where the punishment ironically (as opposite or excess) fits the crime, is strictly Dante's, not the Catholic Church's. After all, this is a work of fiction, and the characters we find placed in certain circles of hell or purgatory are actually placed not by God himself but by Dante the poet, except perhaps for Lucifer. How can we or do we think about justice in the human world, and how does that relate to or not relate to religious beliefs about justice in the afterlife?

What does it mean to be Human? The Medieval worldview had a strictly hierarchical, structured way of thinking about what our "place" is in the world. The Great Chain of Being was widely understood to explain and justify that place. How do we see Dante the poet considering the characters placed in the Inferno within this context? Where and how do we behave as "less than" fully human? Where and how do we and how should we behave or strive to be "more" than fully human?

What is the Good Life? St. Augustine's work was a significant influence on Dante in considering the relationship between the imperfect City of Man compared to the perfect City of God. As a Christian writer, Dante wants his readers to think about this question from a religious perspective, but he also recognizes the ethical conflicts that we face in trying to do so. In the end, how do we think of an individual's idea of a good life versus what a religion "tells" us is a good life?

The Divine Comedy: The Inferno
By Dante Alighieri (1320)
Trans. Robert Langdon[1]

Canto I
Introduction to the Divine Comedy
The Wood and the Mountain

Overview: Dante finds himself lost in a dark wood in a classic mid-life crisis. He sees a mountain (Mountain of Delight) and tries to climb it but is blocked by 3 vicious animals: a Leopard, a Lion, and a she-Wolf. Terrified, he races back down the mountain and meets the spirit of Virgil, a Roman epic poet of long ago who tells him that he will not be able to climb that mountain directly but that his destiny is to travel a different route. Virgil offers to take him partway through the journey, down through Hell and up Mt. Purgatory, where Dante will find another guide, his long lost, deceased love Beatrice, who will guide him through Heaven and back to Earth again.

When half way through the journey of our life	
I found that I was in a gloomy wood,	
because the path which led aright* was lost.	*the right direction
And ah, how hard it is to say just what	
this wild and rough and stubborn woodland was,	5
the very thought of which renews my fear!	
So bitter it is, that death is little worse;	
but of the good to treat which there I found*,	*I found good there as well
I'll speak of what I else discovered there.	
I cannot well say how I entered it,	10

---

1. Dante Alighieri, *The Divine Comedy of Dante Alighieri. The Italian Text with a Translation in English Blank Verse and a Commentary*, trans. Courtney Langdon (Cambridge: Harvard University Press, 1918). Overviews and marginal annotations added by the editor of this text.

so full of slumber* was I at the moment
when I forsook* the pathway of the truth;
but after I had reached a mountain's foot*,
where that vale* ended which had pierced my heart
with fear, I looked on high,
and saw its* shoulders
mantled* already with that planet's rays
which leadeth one aright o'er every path. *
Then quieted a little was the fear,
which in the lake-depths of my heart had lasted
throughout the night I passed so piteously.
And even as he who, from the deep emerged
with sorely troubled breath upon the shore,
turns round, and gazes at the dangerous water;*
even so my mind, which still was fleeing on,
turned back to look again upon the pass
which ne'er permitted any one to live.
When I had somewhat eased my weary body,
over the lone slope I so resumed my way,
that ever the lower was my steady foot.
Then lo, not far from where the ascent began,
a Leopard* which, exceeding light and swift,
was covered over with a spotted hide,
and from my presence did not move away;
nay, rather, she so hindered my advance,
that more than once I turned me to go back.
Some time had now from early morn elapsed,
and with those very stars the sun was rising
that in his* escort were, when Love Divine*
in the beginning moved those beauteous things;
I therefore had as cause for hoping well
of that wild beast with gaily mottled skin,
the hour of daytime and the year's sweet season;*
but not so, that I should not fear the sight,
which next appeared before me, of a Lion*,
— against me this one seemed to be advancing
with head erect and with such raging hunger,
that even the air seemed terrified thereby —

*sleepiness

*gave up or left

*base

*valley

15

*the mountain's

*cloaked/clothed

*long reference to the sun

20

*epic simile comparing swimmer to poet's mind

25

30

*the Leopard is meant to be symbolic of a sin, but scholars argue over which one.

35

*his=the sun, escorted by stars.

*Love Divine=God

40

*I wasn't quite so afraid in the daytime

*the Lion is also meant to be symbolic of a sin

45

and of a she-Wolf*, which with every lust
seemed in her leanness laden, and had caused
many before now to lead unhappy lives. 50
The latter* so oppressed me with the fear
that issued from her aspect, that I lost
the hope I had of winning to the top*.
And such as he is, who is glad to gain,
and who, when times arrive that make him lose, 55
weeps and is saddened in his every thought*;
such did that peaceless animal make me,
which, against me coming, pushed me, step by step,
back to the place where silent is the sun*.
While toward the lowland I was falling fast, 60
the sight of one* was offered to my eyes,
who seemed, through long continued silence, weak.
When him in that vast wilderness I saw,
"Have pity on me," I cried out to him,
"whate'er thou be, or shade*, or very man!" 65
"Not man," he answered, "I was once a man*;
and both my parents were of Lombardy*,
and Mantuans* with respect to fatherland.
Beneath Julius* was I born, though somewhat late,
and under good Augustus' rule I lived 70
in Rome, in days of false and lying gods*.
I was a poet, and of that just man,
Anchises' son, I sang, who came from Troy
after proud Ilion had been consumed*.
But thou, to such sore trouble why return? 75
Why climbst thou not the Mountain of Delight,
which is of every joy the source and cause?"
"Are you that Virgil, then, that fountain-head
which poureth forth so broad a stream of speech?"
I answered him with shame upon my brow. 80
"O light and glory of the other poets,
let the long study, and the ardent love
which made me con* thy book, avail* me now.
Thou art my teacher and authority;
thou only art the one from whom I took 85

*the she-Wolf is also meant to be a symbol

*she-wolf

*top of the mountain, where he's trying to go, but the 3 animals are blocking his path

*epic simile comparing one who knows he has lost to the hopelessness he feels about the 3 animals blocking his path

*back to the dark wood

*person

*an old term for ghost/spirit

*I'm a spirit now

*region in Italy

*city in Lombardy region of Italy

*born in Julius Caesar's reign

*lived under Augustus Caesar

*before Christianity

*Virgil identifies himself here as the writer of the epic Aeneid, describing the fall of Troy and founding of Rome

*learn, read, understand. *help

the lovely manner which hath done me honor.
Behold the beast on whose account I turned;
from her protect me, O thou famous Sage*,   *wise person
for she makes both my veins and pulses tremble!"
"A different course from this must thou pursue,"   90
he answered, when he saw me shedding tears,
"if from this wilderness thou wouldst escape;
for this wild beast, on whose account thou criest,
alloweth none to pass along her way,
but hinders him so greatly, that she kills;   95
and is by nature so malign and guilty,
that never doth she sate* her greedy lust,   *satisfy/satiate
but after food is hungrier than before.
Many are the animals with which she mates,
and still more will there be, until the Hound*   *another symbolic animal   100
shall come, and bring her to a painful death.
He shall not feed on either land or wealth,
but wisdom, love and power shall be his food,
and 'tween two Feltros* shall his birth take place.   *Two cities in Italy surrounding Verona
Of that low Italy he'll be the savior,   105
for which the maid Camilla died of wounds,   *4 characters from *Aeneid* who were
with Turnus, Nisus and Euryalus*.   martyred in founding of Rome
And he shall drive her* out of every town,   *still the she-Wolf who scared Dante
till he have put her back again in Hell,
from which the earliest envy sent her forth.   110
I therefore think and judge it best for thee
to follow me; and I shall be thy guide,
and lead thee hence through an eternal place,
where thou shalt hear the shrieks of hopelessness
of those tormented spirits of old times,   115
each one of whom bewails the second death*;   *Hell
then those shalt thou behold who, though in fire,
contented are, because they hope to come,   *Purgatory is the place where souls go to be
whene'er it be, unto the blessèd folk*;   cleansed and earn their place in Heaven
to whom, thereafter, if thou wouldst ascend,   120
there will be for that a worthier soul than I*.   *Virgil can't take him past Purgatory.
With her at my departure I shall leave thee,   Beatrice will take over.
because the Emperor who rules up there,

since I was not obedient to His law,
wills none shall come into His town* through me.   *heaven   125
He rules as emperor everywhere, and there
as king; there is His town and lofty throne.
O happy he whom He thereto elects!"
And I to him: "O Poet, I beseech thee,
even by the God it was not thine to know,   130
so may I from this ill and worse escape,
conduct me thither where thou said just now,
that I may see Saint Peter's Gate, and those
whom thou describest as so whelmed with woe."
He then moved on, and I behind him kept.   135

The Divine Comedy: The Inferno Canto I. Questions for Discussion

1. The beginning of Canto 1 establishes that Dante is in the middle part of his life when he finds himself in the deep dark wood. Allegorically, what does that mean?

2. What personality traits do we see in Dante in Canto 1? What kind of guy is he? What are his hopes and dreams? What are his fears? How does he handle this strange experience in the woods and on the mountain slope?

3. On the Mountain of Delight path to the light, Dante is blocked by three vicious animals: a Leopard, a Lion, and a she-Wolf. It's clear that these are meant to represent sins, generally Dante's own weaknesses. What sins do they seem to represent to you, based on the way they are described in the poem?

4. As Dante escapes from the animals and runs down the mountain, he encounters Virgil. Why has Virgil been selected to be Dante's guide?

5. Virgil outlines the three stages of the journey that Dante must take. What are those three stages, and who will lead him through each stage? Allegorically, what does this represent?

Canto V

The Second Circle. Sexual Intemperance
The Lascivious* and Adulterers*

*lack of moderation; excess
*showing overt or offensive sexual desire
*having sexual intercourse outside of marriage

Overview: Dante and Virgil travel to the main entry of hell, where condemned souls are sent to their punishments by Minos based on the severity of their crimes: the worse the crime, the deeper they are sent into the pit.

They enter the first circle of hell proper (called Upper Hell), which is the circle of lust. Here they encounter many famous lustful souls from history and mythology. Dante sees two souls (Paolo and Francesca) bound together in the hurricane force winds and asks to speak to them. Francesca tells him their story. Dante is so empathetic to her version of the events that sent them to hell that he faints at the end of the canto.

Thus from the first of circles I went down
into the second, which surrounds less space,
and all the greater pain, which goads to wailing*.
There Minos* stands in horrid guise, and snarls;
inside the entrance he examines sins,
judges, and, as he girds* himself, commits.
I mean that when an ill-born soul appears
before him, it confesses itself wholly;
and thereupon that Connoisseur of sins*
perceives what place in Hell belongs to it,
and girds* him with his tail as many times,
as are the grades* he wishes it sent down.
Before him there are always many standing;
they go to judgment, each one in his turn;
they speak and hear, and then are downward hurled.
"O thou that comest to the inn of woe,"
said Minos, giving up, on seeing me,
the execution of so great a charge,
"see how thou enter, and in whom thou put
thy trust; let not the gate-way's width deceive thee!"*
To him my Leader*: "Why dost thou, too, cry?
Hinder thou not his fate-ordained advance*;
thus is it yonder willed, where there is power

*causes high-pitched cries of pain, grief, anger
*Greek mythological figure; son of Zeus; ruler of Crete; known to be a just ruler   5
*prepares himself for action
*expert judge   10
*wraps
*levels
  15
*Minos isn't used to seeing the living   20
*Virgil responds to Minos's warning: Dante is ordained/fated to make this journey

to do whate'er is willed; so ask no more!"
And now the woeful sounds of actual pain   25
begin to break upon my ears; I now
am come to where much wailing smiteth me*.   *struck me down
I reached a region silent of all light,
which bellows* as the sea doth in a storm,   *roars deep and loudly
if lashed and beaten by opposing winds.   30
The infernal* hurricane, which never stops,   *hellish
carries the spirits onward with its sweep,
and, as it whirls and smites* them, gives them pain. *strikes them down
Whenever they come before the shattered rock,
there lamentations*, moans and shrieks are heard; *weeping   35
there, cursing, they blaspheme* the Power Divine. *curse; speak irreverently about God
I understood that to this kind of pain
are doomed those carnal* sinners, who subject   *relating to sexual needs and activities
their reason to their sensual appetite*.   *focus on bodily desires rather than reason
And as their wings bear starlings on their way,   40
when days are cold, in full and wide-spread flocks;* *epic simile comparing starlings to the spirits
so doth that blast the evil spirits bear;
this way and that, and up and down it leads them;
nor only doth no hope of rest, but none
of lesser suffering, ever comfort them.   45
And even as cranes move on and sing their lays,
forming the while a long line in the air;*   *another epic simile comparing crane song to
thus saw I coming, uttering cries of pain,   sinners wailing in pain
shades* borne along upon the aforesaid storm;   *spirits of the dead
I therefore said: "Who, Teacher, are the people   50
the gloomy air so cruelly chastises*?"   *punishes
"The first of those of whom thou wouldst have news,"
the latter* thereupon said unto me,   *Virgil
"was empress over lands of many tongues.
To sexual vice so wholly was she given,   55
that lust she rendered lawful in her laws,
thus to remove the blame she had incurred.
Semiramis she is, of whom one reads
that she gave suck to Ninus, and became   *Semiramus-mythological queen of Babylon;
his wife; she held the land the Soldan rules. *   known for sexual excess   60

173

The next is she who killed herself through love,*
and to Sichaeus' ashes broke her faith;
the lustful Cleopatra* follows her.
See Helen*, for whose sake so long a time
of guilt rolled by, and great Achilles see,
who fought with love when at the end of life.
Paris and Tristan see;*" and then he showed me,
and pointed out by name, a thousand shades
and more, whom love had from our life cut off.
When I had heard my Leader speak the names
of ladies and their knights of olden times,
pity overcame me, and I almost swooned*.
"Poet," I then began, "I'd gladly talk
with those two yonder* who together go,
and seem to be so light upon the wind. *"
"Thou will see thy chance when nearer us they are;"
said he, "beseech* them then by that same love
which leadeth them along, and they will come."
Soon as the wind toward us had bent their course.
I cried: "O toil-worn souls, come speak with us,
so be it that One Else forbid it not*!"
As doves, when called by their desire, come flying
with raised and steady pinions through the air
to their sweet nest, borne on by their own will;*
so from the band where Dido is they issued,
advancing through the noisome air toward us,
so strong with love the tone of my appeal.
"*O thou benign and gracious living creature,
that goest through the gloomy purple air
to visit us, who stained the world blood-red;*
if friendly were the universal King,
for thy peace would we pray to Him, since pity
thou showest for this wretched woe of ours. *
Of whatsoever it may please you hear
and speak, we will both hear and speak with you,
while yet, as now it is, the wind is hushed.
The town where I was born sits on the shore,
whither the Po descends to be at peace

*Dido—mythological widowed queen of Carthage; killed herself when Aeneas left her

*Queen of Egypt; lover of Mark Antony and Julius Caesar

*Helen "caused" the Trojan War by leaving Meneleus and becoming Paris' lover 65

*Achilles: famous Greek warrior
Paris: Trojan who stole Helen from Greece
Tristan: famous lover in French legend

70

*fainted

*over there

* Paolo and Francesca 75

*ask

80

*as long as God doesn't forbid it

*epic simile comparing doves to 2 lovers Dante is addressing 85

*Francesca speaks here

*surprised to have a live human visit 90
them

*we'd ask God for your grace since you show pity for us

95

together with the streams that follow him. *
Love, which soon seizes on a well-born heart,
seized him* for that fair body's sake, whereof
I was deprived; and still the way offends me.
Love, which absolves from loving none that is loved*,
seized me so strongly for his love of me,*
that, as thou see'st, it doth not leave me yet.
Love to a death in common led us on;
Cain's ice awaiteth him who quenched our life. *"
These words were wafted down to us from them.
When I had heard those sorely troubled souls,
I bowed my head, and long I held it low,
until the Poet said: "What thinkest thou? "
When I made answer I began: "Alas!
how many tender thoughts and what desire
induced these souls to take the woeful step!"*
I then turned back to them again and spoke,
and I began: "Thine agonies, Francesca,
cause me to weep with grief and sympathy.
But tell me: at the time of tender sighs,
whereby and how did Love concede to you
that ye should know each other's veiled desires? "
And she to me: "There is no greater pain
than to remember happy days in days
of misery; and this thy Leader knows.
But if to know the first root of our love
so yearning a desire possesses thee,
I'll do as one who weepeth while he speaks.
One day, for pastime merely, we were reading
of Launcelot, and how love o'erpowered him*;
alone we were, and free from all misgiving.
Oft did that reading cause our eyes to meet,
and often take the color from our faces;
and yet one passage only overcame us.
When we had read of how the longed-for smile
was kissed by such a lover, this one here,
who nevermore shall be divided from me,*
trembling all over, kissed me on my mouth.

*from Ravenna in Italy

100

*Paolo

*love is in control

*I fell in love with him because of his
love for me

105

*the pit of hell is waiting for their murderer:
Francesca's husband/Paolo's brother

110

*How did this happen? !

115

*How did this happen? !   120

125

*Arthurian romance; Lancelot fell in love
with Queen Guinevere, wife of King Arthur

130

*Paolo and Francesca are stuck   135
together in hell for all eternity

A Gallehault* the book, and he who wrote it!   *pander, go-between, "pimp"
No further in it did we read that day."
While one* was saying this, the other spirit*   *Francesca
so sorely wept, that out of sympathy   *Paolo   140
I swooned away as though about to die,
and fell as falls a body that is dead.*   *Dante faints in sympathy for the lovers

The Divine Comedy: The Inferno Canto V. Questions for Discussion

1. How are the lustful being punished in the second Circle of Hell? Why is that punishment appropriate for this sin?

2. Consider the different historical/mythological figures that Dante and Virgil encounter. Why do they provide good "examples" of the sin of lust? What might we learn from them?

3. When Francesca tells her story to Dante, she leaves out some things. What are the things that she leaves out? Why does she leave them out? How does that influence the response that Dante (and the readers) have?

4. Souls in hell cannot see the error of their ways. Because they did not and could not repent for their sins and turn to God during life, they cannot do so in death. Francesca does not take responsibility for her own actions. Who/what does she blame instead?

5. Francesca says, "That day we read no further" (Inferno 5. 138). What did Francesca and Paolo do instead?

6. Does Dante the Pilgrim believe Francesca's version of her story? How do you know? Does Dante the Poet? How can you tell?

Canto XXXIV

The Ninth Circle. Treachery*. Cocytus*
Traitors to their Benefactors*. Lucifer

*betrayal of trust

*Greek river of the underworld

*person who has helped them

Overview: This canto is the last of the *Inferno* and therefore the bottom of
the pit of Hell. Dante is terrified by the vision before him of Lucifer locked
in eternal ice, which is created by Lucifer's wings continually flapping. Lucifer has three heads, all monstrous in their own way, and in each mouth
Lucifer is chewing on one of the three most famous traitors to their lead-
ers:Judas Iscariot, Brutus, and Cassius. After watching this scene, Virgil says
it's time to leave, and Dante climbs onto Virgil's back and they crawl down
Lucifer's thighs. About halfway down, Virgil turns completely around and
starts going up the thigh and crawls out into an underground passageway.
Virgil then explains how Mt. Purgatory arose from Lucifer's fall. Finally,
Virgil and Dante climb out of the passage into the southern hemisphere of
the earth, where they see the stars.

"The banners of the King of Hell advance
toward us; now, therefore, look ahead of thee,"
my Teacher said, "and see if thou perceive him."
As, when a heavy fog is breathed abroad,
or when at night our hemisphere grows dark,   5
a windmill looks when seen from far away;*   *epic simile windmill in fog-Dante seeing
even such a structure seemed I now to see;   structure in the pit of hell vaguely
then, for the wind, I shrank behind my Leader,
for other shelter was there none. I now —
and it is with fear I put it into verse, —   10
was where the shades were wholly covered up,
and visible as is a straw in glass;
some lying are; and some are standing up,
one on his head, the other on his soles;
one, like a bow, bends toward his feet his face.   15
When we had gone so far ahead, that now
it pleased my Teacher to reveal to me
the Creature who once seemed so beautiful,
he stepped from where he was in front of me,
stopped me, and said: "Lo Dis*, and lo the place,   *Lucifer/Satan   20

177

where thou must arm thyself with fortitude*!"   *courage in difficult circumstances
How frozen and how weak I then became,
ask thou not, Reader, for I write it not,
because all speech would be of small avail*.   *useless
I did not die, nor yet remained alive;   25
think for thyself now, hast thou any wit,
what I became, of both of these deprived.
The Emperor of the Realm of Woe* stood forth   *Lucifer/Satan
out of the ice from midway up his breast;
and I compare more closely with a Giant,   30
than merely with his arms the Giants do;
consider now how great that whole must be,
that with such parts as these may be compared.
If, once as beautiful as ugly now,
he still raised up his brows against his Maker*,   *God   35
justly doth every woe proceed from him.
Oh, what a marvel it appeared to me,
when I beheld three faces to his head!
One was in front of us, and that was red;
the other two were to the latter joined   40
right over the middle of each shoulder-blade,
and met each other where he had his crest*;   *crown of the head
that on the right twixt* white and yellow seemed;   *between
the left one such to look at, as are those
who come from there, where valeward* flows the Nile *toward the valley   45
Under each face two mighty wings stretched out*,   *Lucifer was an angel, so these are his wings
of size proportioned to so huge a bird;
sails of the sea I never saw so large.
They had no feathers, but were like a bat's
in fashion; these he flapped in such a way,   50
that three winds issued forth from him; thereby
Cocytus was completely frozen up*.   *Lucifer's wings flap and eternally ice the region of Cocytus
With six eyes he was weeping, and his tears
and bloody slaver* trickled over three chins.   *slobber, saliva
In each mouth, as a heckle* would have done,   *rake   55
a sinner he was crushing with his teeth,
and thus was causing pain to three of them.
To him who was in front of us the biting

was nothing to the clawing, for at times
his back remained completely stripped of skin.   60
"That soul up there which hath the greatest pain
Judas Iscariot* is," my Teacher said,   *Judas betrayed Jesus
"who hath his head within, and plies his legs
without. Of the other two, whose heads are down,
Brutus* is he who from the black snout hangs;   *Julius Caesar's general who   65
see how he writhes, and utters not a word!   conspired to assassinate him
Cassius* the other is, who so big-limbed   *Roman senator who instigated the plot to
appears. But night is coming up again,   assassinate Julius Caesar
and now it is time to leave, for we've seen all."
Then, as it pleased him, I embraced his neck,   70
and he availed* himself of time and place,   *took advantage of
and when the wings were opened wide enough,
he firmly grasped the shaggy flanks, and then
from tuft to tuft he afterward descended
between the matted hair and frozen crusts.   75
When we were come to where the thigh turns round,
just at the thick part of the hips, my Leader
with tiring effort and with stress of breath
turned his head round to where his legs had been,
and seized the hair as one would who ascends;   80
hence* I thought we were going back to Hell.   *therefore
"Hold fast to me, for by such stairs as these"
panting like one worn out, my Teacher said,
"must such great wickedness be left behind."
Then, through an opening in the rock he issued,   85
and, after seating me upon its edge,
over toward me advanced his cautious step.
Raising mine eyes, I thought that I should still
see Lucifer the same as when I left him;
but I beheld him with his legs held up.   90
And thereupon, if I became perplexed,
let those dull people think, who do not see
what kind of point that was which I had passed.
"Stand up" my Teacher said, "upon thy feet!
the way is long and difficult the road,   95
and now to middle-tierce the sun returns."*   *7:30 am

179

It was no palace hallway where we were,
but just a natural passage under ground,
which had a wretched floor and lack of light.
"Before I tear myself from this abyss*,   *big gaping hole (Hell)   100
Teacher," said I on rising, "talk to me
a little, and correct my wrong ideas.
Where is the ice? And how is this one fixed
thus upside down? And in so short a time
how hath the sun from evening crossed to morn?"   105
Then he to me: "Thou thinkest thou art still
beyond the center where I seized the hair
of that bad Worm* who perforates* the world.   *Lucifer   *tears apart
While I was going down, thou wast* beyond it;   *were
but when I turned, thou then didst pass the point   110
to which all weights are drawn on every side;
thou now art come beneath the hemisphere
opposed to that the great dry land overcovers,
and beneath whose zenith was destroyed the Man,
who without sinfulness was born and died*;   *Jesus   115
thy feet thou hast upon the little sphere,
which forms the other surface of Judecca.
It is morning here, whenever evening there;
and he who made our ladder with his hair,
is still fixed fast*, even as he was before.   *stuck   120
He fell on this side out of Heaven; whereat,
the land, which hitherto was spread out here,
through fear of him made of the sea a veil,
and came into our hemisphere; perhaps
to flee from him, what is on this side seen   125
left the place empty here, and upward rushed. *"   *Virgil is explaining how Mt. Purgatory was formed from Lucifer's fall.
There is a place down there, as far removed
from Beelzebub*, as ever his tomb extends,   *Lucifer
not known by sight, but by a brooklet's sound,
which flows down through a hole there in the rock,   130
gnawed in it by the water's spiral course,
which slightly slopes. My Leader then, and I,
in order to regain the world of light,
entered upon that dark and hidden path;

and, without caring for repose*, went up, *rest   135
he going on ahead, and I behind,
till through a rounded opening I beheld
some of the lovely things the sky contains;
thence we came out, and saw again the stars.

The Divine Comedy: The Inferno Canto XXXIV. Questions for Discussion

1. Who is Lucifer? For what crime is he being punished, and what is his punishment? How does the punishment seem to fit his crime?

2. Who are the three sinners that Lucifer is chewing on? Why does their punishment seem to fit their crimes?

3. How do Dante and Virgil get out of the Inferno? Geographically and navigationally, this is quite challenging to conceptualize.

4. How does Dante come to terms with pure evil? How do we?

Introduction to William Shakespeare and
The Tempest

William Shakespeare

You've all heard of William Shakespeare; you've probably read or at least watched a Shakespeare play. He's probably best known in today's age for *Romeo and Juliet*, *Julius Caesar*, and *Hamlet*, all of which are favorites of middle and high school English teachers.

At some point, you've also probably learned a little bit about Shakespeare himself. He was both a playwright and an actor and eventually production manager. He was born in Stratford-upon-Avon in Renaissance England (also known as the Elizabethan Age after Queen Elizabeth I) some time in the late 16th century. He married but wasn't altogether happy in marriage. He helped build the very famous Globe Theater in London. There is a conspiracy theory that William Shakespeare didn't write all of the plays that are attributed to him.

While there are scholars who will debate the point of whether Shakespeare is the single greatest writer in the English language, there is little debate over the quality and insight of Shakespeare's work. It's difficult for us in 21st century America to read Shakespeare, because he wrote in verse, he used words and phrases that are uncommon for us, he liked to invent words, and the English language was less standardized than it is today. However, the richness of his language (even his curses and insults) combined with universal themes make it worth the extra effort to read the lines on the page and figure out what he's saying. It's also a much more enjoyable experience when you are in a community of readers who are all working to make sense of the challenging language.

The Tempest

The Tempest was one of the last plays Shakespeare wrote, and many scholars consider the main character of Prospero to be a stand-in for Shakespeare himself and Prospero's magic to represent Shakespeare's artistic powers.

The play is classified as a Shakespearean comedy, though in some ways it doesn't fit neatly into the genre as a play like *Midsummer Night's Dream* that has lovers and fairies and mythical creatures. Shakespearean comedies work quite a lot like modern romantic comedies—people fall in love; there's some kind of mix-up, misunderstanding, or challenge to the lovers; and then the lovers reconcile and live happily ever after. But one-liners, jokes, and slapstick don't define comedy for this genre. These things do exist in Shakespearean comedy—lots of witty puns and inappropriate jokes, though it's sometimes a struggle to get them. For many of us, that takes a couple extra steps, and by then, the joke might not seem so funny. The term "comedy" for Shakespeare is closer to the ancient Greeks' comedy genre, where the characters are led to believe that they are in control of their own destinies, that they have free will. In that sense, *The Tempest* complicates this idea because there is a mastermind at work who is not a god but rather a human who possesses powers above and beyond the powers and knowledge that the other characters possess.

Power, then, is at the center of this play—who has power over others, what gives a character power over others, who knows that they have power or are under the power of others, and ultimately, what extreme lengths people will go to attain power even if they are stranded on a desert island with few other people.

Shakespeare's plays are all, in one way or another, about order and the re-establishment of order after a period of disorder. Generally in the comedies, civilization represents order, and nature/wilderness/desert islands represent disorder. Crazy things happen in the woods, and love often makes us do crazy things. This is called the pastoral tradition, following an ancient tradition of rustic shepherds and shepherdesses falling into innocent love and representing the simple life. *The Tempest* follows this in strange ways, because the disorder arises in civilization with an unlawful shift of power and then that disorder follows into the natural setting. However, as in both comedies and tragedies, the "natural order" must be restored.

The Tempest takes place wholly on a desert island. While there are some natural springs and sufficient food sources, there is little else there, and that's important to consider because nearly everyone on it is fighting over the island. That setting, according to many Shakespeare scholars, has a remarkable likeness to Bermuda (which is also referenced in the play as Bermoothes), an island situated around 900 miles from the coast of North Carolina. We also have a character in Caliban who, despite all efforts to educate and care for him, ends up being a slave to the main character of the play. So there are serious students of Shakespeare who consider this play to be about race relations and consider Caliban to be a sympathetic character. There are challenges to this interpretation, not only Shakespeare's dedication to the Great Chain of Being but also the ambiguity over Caliban's essential nature as the child of a sea god and a witch; however, given the emphasis on power and claims of ownership of land, the idea is worth serious consideration.

In addition to Caliban and his mother (called his "dam") named Sycorax, who died long before the play begins, there are a number of what we'd now call fantasy elements in the play. Prospero is a powerful sorcerer who possesses items of magical power like a staff, a cloak, and magic books and who has the ability to control other spirits. Only one of these spirits, Ariel, has a major role in the play. While Caliban is more "earthy" than humans, Ariel is a sprite or spirit who is more associated with air and the wind. It is important to note that quite often, it appears that only Prospero knows of Ariel's existence and he's the only one who can speak to and hear Ariel unless Ariel is performing some magical mischief on Prospero's behalf. Obviously, Shakespeare meant to create a fantasy; he was not trying to represent "the real world" here, although we in the real world can learn a lot from this play. In that sense, we are asked as an audience and as readers to suspend our disbelief and enter the story on its own terms. Sometimes, we have to see the world from a totally different vantage point in order to better understand our own.

The Tempest Questions

What is Truth? This play sets up the question of truth/reality versus illusion. Only one character knows exactly what's going on in the play and what the outcome should and will be. In such a world, if you're not that character, how can you tell what is true and what is not true? When can you trust your senses? What constitutes "reality"? And how do we know it when we see/experience it?

What is Justice? Unlike Dante's *Inferno*, justice in *The Tempest* has to do with justice on Earth rather than divine justice. There are aspects of a revenge plot here, and yet who deserves to have revenge, and on whom? What we want isn't always justice just because it's what we want. How can we tell when justice is achieved? What is the relationship between personal justice and societal justice? Is justice achieved at the end of the play? Why or why not?

What does it mean to be Human? Like the medieval world, the Renaissance worldview was strictly hierarchical. The Great Chain of Being was widely understood to explain and justify our place in the world. How do we see Shakespeare's interpretation of the Great Chain of Being in the context of the social classes of Renaissance England? How does this worldview influence people's sense of their place in society, how others view them, and how those factors affect people's behavior? Where and how do our behaviors and motives appear to be "less" than fully human—and why do we behave in those ways?

What is the Good Life? Each character, just like each of us, is looking for the good life. However, it's clear even from the beginning of the play that the good life looks different for each of the characters. Gonzalo, for example, describes a utopia for all humanity, yet no one takes him seriously. Prospero sought the good life through magic and sorcery, yet look where that got him. Antonio sought the good life by taking the dukedom by force, and later tries to persuade his friend Sebastian to follow that same path to power by killing his brother, King Alonso. What does this play say about our individual desires for the good life in relation to the social good?

The Tempest
By William Shakespeare (1610)[1]

CHARACTERS OF THE PLAY:

ALONSO, King of Naples
SEBASTIAN, King's Brother
PROSPERO, the rightful Duke of Milan
ANTONIO, Prospero's Brother / the usurping* Duke of Milan   *overthrew rightful Duke
FERDINAND, Son to the King of Naples
GONZALO, an honest old counsellor
ADRIAN, Lord
FRANCISCO, Lord
CALIBAN, a savage and deformed slave
TRINCULO, a Jester
STEPHANO, a drunken Butler
MASTER OF A SHIP
BOATSWAIN*   *officer in charge of ship's crew
MARINERS
MIRANDA, Daughter to Prospero
ARIEL, an airy Spirit
IRIS, presented by Spirits
CERES, presented by Spirits
JUNO, presented by Spirits
NYMPHS, presented by Spirits
REAPERS, presented by Spirits
Other Spirits attending* on Prospero   *serving

1. William Shakespeare, *The Tempest* (in the public domain). Retrieved from http://shakespeare. mit. edu/tempest/full. html. Scene overviews, line numbers, and annotations added by the editor of this text.

ACT 1
SCENE 1

King Alonso and his retinue, on their return from the marriage of Alonso's daughter Claribel in Tunis, Africa, are caught in a major storm. Rather than staying below deck as passengers should for the safety of all, they keep coming up to the ship's deck and interfering with the boat's crew.

[*On a ship at sea; a tempestuous noise of thunder and lightning heard*]
[*Enter a SHIPMASTER and a BOATSWAIN*]

MASTER
Boatswain!

BOATSWAIN
Here, master: what cheer*?   *what's happening, basically

MASTER
Good! Speak to the mariners: fall to it yarely*, or   *quickly
we run ourselves aground*: bestir*, bestir.   *to the ground *get moving
[*Exit*]
[*Enter MARINERS*]

BOATSWAIN
Heigh*, my hearts! cheerly*, cheerly, my hearts!   *encouraging. *heartily   5
yare*, yare! Take in the topsail. Tend to the master's   *quick
whistle. — Blow till thou burst thy wind, if room enough.
[*Enter ALONSO, SEBASTIAN, ANTONIO, FERDINAND,
GONZALO, and OTHERS*]

ALONSO
Good boatswain, have care. Where's the master?
Play the men*.   *get the men working

BOATSWAIN
I pray now, keep below*.   *Stay below deck   10

ANTONIO
Where is the master, boson?

BOATSWAIN
Do you not hear him? You mar* our labour: *disrupt, interfere with
keep your cabins*: you do assist the storm.   *stay in your cabins.

GONZALO
Nay, good, be patient.

BOATSWAIN
When the sea is. Hence! What cares these   15
roarers for the name of king*? To cabin! Silence! Trouble *The storm doesn't care about the king
us not.

GONZALO
Good, yet remember whom thou hast aboard*.   *King of Naples

BOATSWAIN
None that I more love than myself. You are
counsellor: if you can command these elements to   20
silence, and work the peace of the present, we will not
hand a rope more. Use your authority: if you cannot, give
thanks you have lived so long, and make yourself ready
in your cabin for the mischance* of the hour, if it so   *bad luck
hap*. — Cheerly, good hearts! — Out of our way, I say. *happens   25
[Exit]*   *stage direction; that person leaves

GONZALO
I have great comfort from this fellow. Methinks*   *I think
he hath no drowning mark upon him: his complexion is
perfect gallows*. Stand fast, good Fate, to his hanging! *he looks like the hanging type, not
make the rope of his destiny our cable, for our own doth the drowning type
little advantage! If he be not born to be hang'd, our   30
case is miserable.
[Exeunt]*   *stage direction: everyone leaves
[Re-enter BOATSWAIN]

BOATSWAIN
Down with the topmast! yare! lower, lower!
Bring her to try with th' maincourse. [*A cry within*] A
plague upon this howling*! They are louder than the   *of the passengers
weather or our office—   35
[*Re-enter SEBASTIAN, ANTONIO, and GONZALO*]
Yet again! What do you here? Shall we give o'er, and
drown? Have you a mind to sink?

SEBASTIAN
A pox* o' your throat, you bawling, blasphemous,   *illness; curse
incharitable dog!

BOATSWAIN
Work you, then.   40

ANTONIO
Hang, cur*, hang! You whoreson, insolent* noisemaker,   *dog *rude/disrespectful
we are less afraid to be drowned than thou art*.   *are

GONZALO
I'll warrant* him for drowning, though the ship were   *guarantee
no stronger than a nutshell, and as leaky as an unstanched
wench*.   *girl/woman   45

BOATSWAIN
Lay her a-hold, a-hold! set her two courses: off
to sea again: lay her off.
[*Enter MARINERS, Wet*]

MARINERS
All lost! to prayers, to prayers! all lost!
[*Exeunt*]

BOATSWAIN
What, must our mouths be cold?

GONZALO
The King and Prince at prayers! let us assist them,　　　　　50
For our case is as theirs.

SEBASTIAN
I am out of patience.

ANTONIO
We are merely cheated of our lives by drunkards. —
This wide-chapp'd* rascal—would thou might'st lie drowning　　*wide-mouthed
The washing of ten tides*!　　　*pirates were hanged and left on the beach for a number of tides　　55

GONZALO
He'll be hang'd yet,
Though every drop of water swears against it,
And gape at wid'st to glut him.
[*A confused noise within:* —'Mercy on us!'—'We split, we split!'—'Farewell, my wife
and children!'—'Farewell, brother!'—'We split, we split, we split!'—]

ANTONIO
Let's all sink wi' the King.
[*Exit*]

SEBASTIAN
Let's take leave of him.　　　　　60
[*Exit*]

GONZALO
Now would I give a thousand furlongs* of sea for　　　　　*1/8 of a mile
an acre of barren ground; long heath*, brown furze*, any　　　　*shrubland　*flowering plant
thing. The wills above be done! but I would fain die
a dry death.*　　　　　*I'd rather die on land (not now)
[*Exit*]

SCENE 2

Miranda from her island home sees a ship in distress in a giant storm and races to her father Prospero to ask him if he has caused the storm and to beg him to save the people on the boat. Prospero then explains that no one will be harmed and that she needs to learn of her history as the daughter of the Duke of Milan. He tells of his fascination with magic and learning and how his brother, Antonio, usurped his position. Prospero then lulls Miranda to sleep and discusses his plans with Ariel, who also begs his freedom from Prospero. Prospero wakes Miranda and they go to visit Caliban, their servant, who complains of his treatment. Prospero explains why Caliban has become their slave when before he was their friend. Ariel lures Ferdinand around the island and Prospero makes sure that Miranda sees him and they fall in love at first sight. Prospero pretends to be angry and to make Ferdinand his slave.

[*The Island. Before the cell of PROSPERO*]
[*Enter PROSPERO and MIRANDA*]

MIRANDA

If by your art*, my dearest father, you have   *magic
Put the wild waters in this roar, allay* them.   *put them to rest/stop
The sky, it seems, would pour down stinking pitch*,   *tar
But that the sea, mounting to th'welkin's* cheek,   *sky's
Dashes the fire out. O! I have suffered   5
With those that I saw suffer: a brave vessel,
Who had, no doubt, some noble creatures in her,
Dash'd all to pieces. O! the cry did knock
Against my very heart. Poor souls, they perish'd.
Had I been any god of power, I would   10
Have sunk the sea within the earth, or e'er
It should the good ship so have swallow'd and
The fraughting souls* within her.   *people on board

PROSPERO

Be collected*:   *Calm down
No more amazement: tell your piteous heart   15
There's no harm done.

MIRANDA
O! woe the day!

PROSPERO
No harm.
I have done nothing but in care of thee,
Of thee, my dear one, thee, my daughter, who   20
Art ignorant of what thou art, nought knowing
Of whence I am: nor that I am more better
Than Prospero, master of a full poor cell*,   *dwelling
And thy no greater father.

MIRANDA
More to know   25
Did never meddle* with my thoughts.   *interfere

PROSPERO
'Tis time
I should inform thee farther. Lend thy hand,
And pluck my magic garment from me. —So:
[*Lays down his mantle**]   *cloak
Lie there my art. —Wipe thou thine eyes; have comfort.   30
The direful* spectacle of the wrack, which touch'd   *awful
The very virtue of compassion in thee,
I have with such provision* in mine art   *preparation
So safely ordered that there is no soul—
No, not so much perdition* as an hair   *hell   35
Betid* to any creature in the vessel   *happened
Which thou heard'st cry, which thou saw'st sink. Sit down;
For thou must now know farther.

MIRANDA
You have often
Begun to tell me what I am: but stopp'd,   40
And left me to a bootless inquisition*,   *useless questioning
Conclud
ing 'Stay; not yet.'

192

PROSPERO
The hour's now come,
The very minute bids thee open thine ear;
Obey, and be attentive. Canst thou remember   45
A time before we came unto this cell?
I do not think thou canst: for then thou wast not
Out three years old.

MIRANDA
Certainly, sir, I can.

PROSPERO
By what? By any other house, or person?   50
Of any thing the image, tell me, that
Hath kept with thy remembrance.

MIRANDA
'Tis far off,
And rather like a dream than an assurance*   *certainty/confidence
That my remembrance warrants*. Had I not   *justifies   55
Four, or five, women once, that tended me?

PROSPERO
Thou hadst, and more, Miranda. But how is it
That this lives in thy mind? What seest thou else
In the dark backward and abysm* of time?   *abyss/big gaping hole
If thou rememb'rest aught* ere thou cam'st here,   *anything   60
How thou cam'st here, thou mayst.

MIRANDA
But that I do not.

PROSPERO
Twelve year since, Miranda, twelve year since,
Thy father was the Duke of Milan, and
A prince of power.   65

MIRANDA
Sir, are not you my father?

PROSPERO
Thy mother was a piece of virtue*, and   *virtuous, honorable
She said thou wast my daughter: and thy father
Was Duke of Milan, and his only heir
And princess, —no worse issued*.   *created   70

MIRANDA
O, the heavens!
What foul play had we that we came from thence?
Or blessed was't we did?

PROSPERO
Both, both, my girl.
By foul play, as thou say'st, were we heav'd* thence;   *thrown out   75
But blessedly holp hither*.   *helped here

MIRANDA
O! my heart bleeds
To think o' th' teen* that I have turn'd you to,   *sorrow
Which is from my remembrance. Please you, further.

PROSPERO
My brother and thy uncle, call'd Antonio—   80
I pray thee, mark* me,—that a brother should   *pay attention
Be so perfidious*!—he, whom next thyself,   *deceitful
Of all the world I lov'd, and to him put
The manage of my state*; as at that time   *the management of Milan
Through all the signories* it was the first,   *Italian city-states   85
And Prospero the prime duke*, being so reputed   *first ranked duke
In dignity, and for the liberal arts,
Without a parallel: those being all my study,
The government I cast upon my brother,
And to my state* grew stranger, being transported   *Milan   90
And rapt* in secret studies. Thy false uncle—   *absorbed/obsessed
Dost thou attend me*?   *Are you listening?

MIRANDA
Sir, most heedfully*.   *attentively

PROSPERO
Being once perfected how to grant suits,
How to deny them, who t' advance, and who   95
To trash for over-topping; new created
The creatures that were mine, I say, or chang'd 'em,
Or else new form'd 'em: having both the key
Of officer and office, set all hearts i' th' state
To what tune pleas'd his ear*: that now he was   *Antonio had everyone   100
The ivy which had hid my princely trunk,   following him
And suck'd my verdure* out on't. —Thou attend'st not.   *lush, green vegetation

MIRANDA
O, good sir! I do.

PROSPERO
I pray thee, mark me.
I thus neglecting worldly ends, all dedicated   105
To closeness and the bettering of my mind
With that, which, but by being so retir'd,
O'er-priz'd all popular rate, in my false brother
Awak'd an evil nature; and my trust,
Like a good parent, did beget of him*   *create in him   110
A falsehood, in its contrary as great
As my trust was; which had indeed no limit,
A confidence sans* bound. He being thus lorded,   *without
Not only with what my revenue* yielded,   *income
But what my power might else exact*,—like one   *whatever else could be gotten 115
Who having, into truth, by telling of it,   due to the powerful authority of the
state
Made such a sinner of his memory,
To credit his own lie,—he did believe
He was indeed the Duke; out o' the substitution,
And executing th' outward face of royalty,   120
With all prerogative*. —Hence his ambition growing—   *privilege
Dost thou hear?

MIRANDA
Your tale, sir, would cure deafness.

PROSPERO
To have no screen between this part he play'd
And him he play'd it for, he needs will be   125
Absolute Milan. Me, poor man—my library
Was dukedom large enough: of temporal royalties*   *daily duties of the city-state
He thinks me now incapable; confederates*,—   *allies
So dry he was for sway,—wi' th' King of Naples
To give him annual tribute*, do him homage*;   *payment *respect   130
Subject his coronet* to his crown, and bend   *smaller/lesser crown
The dukedom, yet unbow'd—alas, poor Milan!—
To most ignoble* stooping.   *low

MIRANDA
O the heavens!

PROSPERO
Mark his condition, and the event; then tell me   135
If this might be a brother.

MIRANDA
I should sin
To think but nobly of my grandmother:
Good wombs have borne bad sons.

PROSPERO
Now the condition*.   *terms of agreement   140
This King of Naples, being an enemy
To me inveterate*, hearkens* my brother's suit;   *habitual *gives respectful attention
Which was, that he, in lieu o' the premises*   *previous agreement
Of homage and I know not how much tribute,
Should presently extirpate* me and mine   *remove   145
Out of the dukedom, and confer fair Milan,
With all the honours on my brother: whereon,
A treacherous* army levied*, one midnight   *traitorous   *enlisted/raised
Fated to the purpose, did Antonio open

The gates of Milan; and, i' th' dead of darkness,   150
The ministers* for th' purpose hurried thence   *Antonio's servants
Me and thy crying self.

MIRANDA
Alack, for pity!
I, not rememb'ring how I cried out then,
Will cry it o'er again: it is a hint   155
That wrings mine eyes to't.

PROSPERO
Hear a little further,
And then I'll bring thee to the present business
Which now's upon us; without the which this story
Were most impertinent*.   *irrelevant   160

MIRANDA
Wherefore did they not
That hour destroy us?

PROSPERO
Well demanded, wench*:   *girl
My tale provokes that question. Dear, they durst* not, *dared
So dear the love my people bore me, nor set   165
A mark so bloody on the business; but
With colours fairer painted their foul ends.
In few, they hurried us aboard a bark*,   *small sailing ship
Bore us some leagues* to sea, where they prepared   *distance
A rotten carcass of a boat, not rigg'd,   170
Nor tackle, sail, nor mast: the very rats
Instinctively have quit it. There they hoist* us,   *threw
To cry to th' sea, that roar'd to us: to sigh
To th' winds, whose pity, sighing back again,
Did us but loving wrong.   175

MIRANDA
Alack! what trouble
Was I then to you!

PROSPERO
O, a cherubin*   *angel
Thou wast that did preserve* me! Thou didst smile,   *save
Infused* with a fortitude* from heaven,   *steeped *strength   180
When I have deck'd the sea with drops full salt,
Under my burden groan'd: which rais'd in me
An undergoing stomach, to bear up
Against what should ensue*.   *happen in the future

MIRANDA
How came we ashore?   185

PROSPERO
By Providence divine.
Some food we had and some fresh water that
A noble Neapolitan*, Gonzalo,   *person from Naples
Out of his charity,—who being then appointed
Master of this design*,—did give us, with   *the plan to exile Prospero   190
Rich garments, linens, stuffs, and necessaries,
Which since have steaded* much: so, of his gentleness,   *been so advantageous
Knowing I lov'd my books, he furnish'd me,
From mine own library with volumes that
I prize above my dukedom.   195

MIRANDA
Would I might
But ever see that man!

PROSPERO
Now I arise:—
[*Resumes his mantle*]
Sit still, and hear the last of our sea-sorrow.
Here in this island we arriv'd: and here   200
Have I, thy schoolmaster, made thee more profit
Than other princes can, that have more time
For vainer* hours, and tutors not so careful.   *hours in which to play/waste

MIRANDA
Heavens thank you for't! And now, I pray you, sir,—
For still 'tis beating in my mind,—your reason   205
For raising this sea-storm?

PROSPERO
Know thus far forth.
By accident most strange, bountiful Fortune,
Now my dear lady, hath mine enemies
Brought to this shore; and by my prescience*   *foreknowledge   210
I find my zenith* doth depend upon   *highest point
A most auspicious* star, whose influence   *lucky/fortunate
If now I court not but omit, my fortunes
Will ever after droop. Here cease more questions;
Thou art inclin'd to sleep; 'tis a good dulness,   215
And give it way;—I know thou canst not choose. —
[*MIRANDA sleeps*]
Come away, servant, come! I am ready now.
Approach, my Ariel; Come!
[*Enter ARIEL*]

ARIEL
All hail, great master! grave sir, hail! I come
To answer thy best pleasure; be't to fly,   220
To swim, to dive into the fire, to ride
On the curl'd clouds; to thy strong bidding task
Ariel and all his quality.

PROSPERO
Hast thou, spirit,
Perform'd to point the tempest* that I bade thee?   *storm   225

ARIEL
To every article*.   *in every way
I boarded the King's ship; now on the beak,   *describes how he was on all
Now in the waist, the deck, in every cabin,   parts of the ship
I flam'd amazement; sometime I'd divide,
And burn in many places; on the topmast,   230

The yards, and boresprit, would I flame distinctly,
Then meet and join: Jove's* lightning, the precursors*   *Roman name for the Greek god Zeus
O' th' dreadful thunder-claps, more momentary   *that which comes before
And sight-outrunning were not: the fire and cracks
Of sulphurous* roaring the most mighty Neptune*   *infernal *God of the sea/Poseidon   235
Seem to besiege* and make his bold waves tremble,   *to beset, to cause
Yea, his dread trident* shake.   *3-pronged pitchfork, Neptune's
weapon

PROSPERO
My brave spirit!
Who was so firm, so constant, that this coil*   *uproar
Would not infect his reason?   240

ARIEL
Not a soul
But felt a fever of the mad, and play'd
Some tricks of desperation. All but mariners
Plunged in the foaming brine* and quit the vessel,   *salt water
Then all afire with me: the King's son, Ferdinand,   245
With hair up-staring—then like reeds, not hair—
Was the first man that leapt; cried 'Hell is empty,
And all the devils are here.'

PROSPERO
Why, that's my spirit!
But was not this nigh* shore?   *near   250

ARIEL
Close by, my master.

PROSPERO
But are they, Ariel, safe?

ARIEL
Not a hair perish'd;
On their sustaining garments not a blemish*,   *flaw
But fresher than before: and, as thou bad'st* me,   *requested/ordered   255

In troops I have dispers'd* them 'bout the isle.   *scattered
The king's son have I landed by himself,
Whom I left cooling of the air with sighs
In an odd angle of the isle, and sitting,
His arms in this sad knot.   260

PROSPERO
Of the King's ship
The mariners, say how thou hast dispos'd*,   *taken care of
And all the rest o' th' fleet?

ARIEL
Safely in harbour
Is the King's ship; in the deep nook, where once   265
Thou call'dst me up at midnight to fetch dew
From the still-vex'd Bermoothes*; there she's hid: *Bermuda
The mariners all under hatches stowed*;   *put safely below deck
Who, with a charm join'd to their suff'red labour,
I have left asleep: and for the rest o' th' fleet   270
Which I dispers'd, they all have met again,
And are upon the Mediterranean flote*   *float/boat
Bound sadly home for Naples,
Supposing that they saw the king's ship wrack'd*,   *wrecked
And his great person perish.   275

PROSPERO
Ariel, thy charge
Exactly is perform'd; but there's more work:
What is the time o' th' day?

ARIEL
Past the mid season*.   *past noon

PROSPERO
At least two glasses*. The time 'twixt six and now   *two o'clock   280
Must by us both be spent most preciously.

ARIEL
Is there more toil*? Since thou dost give me pains,   *work
Let me remember thee what thou hast promis'd,
Which is not yet perform'd me.

PROSPERO
How now! moody?   285
What is't thou canst demand?

ARIEL
My liberty.

PROSPERO
Before the time be out! No more!

ARIEL
I prithee,
Remember I have done thee worthy service;   290
Told thee no lies, made no mistakings, serv'd
Without or grudge or grumblings: thou didst promise
To bate* me a full year.   *lessen my time of service

PROSPERO
Dost thou forget
From what a torment I did free thee?   295

ARIEL
No.

PROSPERO
Thou dost; and think'st it much to tread the ooze
Of the salt deep,
To run upon the sharp wind of the north,
To do me business in the veins o' th' earth   300
When it is bak'd with frost.

ARIEL
I do not, sir.

PROSPERO
Thou liest, malignant* thing! Hast thou forgot   *evil
The foul witch Sycorax, who with age and envy
Was grown into a hoop? Hast thou forgot her?   305

ARIEL
No, sir.

PROSPERO
Thou hast. Where was she born?
Speak; tell me.

ARIEL
Sir, in Argier*.   *Algiers in Northern Africa

PROSPERO
O! was she so? I must   310
Once in a month recount* what thou hast been,   *retell the story of
Which thou forget'st. This damn'd witch Sycorax,
For mischiefs manifold*, and sorceries terrible   *many
To enter human hearing, from Argier,
Thou know'st, was banish'd*: for one thing she did   *exiled, kicked out   315
They would not take her life. Is not this true?

ARIEL
Ay, sir.

PROSPERO
This blue-ey'd hag was hither brought with child,
And here was left by the sailors. Thou, my slave,
As thou report'st thyself, wast then her servant: 320
And, for thou wast a spirit too delicate
To act her earthy and abhorr'd* commands,   *hateful, awful
Refusing her grand hests*, she did confine* thee,   *commands *imprison
By help of her more potent* ministers*,   *powerful *helpers
And in her most unmitigable* rage,   *cannot be lessened   325
Into a cloven* pine; within which rift*   *split, divided *divide, fissure
Imprison'd, thou didst painfully remain

A dozen years; within which space she died,
And left thee there, where thou didst vent thy groans
As fast as mill-wheels strike. Then was this island—   330
Save for the son that she did litter here,
A freckl'd whelp*, hag-born—not honour'd with   *boy
A human shape.

ARIEL
Yes; Caliban her son.

PROSPERO
Dull thing, I say so; he, that Caliban,   335
Whom now I keep in service*. Thou best know'st   *as a servant
What torment I did find thee in; thy groans
Did make wolves howl, and penetrate the breasts
Of ever-angry bears: it was a torment
To lay upon the damn'd, which Sycorax   340
Could not again undo; it was mine art*,   *magic
When I arriv'd and heard thee, that made gape*   *opened
The pine, and let thee out.

ARIEL
I thank thee, master.

PROSPERO
If thou more murmur'st, I will rend* an oak   *split   345
And peg* thee in his knotty entrails* till   *put *inside of the oak
Thou hast howl'd away twelve winters.

ARIEL
Pardon, master:
I will be correspondent* to command,   *conform, follow
And do my spriting gently.   350

PROSPERO
Do so; and after two days
I will discharge* thee.   *free

ARIEL
That's my noble master!
What shall I do? Say what? What shall I do?

PROSPERO
Go make thyself like a nymph o' th' sea: be subject   355
To no sight but thine and mine; invisible
To every eyeball else. Go, take this shape,
And hither come in 't: go, hence with diligence*!   *speed, haste
[*Exit ARIEL*]
Awake, dear heart, awake! thou hast slept well;
Awake!   360

MIRANDA
[*Waking*] The strangeness of your story put
Heaviness in me.

PROSPERO
Shake it off. Come on;
We'll visit Caliban my slave, who never
Yields* us kind answer.   *gives   365

MIRANDA
'Tis a villain, sir,
I do not love to look on.

PROSPERO
But as 'tis,
We cannot miss him: he does make our fire,
Fetch in our wood; and serves in offices   370
That profit* us. —What ho! slave! Caliban!   *help
Thou earth, thou! Speak.

CALIBAN
[*Within*] There's wood enough within.

PROSPERO

Come forth, I say; there's other business for thee:

Come, thou tortoise! when?   375

[*Re-enter ARIEL like a water-nymph.*]

Fine apparition*! My quaint Ariel,   *ghost/spirit

Hark* in thine ear.   *listen

ARIEL

My lord, it shall be done.

[*Exit*]

PROSPERO

Thou poisonous slave, got by the devil himself

Upon thy wicked dam*, come forth!   *mother   380

[*Enter CALIBAN*]

CALIBAN

As wicked dew as e'er my mother brush'd

With raven's feather from unwholesome fen*   *swamp

Drop on you both! A south-west blow on ye,

And blister you all o'er!

PROSPERO

For this, be sure, to-night thou shalt have cramps,   385

Side-stitches that shall pen thy breath up; urchins*   *evil spirits

Shall forth at vast* of night that they may work   *big empty stretch

All exercise on thee: thou shalt be pinch'd

As thick as honeycomb, each pinch more stinging

Than bees that made them.   390

CALIBAN

I must eat my dinner.

This island's mine, by Sycorax my mother,

Which thou tak'st from me. When thou cam'st first,

Thou strok'st* me and made much of me; wouldst give me   *petted, treated me well

Water with berries in't; and teach me how   395

To name the bigger light, and how the less,

That burn by day and night: and then I lov'd thee,
And show'd thee all the qualities o' th' isle,
The fresh springs, brine-pits*, barren place, and fertile.   *salt water pits
Curs'd be I that did so! All the charms   400
Of Sycorax, toads, beetles, bats, light on you!
For I am all the subjects* that you have,   *beings to rule
Which first was mine own king; and here you sty* me   *confine, cage
In this hard rock, whiles you do keep from me
The rest o' th' island.   405

PROSPERO
Thou most lying slave,
Whom stripes* may move, not kindness! I have us'd thee,   *whippings, lashes
Filth as thou art, with human care, and lodg'd thee
In mine own cell, till thou didst seek to violate
The honour of my child.   410

CALIBAN
Oh ho! Oh ho! Would it had been done!
Thou didst prevent me; I had peopl'd else
This isle with Calibans.

PROSPERO
Abhorred* slave,   *hated
Which any print of goodness wilt not take,   415
Being capable of all ill! I pitied thee,
Took pains to make thee speak, taught thee each hour
One thing or other: when thou didst not, savage,
Know thine own meaning, but wouldst gabble* like   *speak gibberish
A thing most brutish*, I endow'd* thy purposes   *like an animal *provided   420
With words that made them known: but thy vile* race,   *morally despicable
Though thou didst learn, had that in't which good natures
Could not abide to be with; therefore wast thou
Deservedly confin'd into this rock, who hadst
Deserv'd more than a prison.   425

CALIBAN
You taught me language, and my profit on't
Is, I know how to curse: the red plague rid you,
For learning me your language!

PROSPERO
Hag-seed, hence!
Fetch us in fuel; and be quick, thou 'rt best,   430
To answer other business. Shrug'st thou, malice?
If thou neglect'st, or dost unwillingly
What I command, I'll rack* thee with old cramps,   *cause pain
Fill all thy bones with aches; make thee roar,
That beasts shall tremble at thy din*.   *noise   435

CALIBAN
No, pray thee
[*Aside*]* I must obey. His art is of such power,   *As if speaking to himself
It would control my dam's* god, Setebos,   *mother's
And make a vassal* of him.   *servant

PROSPERO
So, slave: hence!   440
[*Exit CALIBAN*]
[*Re-enter ARIEL invisible, playing and singing;*
FERDINAND following]

[*ARIEL'S* SONG.]
Come unto these yellow sands,
And then take hands:
Curtsied when you have, and kiss'd,—
The wild waves whist,—
Foot it featly here and there;   445
And, sweet sprites, the burden bear.
Hark, hark!
[*Burden: Bow, wow, dispersedly.*]
The watch dogs bark:
[*Burden: Bow, wow, dispersedly.*]   450
Hark, hark! I hear

DELETED TEXT, LINE 437
none of the characters can hear him

The strain of strutting Chanticleer
[*Cry, Cock-a-diddle-dow.*]

FERDINAND
Where should this music be? I' th' air or th' earth?
It sounds no more; and sure it waits upon   455
Some god o' th' island. Sitting on a bank,
Weeping again the king my father's wrack*,   *wreck
This music crept by me upon the waters,
Allaying* both their fury and my passion,   *calming
With its sweet air: thence I have follow'd it,   460
Or it hath drawn* me rather,—but 'tis gone.   *lured
No, it begins again.

[*ARIEL* sings]
Full fathom* five thy father lies: *leagues/miles
Of his bones are coral made:
Those are pearls that were his eyes: 465
Nothing of him that doth fade
But doth suffer a sea-change
Into something rich and strange.
Sea-nymphs hourly ring his knell:
[*Burden: Ding-dong.*]   470
Hark! Now I hear them —ding-dong, bell.

FERDINAND
The ditty* does remember my drown'd father.   *song
This is no mortal business*, nor no sound   *humans couldn't do this
That the earth owes*: —I hear it now above me.   *or anything on earth

PROSPERO
The fringed curtains of thine eye advance,   475
And say what thou seest yond.

MIRANDA
What is't? A spirit?
Lord, how it looks about! Believe me, sir,
It carries a brave form: but 'tis a spirit.

PROSPERO

No, wench*; it eats and sleeps, and hath such senses   *girl   480
As we have, such; this gallant* which thou see'st   *young man of fashion
Was in the wrack*; and but he's something stain'd   *wreck
With grief,—that beauty's canker*,—thou mightst call him *spreading sore
A goodly person: he hath lost his fellows
And strays* about to find 'em.   *wanders   485

MIRANDA

I might call him
A thing divine; for nothing natural
I ever saw so noble.

PROSPERO

[*Aside*]* It goes on, I see,
As my soul prompts it. Spirit, fine spirit! I'll free thee   490
Within two days for this.

FERDINAND

Most sure, the goddess
On whom these airs attend! —Vouchsafe*, my prayer   *grant me
May know if you remain upon this island;
And that you will some good instruction give   495
How I may bear me here: my prime request,
Which I do last pronounce, is, — O you wonder!
If you be maid* or no?   *virgin

MIRANDA

No wonder, sir;
But certainly a maid.   500

FERDINAND

My language! Heavens!
I am the best of them that speak this speech,
Were I but where 'tis spoken.

PROSPERO
How! the best?
What wert thou, if the King of Naples heard thee?   505

FERDINAND
A single thing, as I am now, that wonders
To hear thee speak of Naples. He does hear me;
And, that he does, I weep: myself am Naples*,   *I am now King of Naples
Who with mine eyes, never since at ebb*, beheld   *closed
The King, my father wrack'd.   510

MIRANDA
Alack, for mercy!

FERDINAND
Yes, faith, and all his lords, the Duke of Milan,
And his brave son being twain*.   *two

PROSPERO
[*Aside.*] The Duke of Milan,
And his more braver daughter could control thee,   515
If now 't were fit to do't. At the first sight [*Aside.*]
They have changed eyes*;—delicate Ariel,   *exchanged eyes, fallen in love
I'll set thee free for this! [*To FERDINAND*] A word,
good sir:
I fear you have done yourself some wrong: a word.   520

MIRANDA
[*Aside.*] Why speaks my father so ungently? This
Is the third man that e'er I saw; the first
That e'er I sigh'd for; pity move my father
To be inclin'd my way!

FERDINAND
[*Aside.*] O! if a virgin,   525
And your affection not gone forth*, I'll make you   *if you don't love someone else
The Queen of Naples.

PROSPERO
Soft, sir; one word more —
[*Aside*] They are both in either's powers: but this swift
business I must uneasy make, lest too light winning   530
Make the prize light. [*To FERDINAND*] One word more:
I charge thee
That thou attend me. Thou dost here usurp*   *unlawfully take a position of power
The name thou ow'st* not; and hast put thyself   *you don't own
Upon this island as a spy, to win it   535
From me, the lord on't.

FERDINAND
No, as I am a man.

MIRANDA
There's nothing ill can dwell in such a temple*:   *body
If the ill spirit have so fair a house,
Good things will strive to dwell with't.   540

PROSPERO
[*To FERDINAND*] Follow me —
[*To MIRANDA*] Speak not you for him; he's a traitor —
[*To FERDINAND*] Come;
I'll manacle* thy neck and feet together: *bind
Sea-water shalt thou drink; thy food shall be   545
The fresh-brook mussels, wither'd roots, and husks
Wherein the acorn cradled. Follow.

FERDINAND
No;
I will resist such entertainment till
Mine enemy has more power.   550
[*He draws and is charmed from moving.*]

MIRANDA
O dear father!
Make not too rash a trial of him, for
He's gentle, and not fearful.

PROSPERO
What! I say,
My foot my tutor*? Put thy sword up, traitor;   *do you dare try to teach me? 555
Who mak'st a show, but dar'st not strike, thy conscience
Is so possess'd with guilt: come from thy ward*,   *fighting stance
For I can here disarm thee with this stick
And make thy weapon drop.

MIRANDA
Beseech* you, father!   *I beg you   560

PROSPERO
Hence! Hang not on my garments.

MIRANDA
Sir, have pity;
I'll be his surety*.   *guarantee

PROSPERO
Silence! One word more
Shall make me chide* thee, if not hate thee. What!   *scold   565
An advocate* for an impostor? Hush!   *one who speaks in support of
Thou think'st there is no more such shapes as he,
Having seen but him and Caliban: foolish wench!
To the most of men this is a Caliban,
And they to him are angels.   570

MIRANDA
My affections
Are then most humble; I have no ambition
To see a goodlier man.

PROSPERO
[To FERDINAND] Come on; obey:
Thy nerves are in their infancy again,   575
And have no vigour in them.

FERDINAND
So they are:
My spirits, as in a dream, are all bound up.
My father's loss, the weakness which I feel,
The wrack of all my friends, nor this man's threats,   580
To whom I am subdued*, are but light to me,   *I'm in his power
Might I but through my prison once a day
Behold this maid: all corners else o' th' earth
Let liberty make use of; space enough
Have I in such a prison.   585

PROSPERO
[*Aside*] It works. [*To FERDINAND*] Come on.
[*To ARIEL*] Thou hast done well, fine Ariel!
[*To FERDINAND*] Follow me.
[*To ARIEL*] Hark what thou else shalt do me.

MIRANDA
Be of comfort;   590
My father's of a better nature, sir,
Than he appears by speech: this is unwonted*,   *unusual
Which now came from him.

PROSPERO
Thou shalt be as free
As mountain winds; but then exactly do   595
All points of my command.

ARIEL
To the syllable.

PROSPERO
[*To FERDINAND*] Come, follow. Speak not for him.
[*Exeunt*]

ACT 2
SCENE I

Another part of the island

King Alonso and his company find themselves on the island and believe they are alone and wonder if anyone survived, including Ferdinand. Gonzalo tries to keep the king's hopes up and entertains him, while Sebastian and Antonio criticize him and act cynically and sarcastically. Ariel, invisible, makes Alonso and Gonzalo fall asleep, and Antonio persuades Sebastian to kill the king and Gonzalo so that they can have power over the island. Ariel, invisible, interferes right as they make the attempt, but they cover up their actions by claiming they heard wild animals. They plan to try again at the next opportunity.

[*Enter ALONSO, SEBASTIAN, ANTONIO, GONZALO,*
ADRIAN, FRANCISCO, and OTHERS]

GONZALO

Beseech* you, sir, be merry; you have cause,   *I beg
So have we all, of joy; for our escape
Is much beyond our loss. Our hint of woe*   *unhappiness
Is common: every day, some sailor's wife,
The masters of some merchant and the merchant,   5
Have just our theme of woe; but for the miracle,
I mean our preservation*, few in millions   *survival, saved from death
Can speak like us: then wisely, good sir, weigh
Our sorrow with our comfort.

ALONSO

Prithee*, peace.   *"Pray thee," Please   10

SEBASTIAN

He receives comfort like cold porridge*.   *the king will not be comforted

ANTONIO

The visitor will not give him o'er so*.   *Gonzalo will not allow it

SEBASTIAN

Look, he's winding up the watch of his wit.   * Gonzalo is getting ready to say
By and by it will strike. *   something witty

GONZALO
Sir —   15

SEBASTIAN
One: tell.

GONZALO
When every grief is entertained that's offer'd,   *when a person considers/feels every
Comes to th' entertainer* —   grief that is offered…

SEBASTIAN
A dollar*.   *payment

GONZALO
Dolor* comes to him, indeed: you have spoken   *great sadness   20
truer than you purposed*.   *intended

SEBASTIAN
You have taken it wiselier* than I meant you should.   *wittier/smarter

GONZALO
Therefore, my lord —   25

ANTONIO
Fie, what a spendthrift is he of his tongue*!   *spends his words too freely

ALONSO
I prithee, spare*.   *Spare me; stop talking

GONZALO
Well, I have done: but yet —

SEBASTIAN
[Aside to ANTONIO] He will be talking.

ANTONIO
[Aside to SEBASTIAN] Which, of he or Adrian, for a good wager*,   *bet   30
first begins to crow*?   *talk

SEBASTIAN
The old cock*.

*Gonzalo (old)

ANTONIO
The cockerel*.

*Adrian (young)

SEBASTIAN
Done. The wager?

ANTONIO
A laughter.

35

SEBASTIAN
A match!

ADRIAN
Though this island seem to be desert —

SEBASTIAN
Ha, ha, ha! So, you're paid*.

*Antonio won the bet

ADRIAN
Uninhabitable, and almost inaccessible —

SEBASTIAN
Yet —

40

ADRIAN
Yet —

ANTONIO
He could not miss it.

ADRIAN
It must needs be of subtle, tender, and delicate
temperance.

ANTONIO
Temperance was a delicate wench.   45

SEBASTIAN
Ay, and a subtle, as he most learnedly delivered.

ADRIAN
The air breathes upon us here most sweetly.

SEBASTIAN
As if it had lungs, and rotten ones.

ANTONIO
Or, as 'twere perfumed by a fen*.   *swamp

GONZALO
Here is everything advantageous to life.   50

ANTONIO
True; save means to live.

SEBASTIAN
Of that there's none, or little.

GONZALO
How lush and lusty the grass looks! How green!

ANTONIO
The ground indeed is tawny*.   *brown

SEBASTIAN
With an eye of green in't.   55

ANTONIO
He misses not much.

SEBASTIAN
No; he doth but mistake the truth totally.

GONZALO

But the rarity of it is, which is indeed almost
beyond credit.

SEBASTIAN

As many vouched* rarities are.   *promised   60

GONZALO

That our garments, being, as they were, drenched
in the sea, hold notwithstanding their freshness and
gloss, being rather new-dyed than stain'd with salt
water.

ANTONIO

If but one of his pockets could speak, would it   65
not say he lies?

SEBASTIAN

Ay, or very falsely pocket up his report.

GONZALO

Methinks, our garments are now as fresh as when
we put them on first in Africa, at the marriage of the
king's fair daughter, Claribel, to the King of Tunis.   70

SEBASTIAN

'Twas a sweet marriage, and we prosper well in our
return.

ADRIAN

Tunis was never graced before with such a paragon*   *model of perfection
to their queen.

GONZALO

Not since widow Dido's* time.   *Queen of Carthage, who committed suicide when Aeneas left her   75

ANTONIO
Widow*! A pox o' that! How came that widow in?
Widow Dido!

*she was a widow when she met
Aeneas

SEBASTIAN
What if he had said, widower Aeneas too?
Good Lord, how you take it!

ADRIAN
Widow Dido said you? You make me study of that. She
was of Carthage, not of Tunis*.

80

*Both are in Africa

GONZALO
This Tunis, sir, was Carthage.

ADRIAN
Carthage?

GONZALO
I assure you, Carthage.

ANTONIO
His word is more than the miraculous harp.

85

SEBASTIAN
He hath rais'd the wall, and houses too.

ANTONIO
What impossible matter will he make easy next?

SEBASTIAN
I think he will carry this island home in his
pocket and give it his son for an apple.

ANTONIO
And, sowing the kernels of it in the sea, bring
forth more islands.

90

ALONSO
Ay.

ANTONIO
Why, in good time.

GONZALO
[*To ALONSO.*] Sir, we were talking that our garments seem now
as fresh as when we were at Tunis at the marriage of   95
your daughter, who is now queen.

ANTONIO
And the rarest that e'er came there.

SEBASTIAN
Bate, I beseech you, widow Dido.

ANTONIO
O! widow Dido? Ay, widow Dido.

GONZALO
Is not, sir, my doublet* as fresh as the first day I   *jacket   100
wore it? I mean, in a sort.

ANTONIO
That sort was well fish'd for.

GONZALO
When I wore it at your daughter's marriage?

ALONSO
You cram these words into mine ears against
The stomach of my sense*. Would I had never   *I don't want to hear this   105
Married my daughter there! For coming thence,
My son is lost; and, in my rate, she too,
Who is so far from Italy removed,
I ne'er again shall see her. O thou, mine heir

Of Naples and of Milan! what strange fish   110
Hath made his meal on thee*?   *thinks Ferdinand drowned

FRANCISCO
Sir, he may live:
I saw him beat the surges under him,
And ride upon their backs: he trod the water,
Whose enmity* he flung aside, and breasted   *ill will
115
The surge most swoll'n that met him: his bold head
'Bove the contentious* waves he kept, and oar'd   *argumentative
Himself with his good arms in lusty stroke
To th' shore, that o'er his wave-worn basis bowed,
As stooping to relieve him*. I not doubt   *the shore saved him   120
He came alive to land.

ALONSO
No, no; he's gone.

SEBASTIAN
Sir, you may thank yourself for this great loss,
That would not bless our Europe with your daughter,
But rather lose her to an African;   125
Where she, at least, is banish'd from your eye*,   *you can't see her since she's in Africa
Who hath cause to wet the grief on 't.

ALONSO
Prithee, peace.

SEBASTIAN
You were kneel'd to, and importun'd* otherwise   *begged
By all of us; and the fair soul herself*   *Claribel   130
Weigh'd between loathness* and obedience at   *unwillingness
Which end o' th' beam should bow*. We have lost your son   *which should win
I fear, for ever: Milan and Naples have
More widows in them of this business' making*,   *husbands who died in this storm   135

Than we bring men to comfort them.
The fault's your own.

ALONSO
So is the dearest of the loss.

GONZALO
My lord Sebastian,
The truth you speak doth lack some gentleness   140
And time to speak it in; you rub the sore,
When you should bring the plaster*.   *to soothe/heal the wound

SEBASTIAN
Very well.

ANTONIO
And most chirurgeonly*.   *like a surgeon

GONZALO
It is foul weather in us all, good sir,   145
When you are cloudy.

SEBASTIAN
Foul weather?

ANTONIO
Very foul.

GONZALO
Had I plantation of this isle, my lord —

ANTONIO
He'd sow 't with nettle-seed.   150

SEBASTIAN
Or docks, or mallows.

GONZALO
And were the king on't, what would I do?

SEBASTIAN
'Scape being drunk for want of wine*.

*can't get drunk since there's no wine

GONZALO
I' the commonwealth* I would by contraries*
Execute* all things; for no kind of traffic*
Would I admit; no name of magistrate*;
Letters* should not be known; riches, poverty,
And use of service*, none; contract, succession*,
Bourn*, bound of land, tilth*, vineyard, none;
No use of metal, corn, or wine, or oil;
No occupation; all men idle*, all:
And women too, but innocent and pure;
No sovereignty* —

*nation *contrary to custom
*do things *trade/business   155
*judge
*education
*servants *laws of inheritance
*boundaries. *agriculture
                    160
*no labor

*no king

SEBASTIAN
Yet he would be king on't.

ANTONIO
The latter end of his commonwealth forgets the   165
beginning*.

*Gonzalo has contradicted himself

GONZALO
All things in common nature should produce
Without sweat or endeavour; treason, felony,
Sword, pike, knife, gun, or need of any engine,
Would I not have*; but nature should bring forth,
Of its own kind, all foison*, all abundance,
To feed my innocent people.

*no violence   170
*rich harvest

SEBASTIAN
No marrying 'mong his subjects?

ANTONIO
None, man: all idle; whores and knaves.

GONZALO
I would with such perfection govern, sir,   175
To excel the Golden Age.

SEBASTIAN
Save his Majesty!

ANTONIO
Long live Gonzalo!

GONZALO
And do you mark me*, sir?   *Are you listening?

ALONSO
Prithee, no more: thou dost talk nothing* to me.   *nonsense   180

GONZALO
I do well believe your Highness; and did it to
minister occasion* to these gentlemen, who are of such   *counter-act
sensible and nimble lungs* that they always use to laugh   *so healthy
at nothing.

ANTONIO
'Twas you we laughed at.   185

GONZALO
Who in this kind of merry fooling am nothing to
you; so you may continue, and laugh at nothing still.

ANTONIO
What a blow was there given!

SEBASTIAN
And it had not fallen flat-long.

GONZALO
You are gentlemen of brave mettle*: you would   *strength of spirit   190
lift the moon out of her sphere if she would continue

in it five weeks without changing.
[*Enter ARIEL, invisible, playing solemn music*]

SEBASTIAN
We would so, and then go a-batfowling.

ANTONIO
Nay, good my lord, be not angry.

GONZALO
No, I warrant you; I will not adventure my   195
discretion* so weakly. Will you laugh me asleep? For I am   *lose my sense of judgment
very heavy.

ANTONIO
Go sleep, and hear us.
[*All sleep but ALONSO, SEBASTIAN, and ANTONIO*]

ALONSO
What, all so soon asleep? I wish mine eyes
Would, with themselves, shut up my thoughts: I find   200
They are inclin'd to do so.

SEBASTIAN
Please you, sir,
Do not omit the heavy offer of it:
It seldom visits sorrow; when it doth,
It is a comforter.   205

ANTONIO
We two, my lord,
Will guard your person while you take your rest,
And watch your safety.

ALONSO
Thank you. Wondrous heavy!
[*ALONSO sleeps. Exit ARIEL.*]

SEBASTIAN
What a strange drowsiness possesses them*!

*how did they get so sleepy? 210

ANTONIO
It is the quality o' th' climate.

SEBASTIAN
Why
Doth it not then our eyelids sink? I find not
Myself dispos'd to sleep.

ANTONIO
Nor I: my spirits are nimble*.

*I'm wide awake 215

They fell together all, as by consent;
They dropp'd, as by a thunderstroke. What might,
Worthy Sebastian? O, what might? No more.
And yet methinks I see it in thy face,
What thou shouldst be: The occasion speaks thee; and 220
My strong imagination sees a crown
Dropping upon thy head.

SEBASTIAN
What, art thou waking?

ANTONIO
Do you not hear me speak?

SEBASTIAN
I do: and surely 225
It is a sleepy language, and thou speak'st
Out of thy sleep. What is it thou didst say?
This is a strange repose*, to be asleep

*rest

With eyes wide open — standing, speaking, moving —
And yet so fast asleep. 230

ANTONIO
Noble Sebastian,
Thou let'st thy fortune sleep —die rather: wink'st*   *sleep
Whiles thou art waking.

SEBASTIAN
Thou dost snore distinctly:
There's meaning in thy snores.   235

ANTONIO
I am more serious than my custom; you
Must be so too, if heed me: which to do
Trebles thee o'er*.   *three times over

SEBASTIAN
Well, I am standing water.

ANTONIO
I'll teach you how to flow.   240

SEBASTIAN
Do so: to ebb*,   *recede
Hereditary sloth* instructs me.   *inherited laziness

ANTONIO
O!
If you but knew how you the purpose cherish
Whiles thus you mock it*! how, in stripping it,   *you clearly want it even   245
You more invest it! Ebbing men indeed,   though you joke about it
Most often, do so near the bottom run
By their own fear or sloth.

SEBASTIAN
Prithee, say on:
The setting of thine eye and cheek proclaim*   *praise openly   250
A matter from thee, and a birth, indeed
Which throes* thee much to yield*.   *hurts *give up

ANTONIO
Thus, sir:
Although this lord of weak remembrance, this
Who shall be of as little memory   255
When he is earth'd, hath here almost persuaded —
For he's a spirit of persuasion, only
Professes to persuade —the King his son's alive,
'Tis as impossible that he's undrown'd*   *Ferdinand has to be dead
As he that sleeps here swims.   260

SEBASTIAN
I have no hope
That he's undrown'd. *   *I believe he's drowned

ANTONIO
O! out of that 'no hope'
What great hope have you*! No hope that way is   *how great for you
Another way so high a hope, that even   265
Ambition cannot pierce a wink beyond*,   *better than even ambition imagines
But doubts discovery there. Will you grant with me
That Ferdinand is drown'd?

SEBASTIAN
He's gone.

ANTONIO
Then tell me,   270
Who's the next heir of Naples?

SEBASTIAN
Claribel.

ANTONIO
She that is Queen of Tunis; she that dwells
Ten leagues beyond man's life*; she that from Naples   *she's all the way in Africa
Can have no note, unless the sun were post —   275
The Man i' th' Moon's too slow —till newborn chins

Be rough and razorable*: she that from whom   *she couldn't get here before her kids
We all were sea-swallow'd, though some cast again,   grew up
And by that destiny to perform an act
Whereof what's past is prologue, what to come   280
In yours and my discharge*.   *this is our chance

SEBASTIAN
What stuff is this? How say you?
'Tis true, my brother's daughter's Queen of Tunis;
So is she heir of Naples; 'twixt which regions
There is some space*.   *Claribel is quite far away   285

ANTONIO
A space whose every cubit*   *foot and a half of measurement
Seems to cry out 'How shall that Claribel
Measure us back to Naples? Keep in Tunis,
And let Sebastian wake.' Say this were death
That now hath seiz'd them*; why, they were no worse   *Alonso & Gonzalo   290
Than now they are. There be that can rule Naples
As well as he that sleeps; lords that can prate*   *talk a lot about nothing
As amply and unnecessarily
As this Gonzalo: I myself could make
A chough of as deep chat. O, that you bore   295
The mind that I do! What a sleep were this
For your advancement*! Do you understand me?   *their sleep is your great opportunity

SEBASTIAN
Methinks I do.

ANTONIO
And how does your content
Tender your own good fortune?   300

SEBASTIAN
I remember
You did supplant* your brother Prospero.   *usurp/steal/unlawfully take
                                          the place of

ANTONIO
True,
And look how well my garments sit upon me;
Much feater* than before; my brother's servants   *better   305
Were then my fellows; now they are my men*.   *servants

SEBASTIAN
But, for your conscience?

ANTONIO
Ay, sir; where lies that? If 'twere a kibe*,   *ulcer of the foot
'Twould put me to my slipper: but I feel not
This deity* in my bosom: twenty consciences   *god   310
That stand 'twixt* me and Milan, candied be they   *between
And melt ere they molest*! Here lies your brother,   *bother me
No better than the earth he lies upon,
If he were that which now he's like —that's dead —
Whom I, with this obedient steel*,—three inches of it,—   *knife   315
Can lay to bed for ever; whiles you, doing thus,
To the perpetual wink for aye might put
This ancient morsel, this Sir Prudence*, who   *Gonzalo
Should not upbraid* our course. For all the rest,   *criticize severely
They'll take suggestion as a cat laps milk.   320
They'll tell the clock to any business that
We say befits the hour.

SEBASTIAN
Thy case, dear friend,
Shall be my precedent*: as thou got'st Milan,   *model that came before
I'll come by Naples. Draw thy sword: one stroke   325
Shall free thee from the tribute* which thou pay'st,   *money/loyalty/allegiance
And I the king shall love thee.

ANTONIO
Draw together:
And when I rear* my hand, do you the like,   *raise
To fall it on Gonzalo.   330

SEBASTIAN
O, but one word.
[*They converse apart.*]
[*Music. Re-enter ARIEL, invisible.*]

ARIEL
[*To the sleeping* GONZALO] My master through his art foresees the danger
That you, his friend, are in; and sends me forth —
For else his project dies —to keep thee living.
[*Sings in GONZALO'S ear*]
While you here do snoring lie,   335
Open-ey'd conspiracy*   *plot against the king
His time doth take.
If of life you keep a care,
Shake off slumber and beware.
Awake! Awake!   340

ANTONIO
Then let us both be sudden.

GONZALO
[*waking*] Now, good angels preserve the King!
[*He wakes ALONSO*]

ALONSO
Why, how now! Ho! Awake! Why are you drawn*?   *Why are your weapons drawn?
Wherefore this ghastly looking?

GONZALO
What's the matter?   345

SEBASTIAN
Whiles we stood here securing your repose*,   *protecting you in your sleep
Even now, we heard a hollow burst of bellowing
Like bulls, or rather lions; did't not wake you?
It struck mine ear most terribly.

ALONSO
I heard nothing.   350

ANTONIO
O! 'twas a din* to fright a monster's ear,   *loud noise
To make an earthquake: sure it was the roar
Of a whole herd of lions.

ALONSO
Heard you this, Gonzalo?   355

GONZALO
Upon mine honour, sir, I heard a humming,
And that a strange one too, which did awake me.
I shak'd you, sir, and cried; as mine eyes open'd,
I saw their weapons drawn. There was a noise,
That's verily*. 'Tis best we stand upon our guard,   *true   360
Or that we quit this place: let's draw our weapons.

ALONSO
Lead off this ground: and let's make further search
For my poor son.

GONZALO
Heavens keep him from these beasts!   365
For he is, sure, i' th' island.

ALONSO
Lead away.
[*Exit with the others.*]

ARIEL
Prospero my lord shall know what I have done:
So, king, go safely on to seek thy son.
[*Exit*]

SCENE II

Another part of the island

Caliban is grumbling about his enslavement to Prospero when a thunderstorm arrives. Trinculo notices the storm following him, discovers Caliban, and imagines that he can take him back to Europe and make his fortune by using him as a freak show. He then hides under Caliban's cloak with Caliban. Stephano, who is drunk, comes upon the cloak and also thinks about how to use Caliban to make his fortune. He is reunited with Trinculo after great confusion, and he introduces Caliban to wine. Caliban, thinking Stephano must be a god because of the wine, pledges his allegiance to Stephano and celebrates his freedom from Prospero.

[*Enter CALIBAN, with a burden of wood. A noise of thunder heard*]

CALIBAN

All the infections that the sun sucks up
From bogs*, fens*, flats, on Prosper fall, and make him   *wet, spongy ground   *swamp
By inch-meal* a disease! His spirits hear me,   *inch by inch, slowly
And yet I needs must curse. But they'll nor pinch,
Fright me with urchin-shows, pitch me i' the mire*,   *muck, mud   5
Nor lead me, like a firebrand*, in the dark   *burning wood
Out of my way, unless he bid 'em; but
For every trifle* are they set upon me: *little thing
Sometimes like apes that mow* and chatter at me,   *make faces
And after bite me; then like hedgehogs which   *porcupine   10
Lie tumbling in my barefoot way, and mount
Their pricks at my footfall; sometime am I
All wound with adders*, who with cloven tongues   *poisonous snake
Do hiss me into madness. Lo, now, lo!
Here comes a spirit of his, and to torment me   15
For bringing wood in slowly. I'll fall flat;
Perchance* he will not mind me.   *possibly, maybe

[*He lies down and covers himself with a cloak*]
[*Enter TRINCULO*]

TRINCULO

Here's neither bush nor shrub to bear off any
weather at all, and another storm brewing; I hear it   20
sing i' th' wind; yond* same black cloud, yond huge one,   *over there

looks like a foul bombard* that would shed his liquor*. If   *big leather jug *i. e. rain
it should thunder as it did before, I know not where to
hide my head: yond same cloud cannot choose but fall by
pailfuls. [*Noticing CALIBAN*] What have we here, a man or a fish? Dead or   25
alive? A fish: he smells like a fish: a very ancient and
fish-like smell; a kind of not of the newest poor-John*. A   *fish
strange fish! Were I in England now, as once I was, and
had but this fish painted, not a holiday fool there but
would give a piece of silver: there would this monster   30
make a man*; any strange beast there makes a man. When   *man of standing, wealth
they will not give a doit* to relieve a lame beggar, they   *coin of small value
will lay out ten to see a dead Indian. Legg'd like a
man, and his fins like arms! Warm, o' my troth*! I do now   *truth
let loose* my opinion: hold it no longer; this is no   *speak   35
fish, but an islander, that hath lately suffered by
thunderbolt. [*Thunder*] Alas, the storm is come again! My
best way is to creep under his gaberdine*; there is no   *loose jacket
other shelter hereabout: misery acquaints a man with
strange bedfellows. I will here shroud* till the dregs*   *cover myself up *last effects   40
of the storm be past.
[*He crawls under CALIBAN'S cloak*]
[*Enter STEPHANO singing; a bottle in his hand*]

STEPHANO
I shall no more to sea, to sea,
Here shall I die ashore —
This is a very scurvy* tune to sing at a man's funeral: *obnoxious
Well, here's my comfort*. [*Drinks*]   *alcohol provides comfort   45

The master, the swabber, the boatswain, and I,
The gunner, and his mate,
Loved Mall, Meg, and Marian, and Margery,
But none of us car'd* for Kate: *cared
For she had a tongue with a tang*,   *biting tongue   50
Would cry to a sailor 'Go hang!'
She lov'd not the savour* of tar nor of pitch,   *taste
Yet a tailor might scratch her where'er she did itch.

Then to sea, boys, and let her go hang.
This is a scurvy tune too: but here's my comfort. [*Drinks*]   55

CALIBAN
Do not torment me! O!

STEPHANO
What's the matter? Have we devils here? Do you
put tricks upon us with savages and men of Ind*? Ha! I   *India
have not 'scaped* drowning, to be afeard* now of your four   *escaped *afraid
legs; for it hath been said, 'As proper a man as ever   60
went on four legs cannot make him give ground*,' and it   *back down
shall be said so again, while Stephano breathes at' nostrils.

CALIBAN
The spirit torments me: O!

STEPHANO
This is some monster of the isle with four legs,
who hath got, as I take it, an ague*. Where the devil   *fever, infection   65
should he learn our language*? I will give him some   *Italian (though the play is in English)
relief, if it be but for that; if I can recover him* and   *catch? or help him recover?
keep him tame and get to Naples with him, he's a
present for any emperor that ever trod on neat's leather*.   *cowhide

CALIBAN
Do not torment me, prithee; I'll bring my wood   70
home faster.

STEPHANO
He's in his fit now and does not talk after the
wisest. He shall taste of my bottle: if he have never
drunk wine afore, it will go near to remove his fit*. If   *illness
I can recover him, and keep him tame, I will not take   75
too much for him: he shall pay for him that hath him*,   *I'll take a fair price for him in a sale
and that soundly.

CALIBAN

Thou dost me yet but little hurt. Thou wilt anon*;   *immediately
I know it by thy trembling. Now Prosper works upon thee.

STEPHANO

Come on your ways: open your mouth. Here is   80
that which will give language to you, cat. Open your
mouth: this will shake your shaking, I can tell you, and
that soundly: [*CALIBAN drinks*] you cannot tell
who's your friend: open your chaps* again.   *jaws

TRINCULO

I should know that voice: it should be —but he is   85
drowned; and these are devils. O! defend me.

STEPHANO

Four legs and two voices —a most delicate monster!
His forward voice now is to speak well of his
friend; his backward voice is to utter foul speeches, and
to detract*. If all the wine in my bottle will recover   *farts   90
him, I will help his ague. Come. [*CALIBAN drinks*] Amen!
I will pour some in thy other mouth*.   *back side/behind

TRINCULO
Stephano!

STEPHANO

Doth thy other mouth call me? Mercy! Mercy!
This is a devil, and no monster! I will leave him: I   95
have no long spoon.

TRINCULO

Stephano! If thou beest Stephano, touch me, and
speak to me; for I am Trinculo —be not afeared *—thy   *afraid
good friend Trinculo.

STEPHANO

If thou be'st Trinculo, come forth. I'll pull   100
thee by the lesser legs: if any be Trinculo's legs, these

are they. [*He pulls him out from under CALIBAN'S cloak*]
Thou art very Trinculo indeed! How cam'st thou
to be the siege* of this moon-calf*? Can he vent* Trinculos?   *excrement *monstrosity *fart

TRINCULO
I took him to be kill'd with a thunderstroke*.   *lightning   105
But art thou not drown'd, Stephano? I hope now thou are
not drown'd. Is the storm overblown? I hid me under the
dead moon-calf's gaberdine* for fear of the storm. And   *loose fitting jacket
art thou living, Stephano? O Stephano, two Neapolitans
'scaped*!   *escaped   110

STEPHANO
Prithee, do not turn me about: my stomach is not
constant*.   *is upset (from being drunk)

CALIBAN
[*Aside*] These be fine things, an if they be not sprites*.   *spirits
That's a brave god* and bears celestial liquor*;   *thinks Stephano is a god. *alcohol
I will kneel to him*.   *pledge my allegiance to him   115

STEPHANO
How didst thou 'scape? How cam'st thou hither*? Swear   *here
by this bottle how thou cam'st hither —I escaped upon
a butt* of sack*, which the sailors heaved overboard —by   *large cask/barrel. *wine
this bottle! which I made of the bark of a tree with
mine own hands, since I was cast ashore.   120

CALIBAN
I'll swear upon that bottle to be thy true
subject*, for the liquor is not earthly.   *under your rule

STEPHANO
Here: swear then how thou escapedst.

TRINCULO
Swum ashore, man, like a duck. I can swim like
a duck, I'll be sworn.   125

STEPHANO
[*Passing the bottle*] Here, kiss the book [*gives
TRINCULO a drink*]. Though thou canst swim like a
duck, thou art made like a goose.

TRINCULO
O Stephano! hast any more of this?

STEPHANO
The whole butt*, man. My cellar is in a rock by   *cask   130
the seaside, where my wine is hid. How now, moon-calf!
How does thine ague*?   *fever, illness

CALIBAN
Hast thou not dropped from heaven?

STEPHANO
Out o' the moon, I do assure thee: I was the Man
in the Moon, when time was.   135

CALIBAN
I have seen thee in her, and I do adore thee, my
mistress showed me thee, and thy dog, and thy bush.

STEPHANO
Come, swear to that; kiss the book. I will
furnish it anon with new contents. Swear.

TRINCULO
By this good light, this is a very shallow   140
monster. I afeard of him? —A very weak monster.
The Man i' the Moon! A most poor, credulous*   *gullible, will believe anything
monster! —Well drawn, monster, in good sooth*!   *truth

CALIBAN
I'll show thee every fertile inch o' the island;
And I will kiss thy foot. I prithee, be my god.   145

TRINCULO
By this light, a most perfidious* and drunken
monster: when his god's asleep, he'll rob his bottle.

*faithless, disloyal

CALIBAN
I'll kiss thy foot. I'll swear myself thy subject.

STEPHANO
Come on, then; down, and swear.

TRINCULO
I shall laugh myself to death at this puppy-headed   150
monster. A most scurvy* monster! I could find in
my heart to beat him —

*diseased

STEPHANO
Come, kiss.

TRINCULO
But that the poor monster's in drink: an
abominable* monster!

*horrible, detestable   155

CALIBAN
I'll show thee the best springs; I'll pluck thee berries;
I'll fish for thee and get thee wood enough.
A plague* upon the tyrant* that I serve!
I'll bear him no more sticks*, but follow thee,
Thou wondrous man.

*disease. *Prospero
*firewood
160

TRINCULO
A most ridiculous monster, to make a wonder of
a poor drunkard!

CALIBAN
I prithee, let me bring thee where crabs* grow;
And I with my long nails will dig thee pig-nuts*;
Show thee a jay's nest, and instruct thee how
To snare the nimble marmoset. * I'll bring thee

*crab-apples
*earth nuts (like peanuts)
165
*small monkey

To clust'ring filberts*, and sometimes I'll get thee   *hazelnut
Young scamels* from the rock. Wilt thou go with me?   *birds

STEPHANO
I prithee now, lead the way without any more
talking. —Trinculo, the king and all our company else   170
being drowned, we will inherit* here. —Here, bear my   *take power over the island
bottle. —Fellow Trinculo, we'll fill him by and by
again.

CALIBAN
Farewell, master; farewell, farewell! [*Sings drunkenly*]

TRINCULO
A howling monster, a drunken monster.   175

CALIBAN
No more dams I'll make for fish;
Nor fetch in firing
At requiring,
Nor scrape trenchering, nor wash dish;
'Ban 'Ban, Ca-Caliban,   180
Has a new master. Get a new man.
Freedom, high-day! High-day, freedom! Freedom,
high-day, freedom!

STEPHANO
O brave monster! Lead the way.
[*Exeunt*]

ACT III
SCENE I

Before PROSPERO'S cell
Prospero puts Ferdinand to work, and he and Miranda fall even more in love. Prospero looks on without their knowledge and approves. Prospero then has to go on to other business.

[*Enter FERDINAND bearing a log.*]

FERDINAND
There be some sports are painful, and their labour
Delight in them sets off: some kinds of baseness
Are nobly undergone, and most poor matters
Point to rich ends. This my mean task
Would be as heavy to me as odious*; but   *hateful   5
The mistress which I serve quickens* what's dead,   *revive, bring back to life
And makes my labours pleasures. O, she is
Ten times more gentle than her father's crabbed*,   *grouchy
And he's compos'd of harshness. I must remove
Some thousands of these logs, and pile them up,   10
Upon a sore injunction*: my sweet mistress   *order
Weeps when she sees me work and says such baseness*   *lowness of position/work
Had never like executor*. I forget;   *person doing the work
But these sweet thoughts do even refresh my labours,
Most busy, least when I do it.   15
[*Enter MIRANDA: and PROSPERO behind.*]

MIRANDA
Alas now, pray you,
Work not so hard: I would the lightning had
Burnt up those logs that you are enjoin'd* to pile!   *ordered
Pray, set it down and rest you: when this burns,
'Twill weep for having wearied* you. My father   *tired   20
Is hard at study; pray, now, rest yourself:
He's safe for these three hours.

FERDINAND
O most dear mistress,
The sun will set, before I shall discharge*   *finish
What I must strive* to do.   *devote serious energy   25

MIRANDA
If you'll sit down,
I'll bear* your logs the while. Pray give me that;   *carry
I'll carry it to the pile.

FERDINAND
No, precious creature:
I had rather crack my sinews*, break my back,   *tendons   30
Than you should such dishonour undergo,
While I sit lazy by.

MIRANDA
It would become me
As well as it does you: and I should do it
With much more ease; for my good will is to it,   35
And yours it is against.

PROSPERO
[*Aside*] Poor worm*! Thou art infected: *Ferdinand
This visitation* shows it.   *visit between Ferdinand and
Miranda

MIRANDA
You look wearily.

FERDINAND
No, noble mistress; 'tis fresh morning with me   40
When you are by at night. I do beseech you,
Chiefly that I might set it in my prayers,
What is your name?

MIRANDA
Miranda —O my father!
I have broke your hest* to say so.   *behest, command   45

FERDINAND
Admir'd Miranda!
Indeed, the top of admiration; worth
What's dearest to the world! Full many a lady
I have ey'd with best regard, and many a time
The harmony of their tongues hath into bondage*   *slavery, servitude   50
Brought my too diligent* ear: for several virtues   *eager
Have I lik'd several women; never any

243

With so full soul but some defect* in her   *flaw
Did quarrel* with the noblest grace she ow'd,   *argue
And put it to the foil*: but you, O you!   *contrast   55
So perfect and so peerless*, are created   *without peer or equal
Of every creature's best.

MIRANDA
I do not know
One of my sex; no woman's face remember,
Save, from my glass*, mine own; nor have I seen   *mirror   60
More that I may call men than you, good friend,
And my dear father: how features are abroad,
I am skillless of; but, by my modesty —
The jewel in my dower* —I would not wish   *dowry, the wealth that a woman brings
Any companion in the world but you;   to a marriage from her family   65
Nor can imagination form a shape,
Besides yourself, to like of. But I prattle
Something too wildly, and my father's precepts*   *commands
I therein do forget.

FERDINAND
I am, in my condition,   70
A prince, Miranda; I do think, a king —
I would not so! —and would no more endure
This wooden slavery than to suffer
The flesh-fly* blow my mouth. Hear my soul speak: *fly whose maggots feed on flesh
The very instant that I saw you, did   75
My heart fly to your service; there resides,
To make me slave to it; and for your sake
Am I this patient log-man.

MIRANDA
Do you love me?

FERDINAND
O Heaven! O Earth! Bear witness to this sound,   80
And crown what I profess with kind event,
If I speak true: if hollowly, invert*   *reverse

What best is boded* me to mischief! I,   *foretold
Beyond all limit of what else i' the world,
Do love, prize, honour you.   85

MIRANDA
I am a fool
To weep at what I am glad of.

PROSPERO
[*Aside*] Fair encounter
Of two most rare affections! Heavens rain grace
On that which breeds* between them!   *grows   90

FERDINAND
Wherefore weep you?

MIRANDA
At mine unworthiness, that dare not offer
What I desire to give; and much less take
What I shall die to want. But this is trifling*;   *small concern
And all the more it seeks to hide itself,   95
The bigger bulk it shows. Hence, bashful cunning*!   *trickery
And prompt me, plain and holy innocence!
I am your wife, if you will marry me;
If not, I'll die your maid: to be your fellow*   *mate
You may deny me; but I'll be your servant,   100
Whether you will or no.

FERDINAND
My mistress*, dearest, and I thus humble ever.   *unmarried woman

MIRANDA
My husband, then?

FERDINAND
Ay, with a heart as willing
As bondage* e'er of freedom: here's my hand.   *slavery, servitude 105

MIRANDA
And mine, with my heart in 't: and now farewell
Till half an hour hence.

FERDINAND
A thousand thousand!
[*Exeunt FERDINAND and MIRANDA severally.*]

PROSPERO
So glad of this as they I cannot be,
Who are surpris'd withal; but my rejoicing   110
At nothing can be more. I'll to my book;
For yet, ere suppertime, must I perform
Much business appertaining*.   *connected to this
[*Exit*]

SCENE II

Another part of the island
Stephano enjoys his power over Caliban, and Ariel interferes, creating conflict be-
tween Stephano and Trinculo. Caliban explains what they'll have to do to kill Cali-
ban's master, Prospero, and promises Stephano marriage to Miranda. Stephano and
Trinculo make up. Ariel leaves to warn Prospero of the plan.
[*Enter CALIBAN, with a bottle, STEPHANO, and TRINCULO.*]

STEPHANO
Tell not me: —when the butt is out we will drink
water; not a drop before. Therefore bear up and board
'em. —Servant-monster, drink to me.

TRINCULO
Servant-monster! The folly of* this island! They   *foolishness about
say there's but five* upon this isle; we are three of   *people   5
them; if th' other two be brained* like us, the state   *intelligence
totters*.   *is unstable

STEPHANO
Drink, servant-monster, when I bid thee: thy
eyes are almost set in thy head*.

*you're drunk

TRINCULO
Where should they be set else? He were a brave   10
monster indeed, if they were set in his tail.

STEPHANO
My man-monster hath drown'd his tongue in
sack*. For my part, the sea cannot drown me; I swam, ere   *Caliban is drunk
I could recover the shore, five-and-thirty leagues, off
and on, by this light. Thou shalt be my lieutenant,   15
monster, or my standard*.   *soldier who bears the military's flag

TRINCULO
Your lieutenant, if you list. He's no standard.   *like

STEPHANO
We'll not run, Monsieur Monster.

TRINCULO
Nor go neither: but you'll lie like dogs, and
yet say nothing neither.   20

STEPHANO
Moon-calf, speak once in thy life, if thou be'st
a good moon-calf.

CALIBAN
How does thy honour? Let me lick thy shoe.
I'll not serve him: he is not valiant*.   *noble

TRINCULO
Thou liest, most ignorant monster: I am in case   25
to justle a constable*. Why, thou debauched* fish thou,   *officer of the law *excessive pleasure in
was there ever man a coward that hath drunk so much   partying (drugs, alcohol, sex)

sack as I today? Wilt thou tell a monstrous lie, being but
half fish and half a monster?

CALIBAN
Lo, how he mocks me! wilt thou let him, my lord?   30

TRINCULO
'Lord' quoth he! That a monster should be such
a natural*!   *person born without
                                                                     intelligence/reason

CALIBAN
Lo, lo again! Bite him to death, I prithee.

STEPHANO
Trinculo, keep a good tongue in your head: if
you prove a mutineer*, the next tree! The poor monster's *person who rises up against authority 35
my subject, and he shall not suffer indignity*.   *insult, humiliation

CALIBAN
I thank my noble lord. Wilt thou be pleas'd to
hearken* once again to the suit* I made to thee?   *hear *appeal, request

STEPHANO
Marry will I; kneel, and repeat it: I will stand,
and so shall Trinculo.   40
[Enter ARIEL, invisible]

CALIBAN
As I told thee before, I am subject to a tyrant,
sorcerer, that by his cunning* hath cheated me of the   *trickery
island.

ARIEL
Thou liest.

CALIBAN
Thou liest, thou jesting* monkey, thou;   *joking   45
I would my valiant* master would destroy thee;   *noble, brave
I do not lie.

STEPHANO
Trinculo, if you trouble him any more in his tale,
by this hand, I will supplant* some of your teeth.   *knock out

TRINCULO
Why, I said nothing.   50

STEPHANO
Mum, then, and no more. [*To CALIBAN*] Proceed.

CALIBAN
I say, by sorcery he got this isle;
From me he got it: if thy greatness will ,
Revenge it on him* —for I know, thou dar'st*;   *get revenge for me *dare
But this thing* dare not —   *Trinculo   55

STEPHANO
That's most certain.

CALIBAN
Thou shalt be lord of it and I'll serve thee.

STEPHANO
How now shall this be compassed*? Canst thou   *achieved
bring me to the party?

CALIBAN
Yea, yea, my lord. I'll yield* him thee asleep,   *bring you to him   60
Where thou may'st knock a nail into his head.

ARIEL
Thou liest: thou canst not. *   *Ariel, invisible, speaks in Trinculo's voice

CALIBAN
What a pied ninny's* this! —Thou scurvy patch*! — *fool in multi-colored dress *diseased clown
I do beseech thy greatness, give him blows
And take his bottle from him: when that's gone   65
He shall drink nought but brine*; for I'll not show him   *salt water
Where the quick freshes* are.   *fresh water

STEPHANO
Trinculo, run into no further danger: interrupt the
monster one word further and, by this hand, I'll turn
my mercy out o' doors, and make a stockfish* of thee.   *dried fish, softened by beating 70

TRINCULO
Why, what did I? I did nothing. I'll go farther off.

STEPHANO
Didst thou not say he lied?

ARIEL
Thou liest.

STEPHANO
Do I so? Take thou that. [*Strikes TRINCULO.*]
As you like this, give me the lie another time*.   *calling Trinculo the liar 75

TRINCULO
I did not give the lie: —out o' your wits and
hearing too? —A pox* o' your bottle! this can sack and   *disease (curse)
drinking do*. —A murrain* on your monster, and the devil *drinking does this to a man *plague
take your fingers!

CALIBAN
Ha, ha, ha!   80

STEPHANO
Now, forward with your tale. —Prithee stand
further off.

CALIBAN
Beat him enough: after a little time, I'll beat
him too.

STEPHANO
Stand farther. Come, proceed.   85

CALIBAN
Why, as I told thee, 'tis a custom with him
I' th' afternoon to sleep: there thou may'st brain* him,   *kill by smashing the skull
Having first seiz'd his books; or with a log
Batter his skull, or paunch* him with a stake,   *stab in the belly
Or cut his weasand* with thy knife. Remember   *windpipe   90
First to possess his books; for without them
He's but a sot*, as I am, nor hath not   *a drunk
One spirit to command: they all do hate him
As rootedly* as I. Burn but his books;   *at the root or heart
He has brave utensils* —for so he calls them,—   *tools   95
Which, when he has a house, he'll deck* withal: *decorate
And that most deeply to consider is
The beauty of his daughter; he himself
Calls her a nonpareil*: I never saw a woman   *without peer, without equal
But only Sycorax my dam* and she;   *mother   100
But she as far surpasseth* Sycorax   *to surpass, to be superior to
As great'st does least.

STEPHANO
Is it so brave a lass*?   *girl

CALIBAN
Ay, lord: she will become thy bed, I warrant,
And bring thee forth brave brood*.   *children   105

STEPHANO
Monster, I will kill this man; his daughter and I
will be king and queen —save our graces! —and Trinculo
and thyself shall be viceroys*. Dost thou like the plot*,   *governors *plan
Trinculo?

TRINCULO
Excellent.   110

STEPHANO
Give me thy hand: I am sorry I beat thee; but
while thou livest, keep a good tongue in thy head.

CALIBAN
Within this half hour will he be asleep;
Wilt thou destroy him then?

STEPHANO
Ay, on mine honour.   115

ARIEL
This will I tell my master.

CALIBAN
Thou mak'st me merry: I am full of pleasure.
Let us be jocund*: will you troll the catch*   *merry, happy *sing the song
You taught me but while-ere*?   *just now

STEPHANO
At thy request, monster, I will do reason, any   120
reason. Come on, Trinculo, let us sing.
[*Sings*]
Flout 'em and scout 'em;
And scout 'em and flout 'em!
Thought is free.

CALIBAN
That's not the tune.   125
[*ARIEL plays the tune on a Tabor and Pipe.*]

STEPHANO
What is this same?

TRINCULO
This is the tune of our catch, played by the
picture of Nobody*. ^they can't see anyone playing the music

STEPHANO
If thou be'st a man, show thyself in thy ^show yourself if you're a man
likeness*: if thou beest a devil, take't as thou list*. ^do what you want if you're a devil
130

TRINCULO
O, forgive me my sins!

STEPHANO
He that dies pays all debts: I defy thee. —Mercy
upon us!

CALIBAN
Art thou afeard?

STEPHANO
No, monster, not I. 135

CALIBAN
Be not afeard: the isle is full of noises,
Sounds, and sweet airs, that give delight, and hurt not.
Sometimes a thousand twangling* instruments ^plucking
Will hum about mine ears; and sometimes voices,
That, if I then had wak'd after long sleep, 140
Will make me sleep again: and then, in dreaming,
The clouds methought would open and show riches
Ready to drop upon me; that, when I wak'd,
I cried to dream again.

STEPHANO
This will prove a brave kingdom to me, where I 145
shall have my music for nothing*. ^free of charge

CALIBAN
When Prospero is destroyed.

STEPHANO
That shall be by and by: I remember the story.

TRINCULO
The sound is going away: let's follow it, and
after do our work.   150

STEPHANO
Lead, monster: we'll follow. —I would I could see
this taborer*! He lays it on. Wilt come?   *drummer

TRINCULO
I'll follow, Stephano.
[*Exeunt*]

SCENE III

Another part of the island

Tired of searching the island for Ferdinand, the royal group stops. Antonio and
Sebastian determine that they will try their assassination plot later. Suddenly, they
come upon a magical feast. Just as they are deciding to eat, Ariel comes down in the
form of a harpy and terrifies them by telling them of their sins against Prospero and
that they are now being punished. Gonzalo does not see what the others are seeing
and is very confused.

[*Enter ALONSO, SEBASTIAN, ANTONIO, GONZALO,
ADRIAN, FRANCISCO, and OTHERS.*]

GONZALO
By 'r lakin*, I can go no further, sir.   *By our lady (i. e. Virgin Mary)
My old bones ache: here's a maze trod*, indeed,   *we've traveled a maze
Through forth-rights and meanders*! By your patience,   *gone straight and crooked
I needs must rest me*.   *I've got to rest

ALONSO

Old lord, I cannot blame thee,   5
Who am myself attach'd* with weariness   *I'm so tired my spirits are dull
To th' dulling of my spirits: sit down, and rest.
Even here I will put off my hope, and keep it
No longer for my flatterer: he* is drown'd   *Ferdinand
Whom thus we stray* to find; and the sea mocks   *wander about   10
Our frustrate* search on land. Well, let him go.   *frustrated, fruitless

ANTONIO

[*Aside to SEBASTIAN*] I am right glad that he's
so out of hope.
Do not, for one repulse*, forgo the purpose   *rejection, failure
That you resolv'd to effect*.   *plot to kill Alonso & Gonzalo 15

SEBASTIAN

[*Aside to ANTONIO*] The next advantage
Will we take throughly*.   *thoroughly

ANTONIO

[*Aside to SEBASTIAN*] Let it be tonight;
For, now they are oppress'd* with travel, they   *exhausted, burdened
Will not, nor cannot, use such vigilance*   *alertness, caution around danger
20
As when they are fresh*.   *rested, fully awake

SEBASTIAN

[*Aside to ANTONIO*] I say, tonight: no more.
[*Solemn and strange music: and PROSPERO above,
invisible. Enter several strange Shapes, bringing in a
banquet: they dance about it with gentle actions of
salutation; and inviting the KING, &c. , to eat, they
depart.*]

ALONSO

What harmony is this? My good friends, hark!

GONZALO
Marvellous sweet music!

ALONSO
Give us kind keepers, heavens! What were these?   25

SEBASTIAN
A living drollery*. Now I will believe   *puppet show
That there are unicorns; that in Arabia
There is one tree, the phoenix' throne; one phoenix*   *bird that could burn itself up and then
At this hour reigning there.   regenerate out of its own ashes.

ANTONIO
I'll believe both;   30
And what does else want credit*, come to me,   *to be proven true
And I'll be sworn 'tis true: travellers ne'er did lie,
Though fools at home condemn them.

GONZALO
If in Naples
I should report this now, would they believe me?   35
If I should say, I saw such islanders,—
For, certes*, these are people of the island,—   *certainly
Who, though, they are of monstrous shape, yet, note,
Their manners are more gentle, kind, than of
Our human generation you shall find   40
Many, nay, almost any.

PROSPERO
[*Aside*] Honest lord,
Thou hast said well; for some of you* there present   *Antonio, Sebastian, even Alonso
Are worse than devils.

ALONSO
I cannot too much muse*   *wonder, marvel   45
Such shapes, such gesture, and such sound, expressing —
Although they want the use of tongue* —a kind   *the scene is silent
Of excellent dumb discourse*.   *silent communication

PROSPERO
[*Aside*] Praise in departing.

FRANCISCO
They vanish'd strangely.   50

SEBASTIAN
No matter, since
They have left their viands* behind; for we have stomachs*.   *tasty food *are hungry
—

Will't please you taste of what is here?

ALONSO
Not I.

GONZALO
Faith, sir, you need not fear. When we were boys,   55
Who would believe that there were mountaineers
Dewlapp'd* like bulls, whose throats had hanging at them   *skin hanging from their necks
Wallets of flesh*? or that there were such men   *bag/folder of skin
Whose heads stood in their breasts? which now we find
Each putter-out of five for one will bring us   60
Good warrant of*.   *travelers who insured themselves
for travel

ALONSO
I will stand to, and feed,
Although my last; no matter, since I feel
The best is past. —Brother, my lord the duke,
Stand to and do as we*.   *be ready and follow our lead   65
[*Thunder and lightning. Enter ARIEL, like a harpy*; claps   *Greek mythology—evil creature
his wings upon the table; and, with a quaint device, the   that is half human woman, half bird
banquet vanishes*]

ARIEL
You are three men of sin, whom Destiny,
That hath to instrument this lower world*   *that rules this lower world=earth
And what is in't —the never-surfeited* sea   *never full

257

Hath caused to belch up you; and on this island
Where man doth not inhabit; you 'mongst men   70
Being most unfit to live. I have made you mad*:   *crazy, insane
[Seeing ALONSO, SEBASTIAN, & ANTONIO draw their swords]
And even with such-like valour* men hang and drown   *courage
Their proper selves.
You fools! I and my fellows
Are ministers of fate: the elements
Of whom your swords are temper'd* may as well   *composed   75
Wound the loud winds, or with bemock'd-at* stabs   *mocked-at, pathetic
Kill the still-closing waters, as diminish
One dowle* that's in my plume*; my fellow-ministers   *bit of down *feathers
Are like invulnerable*. If you could hurt,   *incapable of being injured
Your swords are now too massy* for your strengths,   *massive, heavy   80
And will not be uplifted. But, remember —
For that's my business to you —that you three
From Milan did supplant* good Prospero;   *uproot, overthrow
Expos'd unto the sea, which hath requit* it,   *avenged the crime
Him, and his innocent child: for which foul deed   85
The powers, delaying, not forgetting, have
Incens'd* the seas and shores, yea, all the creatures,   *enraged, angered
Against your peace. Thee of thy son, Alonso,
They have bereft*; and do pronounce, by me   *deprived
Lingering perdition*, —worse than any death   *hell   90
Can be at once, —shall step by step attend*   *follow
You and your ways; whose wraths* to guard you from —   *rage, angers
Which here, in this most desolate isle, else* falls   *otherwise
Upon your heads, —is nothing but heart-sorrow*,   *only repentance can save you
And a clear life ensuing.   95
[He vanishes in thunder: then, to soft music, enter the
Shapes again, and dance, with mocks and mows*, and   *angry facial and hand gestures
carry out the table]

PROSPERO
[Aside] Bravely the figure of this harpy hast thou
Perform'd, my Ariel; a grace it had, devouring*;   *making the banquet vanish
Of my instruction hast thou nothing bated*   *omitted, left out
In what thou hadst to say: so, with good life

And observation strange*, my meaner ministers*   *careful attention to my wishes   100
Their several kinds have done. My high charms work,   *lesser spirits than Ariel
And these mine enemies are all knit up*   *tied up, preoccupied
In their distractions; they now are in my power;
And in these fits I leave them, while I visit
Young Ferdinand —whom they suppose is drown'd—   105
And his and mine lov'd darling.
[*Exit above*]

GONZALO
I' the name of something holy, sir, why stand you
In this strange stare? *   *Gonzalo did not see or hear the harpy Ariel

ALONSO
O, it is monstrous! monstrous!
Methought the billows* spoke, and told me of it;   *waves   110
The winds did sing it to me; and the thunder,
That deep and dreadful organ-pipe, pronounc'd
The name of Prosper*: it did bass my trespass*.   *Prospero *made me see my sin against
him
Therefore my son i' th' ooze is bedded*; and   *dead at the bottom of the ocean
I'll seek him deeper than e'er plummet sounded*,   *deeper than what can be measured   115
And with him there lie mudded*.   *in the mud at the bottom of the ocean
[*Exit*]

SEBASTIAN
But one fiend at a time,
I'll fight their legions o'er.

ANTONIO
I'll be thy second.
[*Exeunt SEBASTIAN and ANTONIO*]

GONZALO
All three of them are desperate: their great guilt,   120
Like poison given to work a great time after,
Now 'gins to bite the spirits*. I do beseech you   *their guilt begins to gnaw at them now
That are of suppler joints*, follow them swiftly   *younger and faster

And hinder them from what this ecstasy*   *insanity
May now provoke* them to.   *make them do   125

ADRIAN
Follow, I pray you.
[*Exeunt*]

ACT 4
SCENE I

Before PROSPERO'S cell

Prospero explains to Ferdinand and Miranda that they have passed his test and that they have his blessing to marry. Ariel appears and tells Prospero of Caliban's plot to kill him. Prospero puts on a show with his spirits for their entertainment. Then he remembers that he has to deal with Caliban's plot to kill him and acts strangely before getting philosophical with them. Meanwhile, Caliban, Trinculo, and Stephano fall for Prospero's trap and get hunted down by Ariel in the form of hell hounds.
[*Enter PROSPERO, FERDINAND, and MIRANDA*]

PROSPERO
If I have too austerely* punish'd you,   *severely
Your compensation* makes amends: for   *I'll make up for it now with kindness
Have given you here a third of mine own life*, *Miranda is ⅓ of his life
Or that for which I live; who once again
I tender to thy hand: all thy vexations*   *troubles, irritations, problems   5
Were but my trials of thy love, and thou
Hast strangely stood the test: here, afore Heaven,
I ratify this my rich gift*. O Ferdinand!   *formally approve Miranda as my gift to you
Do not smile at me that I boast her off,
For thou shalt find she will outstrip all praise*, *she's better than any praise   10
And make it halt behind her*.   *praise will limp behind the real Miranda

FERDINAND
I do believe it   *even a bad prophecy won't make me believe
Against an oracle*.   otherwise about her

PROSPERO

Then, as my gift and thine own acquisition*   *possession
Worthily purchas'd*, take my daughter: but   *by falling in love and earning her love 15
If thou dost break her virgin knot* before   *virginity
All sanctimonious* ceremonies may   *holy
With full and holy rite be minister'd*,   *administered (by a priest)
No sweet aspersion* shall the heavens let fall   *blessing
To make this contract* grow; but barren hate,   *marriage become fruitful   20
Sour-ey'd disdain, and discord, shall bestrew
The union of your bed with weeds so loathly
That you shall hate it both*: therefore take heed, *hate the bed/marriage/each other
As Hymen's* lamps shall light you.   *Greek god of marriage, carried torch to bless

FERDINAND

As I hope   25
For quiet days, fair issue*, and long life,   *progeny, children
With such love as 'tis now, the murkiest den*,   *cave/dwelling
The most opportune place, the strong'st suggestion
Our worser genius can, shall never melt
Mine honour into lust, to take away   30
The edge of that day's celebration,
When I shall think, or Phoebus' steeds are founder'd*, *day will never end
Or Night kept chain'd below*.   *night will never come

PROSPERO

Fairly spoke:
Sit, then, and talk with her. She is thine own.   35
What, Ariel! My industrious* servant, Ariel!   *hard-working
[Enter ARIEL]

ARIEL

What would my potent* master? here I am.   *powerful

PROSPERO

Thou and thy meaner* fellows your last service   *lesser spirits
Did worthily perform; and I must use you
In such another trick. Go bring the rabble*,   *lowest class of people   40
O'er whom I give thee power, here to this place;

Incite* them to quick motion; for I must   *stir up, rouse
Bestow* upon the eyes of this young couple   *give as a gift
Some vanity* of mine art: it is my promise,   *little show (of magic)
And they expect it from me.   45

ARIEL
Presently?

PROSPERO
Ay, with a twink.

ARIEL
Before you can say 'Come' and 'Go,'
And breathe twice; and cry 'so, so,'
Each one, tripping on his toe,   50
Will be here with mop and mow.
Do you love me, master? No?

PROSPERO
Dearly, my delicate Ariel. Do not approach
Till thou dost hear me call.

ARIEL
Well, I conceive.   55
[*Exit*]

PROSPERO
Look, thou be true; do not give dalliance*   *love play
Too much the rein*: the strongest oaths are straw   *too much play
To th' fire i' the blood*: be more abstemious*,   *passion overrules promises *restrained
Or else good night your vow*!   *promise to keep Miranda's virginity intact

FERDINAND
I warrant* you, sir;   *promise   60
The white-cold virgin snow upon my heart
Abates* the ardour of my liver*.   *lessens *passion of my liver (seat of passion)

PROSPERO
Well —
Now come, my Ariel! Bring a corollary*,   *parallel/another spirit
Rather than want a spirit: appear, and pertly*.   *in a lively manner   65
No tongue! All eyes! Be silent.
[*Soft music*]
[*A Masque*. Enter IRIS*]²   *dramatic entertainment/skit

IRIS*   *goddess of rainbow/messenger goddess
Ceres*, most bounteous lady, thy rich leas   *Roman goddess of agriculture (fertility)
Of wheat, rye, barley, vetches, oats, and peas;
Thy turfy mountains, where live nibbling sheep,
And flat meads thatch'd with stover, them to keep;   70
Thy banks with pioned and twilled brims,
Which spongy April at thy hest betrims,
To make cold nymphs chaste crowns; and thy broom groves,
Whose shadow the dismissed bachelor loves,
Being lass-lorn: thy pole-clipt vineyard;   75
And thy sea-marge, sterile and rocky-hard,
Where thou thyself dost air: the Queen o' the sky,
Whose watery arch and messenger am I,
Bids thee leave these; and with her sovereign grace,
Here on this grass-plot, in this very place,   80
To come and sport; her peacocks fly amain:
Approach, rich Ceres, her to entertain.
[*Enter CERES*]

CERES
Hail, many-colour'd messenger, that ne'er
Dost disobey the wife of Jupiter;
Who with thy saffron wings upon my flowers   85
Diffusest honey drops, refreshing showers:

2. Lines 67–151 are a vision that is created by Prospero for Ferdinand and Miranda. It's an illusion that is intended to entertain them but also to bless their union. Iris, the messenger goddess, calls Ceres, Roman goddess
of agriculture and fertility, to bless the union in advance of the marriage, and the couple is reminded that they
must be married before engaging in sexual intercourse. Juno, Roman queen of the gods who is also goddess of
women and marriage, then blesses the two and any offspring that come. Finally, Iris calls on the Naiads, nymphs
or lower order female divinities who are associated with fresh water, to dance with farmers (reapers of wheat)
in celebration. The masque or vision is abruptly ended when Prospero remembers Caliban's plot to kill him.

And with each end of thy blue bow dost crown
My bosky acres and my unshrubb'd down,
Rich scarf to my proud earth; why hath thy queen
Summon'd me hither to this short-grass'd green?   90

IRIS
A contract of true love to celebrate,
And some donation freely to estate
On the blest lovers.

CERES
Tell me, heavenly bow,
If Venus or her son, as thou dost know,   95
Do now attend the queen? Since they did plot
The means that dusky Dis my daughter got*,   *This is Proserpina (Greek=Persephone), who
Her and her blind boy's scandal'd company   was taken down to the underworld to be the wife
I have forsworn.   of Dis (Greek=Hades)

IRIS
Of her society   100
Be not afraid. I met her deity
Cutting the clouds towards Paphos and her son
Dove-drawn with her. Here thought they to have done
Some wanton charm upon this man and maid,
Whose vows are, that no bed-rite shall be paid   105
Till Hymen's torch be lighted;* but in vain.   *They can't have sex until after marriage
Mars's hot minion is return'd again;
Her waspish-headed son has broke his arrows,
Swears he will shoot no more, but play with sparrows,
And be a boy right out.   110

CERES
Highest Queen of State,
Great Juno comes; I know her by her gait.
[Enter JUNO.]

JUNO*   *Roman queen of heaven, and goddess of light, birth, women, and marriage (Greek=Hera)

How does my bounteous sister? Go with me
To bless this twain, that they may prosperous be,
And honour'd in their issue*.   *offspring, children   115
[*singing*]

JUNO.
Honour, riches, marriage-blessing,
Long continuance, and increasing,
Hourly joys be still upon you!
Juno sings her blessings on you.

CERES
Earth's increase, foison plenty,   120
Barns and gamers never empty;
Vines with clust'ring bunches growing;
Plants with goodly burden bowing;
Spring come to you at the farthest,
In the very end of harvest!   125
Scarcity and want shall shun you;
Ceres' blessing so is on you.

FERDINAND
This is a most majestic vision*, and   *show
Harmonious charmingly; may I be bold
To think these spirits*?   *this isn't real, right?   130

PROSPERO
Spirits, which by mine art
I have from their confines* call'd to enact*   *regular work *act out, perform
My present fancies*.   *desire to put on this show for you

FERDINAND
Let me live here ever:
So rare a wonder'd father and a wise,   135
Makes this place paradise.
[*JUNO and CERES whisper, and send IRIS on employment.*]

PROSPERO
Sweet now, silence!
Juno and Ceres whisper seriously,
There's something else to do: hush, and be mute*,   *silent
Or else our spell is marr'd*.   *interrupted, damaged   140

IRIS
You nymphs, call'd Naiads, of the windring brooks,
With your sedg'd crowns and ever-harmless looks,
Leave your crisp channels, and on this green land
Answer your summons: Juno does command.
Come, temperate nymphs, and help to celebrate   145
A contract of true love: be not too late.
[*Enter certain NYMPHS*]
You sun-burn'd sicklemen*, of August weary,   *farmers who are harvesting grain
Come hither from the furrow, and be merry:
Make holiday: your rye-straw hats put on,
And these fresh nymphs encounter every one   150
In country footing.
[*Enter certain Reapers*, properly habited: they join with the Nymphs in a graceful
dance; towards the end whereof PROSPERO starts suddenly, and speaks; after which, to
a strange, hollow, and confused noise, they heavily vanish.]*   *the same farmers as the "sicklemen"

PROSPERO
[*Aside*] I had forgot that foul conspiracy*   *plot to overthrow him
Of the beast Caliban and his confederates*   *allies in the plot
Against my life: the minute of their plot
Is almost come. [*To the Spirits.*] Well done! Avoid; no more!   155

FERDINAND
This is strange: your father's in some passion*   *emotional disturbance
That works him strongly.

MIRANDA
Never till this day
Saw I him touch'd with anger so distemper'd*.   *out of order, unsettled

PROSPERO

You do look, my son, in a mov'd sort*,   *troubled mood   160
As if you were dismay'd: be cheerful, sir:
Our revels* now are ended. These our actors*,   *party/entertainment *in the vision
As I foretold you, were all spirits and
Are melted into air, into thin air:
And, like the baseless fabric of this vision*,   *play he put on for them   165
The cloud-capp'd towers, the gorgeous palaces,
The solemn temples, the great globe itself,
Yea, all which it inherit, shall dissolve*   *like this entertainment, everything on earth will crumble/die
And, like this insubstantial pageant faded*,   *entertainment dissolves
Leave not a rack behind* We are such stuff   *not even a cloud will be left   170
As dreams are made on, and our little life
Is rounded with a sleep*. —Sir, I am vex'd*:   *before birth/sleep as mini-death *distressed
Bear with my weakness; my old brain is troubled.
Be not disturb'd with my infirmity*.   *illness, disability
If you be pleas'd, retire into my cell*   *place of residence, abode   175
And there repose*: a turn or two I'll walk,   *rest
To still my beating* mind.   *unsettled,

FERDINAND, MIRANDA

We wish your peace.
[*Exeunt.*]

PROSPERO

Come, with a thought. [*To them.*] I thank thee.
Ariel, come!   180
[*Enter ARIEL.*]

ARIEL

Thy thoughts I cleave* to. What's thy pleasure?   *hang on

PROSPERO

Spirit,
We must prepare to meet with Caliban.

ARIEL

Ay, my commander; when I presented Ceres,
I thought to have told thee of it: but I fear'd   185
Lest* I might anger thee.   *in case

PROSPERO

Say again, where didst thou leave these varlets*?   *lower class people

ARIEL

I told you, sir, they were red-hot with drinking;
So full of valour* that they smote* the air   *false courage *struck
For breathing in their faces; beat the ground   190
For kissing of their feet; yet always bending
Towards their project. Then I beat my tabor*;   *drum
At which, like unback'd colts*, they prick'd* their ears,   *unbroken young horses *stood up
Advanc'd their eyelids*, lifted up their noses   *lifted up their eyelids
As they smelt music: so I charm'd their ears,`   195
That, calf-like, they my lowing* follow'd through   *sounding like a calf
Tooth'd briers, sharp furzes, pricking gorse and thorns*,   *led them through prickers and briars
Which enter'd their frail shins*: at last I left them   *which stabbed their shins
I' the filthy-mantled* pool beyond your cell,   *scum-covered
There dancing up to the chins, that the foul lake   200
O'erstunk their feet.

PROSPERO

This was well done, my bird.
Thy shape invisible retain thou still*:   *stay invisible
The trumpery* in my house, go bring it hither   *trivial articles (but showy)
For stale* to catch these thieves.   *decoy/trap   205

ARIEL

I go, I go.
[*Exit*]

PROSPERO

A devil, a born devil, on whose nature
Nurture can never stick*; on whom my pains,   *nurturing can't transform him from
Humanely taken, all, all lost, quite lost;   evil to good

And as with age his body uglier grows,   210
So his mind cankers*. I will plague* them all,   *becomes corrupted *to afflict with disease
Even to roaring*.   *until they scream
[*Re-enter ARIEL, loaden with glistering* apparel, etc.*] *glittering
Come, hang them on this line.
[*PROSPERO and ARIEL remain invisible. Enter
CALIBAN, STEPHANO, and TRINCULO, all wet*]

CALIBAN
Pray you, tread* softly, that the blind mole* may not   *walk *Prospero
Hear a foot fall*: we now are near his cell.   *footsteps   215

STEPHANO
Monster, your fairy, which you say is a harmless
fairy, has done little better than played the
Jack with us.

TRINCULO
Monster, I do smell all horse piss, at which my
nose is in great indignation*.   *stinks/offensive smell   220

STEPHANO
So is mine. —Do you hear, monster? If I should
take a displeasure against you, look you —

TRINCULO
Thou wert but a lost monster.

CALIBAN
Good my lord, give me thy favour still:
Be patient, for the prize I'll bring thee to   225
Shall hoodwink* this mischance*: therefore speak softly;   *hide/overlook *misfortune
All's hush'd as midnight yet.

TRINCULO
Ay, but to lose our bottles in the pool*!   *they lost their alcohol in the swamp

STEPHANO
There is not only disgrace and dishonour in
that, monster, but an infinite loss.   230

TRINCULO
That's more to me than my wetting*: yet this is   *my getting wet
your harmless fairy, monster.

STEPHANO
I will fetch off my bottle, though I be o'er
ears for my labour*.   *even if I'm up to my ears in water

CALIBAN
Prithee, my king, be quiet. Seest thou here,   235
This is the mouth* o' the cell: no noise and enter.   *entrance
Do that good mischief which may make this island
Thine own for ever, and I, thy Caliban,
For aye thy foot-licker*.   *suck-up, boot-licker

STEPHANO
Give me thy hand: I do begin to have bloody thoughts.   240

TRINCULO
O King Stephano! O peer*! O worthy Stephano!   *companion
Look what a wardrobe* here is for thee!   *fancy clothes

CALIBAN
Let it alone, thou fool; it is but trash.

TRINCULO
O, ho, monster! we know what belongs to a
frippery*. O King Stephano!   *2nd hand store for clothes   245

STEPHANO
Put off that gown, Trinculo; by this hand, I'll
have that gown.

TRINCULO
Thy Grace shall have it.

CALIBAN
The dropsy* drown this fool! What do you mean   *excess fluid in the body
To dote thus on such luggage*? Let's along,   *useless items   250
And do the murder first. If he awake,
From toe to crown he'll fill our skins with pinches*;   *curse us with cramps
Make us strange stuff.

STEPHANO
Be you quiet, monster. —Mistress line, is not   *this is a set of puns
this my jerkin? Now is the jerkin under the line: now,   255
jerkin, you are like to lose your hair, and prove a bald
jerkin*.

TRINCULO
Do, do: we steal by line and level, an 't like
your Grace.

STEPHANO
I thank thee for that jest*: here's a garment*   *joke *article of clothing
for't: wit shall not go unrewarded while I am king of   260
this country: 'Steal by line and level,' is an excellent
pass of pate*: there's another garment for't.   *witty statement

TRINCULO
Monster, come, put some lime* upon your fingers,   *sticky substance (thieves have
and away with the rest.   sticky fingers

CALIBAN
I will have none on't. We shall lose our time,   265
And all be turn'd to barnacles*, or to apes   *crustacean
With foreheads villainous low.

STEPHANO

Monster, lay to your fingers: help to bear this
away where my hogshead of wine is, or I'll turn you out
of my kingdom. Go to; carry this.   270

TRINCULO

And this.

STEPHANO

Ay, and this.
[*A noise of hunters heard. Enter divers Spirits, in shape
of hounds, and hunt them about; PROSPERO and ARIEL
setting them on*]

PROSPERO

Hey, Mountain, hey!

ARIEL

Silver! here it goes, Silver!

PROSPERO

Fury, Fury! There, Tyrant, there! Hark, Hark!   275
[*CALIBAN, STEPHANO, and TRINCULO are driven
out.*]
Go, charge my goblins that they grind their joints
With dry convulsions*; shorten up their sinews   *seizures
With aged cramps*, and more pinch-spotted make them   *cause cramps in their tendons
Than pard*, or cat o' mountain.   *leopard

ARIEL

Hark, they roar.   280

PROSPERO

Let them be hunted soundly. At this hour
Lies at my mercy all mine enemies;
Shortly shall all my labours end, and thou
Shalt have the air at freedom; for a little
Follow and do me service*.   *continue to serve me   285

[*Exeunt*]

ACT 5
SCENE I

Before the cell of PROSPERO

Prospero feels that all is going well and gets an update from Ariel. King Alonso and all his followers are bound up in guilt and remorse from Ariel's trick, and Ariel says he feels sorry for them if he were human. Prospero agrees and says that mercy is better than revenge. He has Ariel lead the group to him. Prospero speaks to the spirits he has worked with all this time, and promises that after these last few magical feats, he will give up his magic. He undoes his spell over them, and they begin to regain their senses. Alonso begs forgiveness and returns the dukedom to Prospero. Prospero forgives Antonio and Sebastian even if they don't deserve it and says he knows what they tried to do to Alonso but that he won't tell Alonso at this time. He brings the group to see Ferdinand and Miranda, and Miranda is amazed by this beautiful group of people from what she calls "the new world," which is really Old Europe. The boat's crew arrives and Prospero promises to tell his story and help them get home safely. Ariel brings Stephano, Trinculo, and Caliban, and Prospero explains what they've been doing and that Stephano and Trinculo need to be managed by their masters and that he will have to deal with Caliban. Caliban knows he was a fool to take Stephano for a god and fears Prospero's punishment.

[*Enter PROSPERO in his magic robes; and ARIEL.*]

PROSPERO

Now does my project gather to a head*:   *everything is coming together
My charms crack not*; my spirits obey, and time   *my charms are working
Goes upright with his carriage*. How's the day?   *time isn't against me

ARIEL

On the sixth hour; at which time, my lord,
You said our work should cease.   5

PROSPERO

I did say so,
When first I rais'd the tempest. Say, my spirit,
How fares* the King and 's followers?   *how is the king's group

ARIEL
Confin'd together*   *held together
In the same fashion as you gave in charge*;   *as you ordered   10
Just as you left them: all prisoners, sir,
In the line-grove which weather-fends your cell*;   *protective trees around your home
They cannot budge till your release. The king,
His brother, and yours, abide all three distracted*,   *disturbed, confused
And the remainder mourning over them*,   *upset (not actual mourning)   15
Brim full of sorrow and dismay; but chiefly
Him you term'd*, sir, 'the good old lord, Gonzalo':   *described as
His tears run down his beard, like winter's drops
From eaves of reeds; your charm so strongly works them,
That if you now beheld them, your affections   20
Would become tender*.   *you'd feel sorry for them

PROSPERO
Dost thou think so, spirit?

ARIEL
Mine would, sir, were I human.

PROSPERO
And mine shall.
Hast thou, which art but air, a touch, a feeling   25
Of their afflictions*, and shall not myself,   *suffering
One of their kind, that relish* all as sharply,   *to enjoy
Passion as they, be kindlier mov'd than thou art*?   *won't I be more sympathetic to them?
Though with their high wrongs* I am struck to the quick*, *sins against me *core
Yet with my nobler reason 'gainst my fury   30
Do I take part*: the rarer action is   *I choose reason over revenge
In virtue than in vengeance: they being penitent*,   *remorseful, repentant
The sole drift of my purpose doth extend
Not a frown further*. Go release them, Ariel.   *I will not punish them even with a
frown
My charms I'll break, their senses I'll restore,   35
And they shall be themselves*.   *they'll be back to their original nature

ARIEL
I'll fetch them, sir.
[*Exit.*]

PROSPERO
Ye elves* of hills, brooks, standing lakes, and groves;   *he's speaking to the spirits of the island
And ye that on the sands with printless foot*   *leave no footprints (as they are spirits)
Do chase the ebbing Neptune*, and do fly him   *Roman god of the sea (Poseidon)   40
When he comes back; you demi-puppets that
By moonshine do the green sour ringlets make*,   *fairy rings
Whereof the ewe* not bites; and you whose pastime   *female sheep
Is to make midnight mushrooms, that rejoice
To hear the solemn curfew*; by whose aid*,—   *midnight *the spirits helped me   45
Weak masters though ye be,—I have bedimm'd*   *made dim *eclipse
The noontide sun*, call'd forth the mutinous winds*,   *set winds fighting against each other
And 'twixt the green sea and the azur'd vault
Set roaring war*: to the dread rattling thunder   *set sea and sky against each other
Have I given fire*, and rifted Jove's stout oak*   *head god (Zeus)   50
With his own bolt*: the strong-based promontory*   *split the oak with lightning *high point
Have I made shake*; and by the spurs pluck'd up   of land *earthquake
The pine and cedar*: graves at my command   *uprooted trees
Have wak'd their sleepers, op'd, and let them forth*   *raised the dead
By my so potent art*. But this rough magic   *with my magic   55
I here abjure*; and, when I have requir'd   *I'm giving up my magic
Some heavenly music,—which even now I do,—
To work mine end upon their senses that
This airy charm is for*, I'll break my staff*,   *after I restore everyone *magic cane
Bury it certain fathoms in the earth*,   *deep   60
And deeper than did ever plummet sound*   *than we can determine depth
I'll drown my book*.   *staff and book=Prospero's magic
[*Solemn music*]
[*Re-enter ARIEL: after him, ALONSO, with frantic gesture, attended by GONZALO; SEBASTIAN and ANTONIO in like manner, attended by ADRIAN and FRANCISCO: they all enter the circle which PROSPERO had made, and there stand charmed: which PROSPERO observing, speaks.*]

A solemn air*, and the best comforter   *music
To an unsettled fancy*, cure thy brains,   *imagination
Now useless, boil'd within thy skull*! There stand,   *brains are like mush   65
For you are spell-stopp'd*.   *paralyzed by my spell
Holy Gonzalo, honourable man,
Mine eyes, even sociable to the show of thine,   *Gonzalo sheds tears for the group
Fall fellowly drops*. The charm dissolves* apace*;   *fades away *swiftly
And as the morning steals upon the night*,   *as dawn comes   70
Melting the darkness, so their rising senses
Begin to chase the ignorant fumes* that mantle*   *vapors/confused senses *cloak, cover
Their clearer reason. —O good Gonzalo!
My true preserver*, and a loyal sir   *life saver
To him thou follow'st*, I will pay thy graces   *you're loyal to your employer   75
Home*, both in word and deed. —Most cruelly   *when we get home
Didst thou, Alonso, use me and my daughter:
Thy brother was a furtherer in the act;—
Thou'rt pinch'd* for't now, Sebastian. —Flesh and blood,   *suffering
You, brother mine, that entertain'd ambition*,   *desire to take over my position   80
Expell'd remorse* and nature*, who, with Sebastian, —   *self-reproach *brotherly nature
Whose inward pinches* therefore are most strong, —   *suffering of conscience
Would here have kill'd your king*; I do forgive thee,   *assassination attempt on Alonso
Unnatural* though thou art! Their understanding   *against proper place and human nature
Begins to swell, and the approaching tide*   *tide of their reason and awareness 85
Will shortly fill the reasonable shores
That now lie foul and muddy*. Not one of them   *cloudy reasoning
That yet looks on me or would know* me. —Ariel,   *they won't recognize me
Fetch me the hat and rapier* in my cell.   *sword
[*Exit ARIEL*]
I will discase* me, and myself present,   *undress   90
As I was sometime Milan*. —Quickly, spirit;   *present myself as I appeared in Milan
Thou shalt ere long be free.
[*ARIEL re-enters, singing, and helps to attire
PROSPERO.*]

ARIEL
Where the bee sucks, there suck I:
In a cowslip's bell I lie;
There I couch when owls do cry.   95

On the bat's back I do fly
After summer merrily:
Merrily, merrily shall I live now
Under the blossom that hangs on the bough.

PROSPERO
Why, that's my dainty Ariel! I shall miss thee;   100
But yet thou shalt have freedom —so, so, so —
To the king's ship, invisible as thou art*: *Go invisible to the hidden ship
There shalt thou find the mariners asleep
Under the hatches*; the master and the boatswain *everyone is asleep below deck
Being awake, enforce them to this place*, *bring them all here 105
And presently*, I prithee. *now

ARIEL
I drink the air before me, and return
Or ere your pulse twice beat*. *before your heart beats twice
[*Exit*]

GONZALO
All torment, trouble, wonder and amazement
Inhabits here*. Some heavenly power guide us *I'm so confused 110
Out of this fearful country!

PROSPERO
Behold, sir king,
The wronged Duke of Milan, Prospero.
For more assurance* that a living prince *proof
Does now speak to thee, I embrace thy body*; *give you a hug 115
And to thee and thy company I bid
A hearty welcome.

ALONSO
Whe'er* thou be'st he or no, *Whether
Or some enchanted trifle* to abuse me, *spirit
As late I have been, I not know: thy pulse 120
Beats, as of flesh and blood; and, since I saw thee,
Th' affliction of my mind amends*, with which, *corrects, fixes

I fear, a madness* held me: this must crave,   *insanity
An if this be at all —a most strange story*.   *I want to hear this story
Thy dukedom I resign*, and do entreat   *I give your dukedom back to you   125
Thou pardon me my wrongs*. —But how should   *I beg your forgiveness
Prospero Be living and be here?

PROSPERO
First, noble friend,
Let me embrace thine age*; whose honour cannot   *I'd like to hug your honor
Be measur'd or confin'd.   130

GONZALO
Whether this be
Or be not, I'll not swear.

PROSPERO
You do yet taste
Some subtleties o' the isle, that will not let you
Believe things certain*. —Welcome, my friends all.   *can't determine what's real   135
[*Aside to SEBASTIAN and ANTONIO*] But you, my
brace* of lords, were I so minded,   *pair (Sebastian and Antonio)
I here could pluck his highness' frown upon you*,   *I could get Alonso really mad at you
And justify* you traitors: at this time   *prove
I will tell no tales*.   *I won't tell on you right now   140

SEBASTIAN
[*Aside*] The devil speaks in him*.   *he speaks evil

PROSPERO
No.
For you, most wicked sir, whom to call brother
Would even infect my mouth, I do forgive
Thy rankest fault*; all of them; and require   *worst faults, sins against me   145
My dukedom of thee*, which, perforce*, I know   *give me my dukedom back *by necessity
Thou must restore*.   *return to me

ALONSO
If thou be'st Prospero,
Give us particulars of thy preservation*;   *survival
How thou hast met us here, whom three hours since   150
Were wrack'd upon this shore*; where I have lost —   *we wrecked here three hours ago
How sharp the point of this remembrance is!
My dear son Ferdinand.

PROSPERO
I am woe* for't, sir.   *sad, sorry

ALONSO
Irreparable* is the loss, and patience   *loss cannot be recovered   155
Says it is past her cure*.   *patience can't fix it either

PROSPERO
I rather think
You have not sought her* help; of whose soft grace,   *help of patience
For the like loss I have her sovereign* aid,   *queenly
And rest myself content*.   *she's made me content   170

ALONSO
You the like loss*!   *you've experienced the same loss?

PROSPERO
As great to me, as late; and, supportable
To make the dear loss, have I means much weaker
Than you may call to comfort you, for I
Have lost my daughter*.   *to Ferdinand in promise   175

ALONSO
A daughter?
O heavens! that they were living both in Naples,
The king and queen there! That they were, I wish
Myself were mudded in that oozy bed
Where my son lies*. When did you lose your daughter?   *I wish I had died instead   180

PROSPERO

In this last tempest. I perceive, these lords
At this encounter do so much admire
That they devour their reason, and scarce think
Their eyes do offices of truth*, their words   *they can't believe their eyes
Are natural breath; but, howsoe'er you have   185
Been justled from your senses, know for certain
That I am Prospero, and that very duke
Which was thrust forth of Milan; who most strangely
Upon this shore, where you were wrack'd, was landed
To be the lord on't. No more yet of this;   190
For 'tis a chronicle* of day by day,   *long story
Not a relation for a breakfast nor
Befitting this first meeting*. Welcome, sir: *better for another day
This cell's my court*: here have I few attendants*   *duke's home *servants
And subjects none* abroad: pray you, look in.   *people to rule   195
My dukedom since you have given me again,
I will requite you with as good a thing;
At least bring forth a wonder, to content ye*   *you'll see something that will content
As much as me my dukedom.   you just as much as my return to the dukedom
[*The entrance of the cell opens, and discovers
FERDINAND and MIRANDA playing at chess.*]

MIRANDA

Sweet lord, you play me false*.   *you're cheating   200

FERDINAND

No, my dearest love,
I would not for the world.

MIRANDA

Yes, for a score of kingdoms you should wrangle*,   *bicker
And I would call it fair play.

ALONSO

If this prove   205
A vision of the island*, one dear son   *if this is just an illusion
Shall I twice lose.

SEBASTIAN
A most high miracle!

FERDINAND
Though the seas threaten, they are merciful:
I have curs'd them without cause*.   *his father is still alive   210
[*Kneels to ALONSO.*]

ALONSO
Now all the blessings
Of a glad father compass* thee about!   *I'll surround you with blessings
Arise, and say how thou cam'st here*.   *tell me how you got here

MIRANDA
O, wonder!
How many goodly creatures are there here!   215
How beauteous mankind is! O, brave new world
That has such people in't!

PROSPERO
'Tis new to thee.

ALONSO
What is this maid, with whom thou wast at play?
Your eld'st acquaintance cannot be three hours: 220
Is she the goddess* that hath sever'd us,   *Is Miranda a goddess who separated us?
And brought us thus together?

FERDINAND
Sir, she is mortal;
But by immortal Providence she's mine*.   *she belongs to me now
I chose her when I could not ask my father   225
For his advice, nor thought I had one*. She   *thought you were dead
Is daughter to this famous Duke of Milan,
Of whom so often I have heard renown*,   *famous
But never saw before; of whom I have
Receiv'd a second life*: and second father   *i. e. Miranda   230
This lady makes him to me*.   *Prospero is now my second father

ALONSO

I am hers: *I am now Miranda's 2nd father
But, O! how oddly will it sound that I
Must ask my child forgiveness!

PROSPERO

There, sir, stop: 235
Let us not burden our remembrances with
A heaviness that's gone.

GONZALO

I have inly wept,
Or should have spoke ere* this. Look down, you gods,   *before
And on this couple drop a blessed crown*;   *alliance between Naples & Milan 240
For it is you* that have chalk'd* forth the way   *gods *outlined
Which brought us hither.

ALONSO

I say, Amen, Gonzalo!

GONZALO

Was Milan thrust from Milan*, that his issue*   *Prospero exiled *descendants
Should become kings of Naples? O, rejoice   245
Beyond a common joy, and set it down
With gold on lasting pillars. In one voyage
Did Claribel her husband find at Tunis*,   *we married Claribel in Tunis
And Ferdinand, her brother, found a wife   *Ferdinand found wife in shipwreck
Where he himself was lost*; Prospero his dukedom* *Prospero got his dukedom back 250
In a poor isle; and all of us ourselves*,   *we all returned to normal
When no man was his own*.   *when we had all lost our senses

ALONSO

[To FERDINAND and MIRANDA] Give me your hands.
Let grief and sorrow still embrace his heart
That doth not wish you joy!   255

GONZALO

Be it so. Amen!

[*Re-enter ARIEL, with the Master and Boatswain amazedly following.*]
O look, sir! look, sir! Here are more of us.
I prophesied*, if a gallows were on land,   *I predicted this guy would not drown
This fellow could not drown*. —Now, blasphemy*,   *you swore blasphemy on the goat
That swear'st grace o'erboard, not an oath on shore*?   *do you have nothing to say now?   260
Hast thou no mouth by land? What is the news?

BOATSWAIN
The best news is that we have safely found
Our king and company; the next, our ship —
Which but three glasses* since we gave out split* —   *hours *declared it was split in half
Is tight and yare, and bravely rigg'd* as when   *is now in ship shape, ready to sail   265
We first put out to sea.

ARIEL
[*Aside to PROSPERO*] Sir, all this service
Have I done since I went.

PROSPERO
[*Aside to ARIEL*] My tricksy spirit!

ALONSO
These are not natural events; they strengthen*   *grow   270
From strange to stranger. Say, how came you hither*?   *here

BOATSWAIN
If I did think, sir, I were well awake,
I'd strive to tell you. We were dead of sleep*,   *fully asleep
And,—how, we know not,—all clapp'd under hatches*, *latched below deck
Where, but even now, with strange and several noises   275
Of roaring, shrieking, howling, jingling chains,
And more diversity of sounds, all horrible,
We were awak'd; straightway, at liberty*:   *freed from the hold
Where we, in all her trim, freshly beheld*   *saw
Our royal, good, and gallant ship; our master   280
Cap'ring to eye her*. On a trice*, so please you,   *leaped or danced to see the ship *instantly
Even in a dream, were we divided from them*,   *separated from the ship
And were brought moping* hither.   *in a daze

ARIEL
[*Aside to PROSPERO*] Was't well done?

PROSPERO
[*Aside to ARIEL*] Bravely, my diligence*. Thou   *speedy, hasty one   285
shalt be free.

ALONSO
This is as strange a maze as e'er men trod*,   *walked
And there is in this business more than nature
Was ever conduct* of. Some oracle*   *could do alone *prophet
Must rectify* our knowledge.   *set right   290

PROSPERO
Sir, my liege*,   *king
Do not infest* your mind with beating* on   *worry *figuring out
The strangeness of this business: at pick'd* leisure,   *selected
Which shall be shortly, single I'll resolve* you,   *help you resolve confusion
Which to you shall seem probable, of every   295
These happen'd accidents*; till when, be cheerful   *events that turned out well
And think of each thing well. [*Aside to ARIEL*] Come
hither, spirit;
Set Caliban and his companions free.
Untie* the spell.   *undo   300
[*Exit ARIEL*]
[*To ALONSO*] How fares* my gracious sir?   *How do you get along?
There are yet missing of your company
Some few odd lads* that you remember not.   *boys (men, but they are servants)
[*Re-enter ARIEL, driving in CALIBAN, STEPHANO, and TRINCULO, in their
stolen apparel.*]

STEPHANO
Every man shift for all the rest*, and let no   *every man for himself
man take care for himself, for all is but fortune. Coragio*!   *courage   305
bully-monster*, Coragio!   *Caliban

TRINCULO
If these be true spies which I wear in my head*,   *If my eyes see correctly
here's a goodly sight.

CALIBAN
O Setebos*, these be brave spirits indeed.   *the god of Caliban's mother
How fine my master is! I am afraid   310
He will chastise * me.   *punish

SEBASTIAN
Ha, ha!
What things are these, my lord Antonio?
Will money buy them?

ANTONIO
Very like; one of them   315
Is a plain fish, and, no doubt, marketable*.   *Antonio sees Caliban as "marketable"

PROSPERO
Mark but the badges* of these men, my lords,   *stolen clothes
Then say if they be true*. This misshapen knave*,   *honest *Caliban as deformed, lower class
His mother was a witch; and one so strong
That could control the moon, make flows and ebbs,   320
And deal in her command without her power.
These three have robb'd me*; and this demi-devil —   *clothes he set out to lure/distract them
For he's a bastard one —had plotted with them
To take my life*. Two of these fellows you   *Caliban, Stephano, Trinculo
Must know and own*. This thing of darkness I   *masters are responsible for their   325
Acknowledge mine*.   servants. *I am responsible for Caliban

CALIBAN
I shall be pinch'd to death.

ALONSO
Is not this Stephano, my drunken butler?

SEBASTIAN
He is drunk now: where had he wine*?   *where did he find wine?

285

ALONSO

And Trinculo is reeling ripe*. Where should they   *drunk   330
Find this grand liquor that hath gilded them*?   *got them drunk
How cam'st thou in this pickle?   *awkward situation

TRINCULO

I have been in such a pickle since I saw you
last that, I fear me, will never out of my bones. I
shall not fear fly-blowing*.   *contamination   355

SEBASTIAN

Why, how now, Stephano!

STEPHANO

O, touch me not! I am not Stephano, but a cramp.

PROSPERO

You'd be king o' the isle, sirrah*?   *person of inferior rank

STEPHANO

I should have been a sore one, then.

ALONSO

[*Pointing to CALIBAN*] This is as strange a thing as e'er I look'd on.   360

PROSPERO

He is as disproportioned in his manners   *he is deformed in body and in

manners

As in his shape*. —Go, sirrah, to my cell.
Take with you your companions*: as you look   *Stephano and Trinculo
To have my pardon*, trim it handsomely*.   *to be forgiven by me *do it well

CALIBAN

Ay, that I will; and I'll be wise hereafter,   365
And seek for grace*. What a thrice-double ass*   *forgiveness *stupid
Was I, to take this drunkard for a god*,   *Stephano for a god
And worship this dull fool!

PROSPERO
Go to. Away!

ALONSO
Hence, and bestow your luggage* where you found it.   *stolen goods   370

SEBASTIAN
Or stole it, rather.
[*Exeunt CALIBAN, STEPHANO, and TRINCULO.*]

PROSPERO
Sir, I invite your Highness and your train*   *retinue, group
To my poor cell, where you shall take your rest
For this one night; which, part of it, I'll waste
With such discourse* as, I not doubt, shall make it   *tell you my story   375
Go quick away; the story of my life
And the particular accidents* gone by   *events
Since I came to this isle. And in the morn
I'll bring you to your ship, and so to Naples,
Where I have hope to see the nuptial*   *marriage   380
Of these our dear-belov'd solemnized*;
And thence retire me to my Milan*, where   *return to Milan
Every third thought shall be my grave*.   *ponder death

ALONSO
I long
To hear the story of your life, which must   385
Take the ear* strangely.   *will sound very strange

PROSPERO
I'll deliver all;
And promise you calm seas, auspicious gales*   *encouraging, promising winds,
And sail so expeditious* that shall catch   *efficient
Your royal fleet far off*.
[*Aside to ARIEL*] My Ariel, chick,   *we'll catch the rest of the fleet fast   390
That is thy charge: then to the elements
Be free, and fare thou well!

[*To the others*] Please you, draw near*.   *come closer
[*Exeunt*]

EPILOGUE

An epilogue takes place after the conclusion of the events of the play. Prospero comes out and addresses the audience directly, acknowledging that we've been watching a play, a work of illusion and fiction, all this time. Here, Prospero says he's given up all his powers and thus he's in the audience's power to return to Naples (Italy) with our blessing—our good wishes, positive praise for the play, and clapping of our hands. [*Spoken by* PROSPERO]

Now my charms are all o'erthrown*,   *I've given up my magic
And what strength I have's mine own;   *I only have my own power, not supernatural
Which is most faint*; now 'tis true,   *weak
I must be here confin'd by you*,   *kept here *the audience of the play
Or sent to Naples. Let me not,   5
Since I have my dukedom got,
And pardon'd the deceiver*, dwell   *forgiven my enemies
In this bare island by your spell*,   *kept here by your magic
But release me from my bands*   *chains, constraints
With the help of your good hands*.   *your applause   10
Gentle breath of yours my sails
Must fill,* or else my project fails,   *praise the play
Which was to please*. Now I want   *I intended to entertain you
Spirits to enforce, art to enchant*   *I have no magic to make it happen
And my ending is despair,   15
Unless I be reliev'd by prayer,   *my request
Which pierces so that it assaults
Mercy itself, and frees all faults.
As you from crimes would pardon'd be*,   *just like you want to be forgiven for your sins
Let your indulgence set me free*.   *indulge me and set me free   20

The Tempest. Questions for Discussion

1. It's quite clear by the end of the play that Prospero has far more power than anyone else. To what degree does it appear that he abuses his power? To what degree does he use it toward the good of everyone? How do we determine the "right" use of power and keep the powerful from becoming corrupted by that power?

2. A large majority of characters in the play seek power over others and to establish ownership and authority over this desert island. Is Shakespeare here following St. Augustine's concern that human nature by design makes people seek dominion over others? Or is he trying to show us something else about human nature and power?

3. Shakespeare's plays all establish the medieval way of thinking about the natural order of things. Both the tragedies and the comedies restore the social and the natural order by the end, although they do so in different ways. Generally, this play follows that natural order, though there are some challenges—for example, we don't find out exactly what happens to Caliban. Prospero promises to set Ariel free, though we don't actually witness Ariel's true freedom within the play. Prospero promises to give up his magic *after* the last night on the island, and we don't see the return to Italy. Is justice fully served in this play? What are your best reasons for your response? Why do you think that Shakespeare chose to end one of his very last plays in this way?

4. Ariel and Caliban are not fully human characters in the play. However, they indirectly and directly comment on the nature of humanity and of civilization. How do they separately and together show us something about what it means to be human?

5. The world of *The Tempest* is a fantasy world that includes magic, sorcery, and spirits. Magic is at its very heart the effort to create illusion, to show us something that isn't "really" there or to make us see something that has a deceptive appearance. In what ways do we in the modern world create or fall victim to illusions, and what are the technologies that are used to facilitate such "magic"? What do you think Shakespeare is trying to show us about the relationship between reality and illusion, indeed about the very nature of Truth?

The Age of Exploration,
the Rise of the Atlantic Slave Trade, and
the Age of Revolutions

The Age of Exploration, The Rise of the Atlantic Slave Trade, and the Age of Revolutions: Overview
(16th–19th Centuries CE)

The Age of Exploration and the Rise of the Atlantic Slave Trade

As new ideas and innovations flourished during the Renaissance, new technologies, inspirations to travel, and need for resources encouraged European countries to journey on long exploratory expeditions across the globe. Portuguese explorers, including Prince Henry the Navigator, Vasco da Gama, Ferdinand Magellan, and Spanish explorers, including Hernán Cortés, Juan Ponce de León, and Christopher Columbus, embarked on early quests in the 15th and 16th centuries. Their goals included finding new trade routes, colonizing new lands, and extracting resources for the benefit and wealth of the home country. Other nations followed, including the Netherlands, Britain, France, and Germany. Because this time period overlaps with the Age of Revolutions, in *Frankenstein*, for example, the explorations of Robert Walton at the beginning and end of the novel highlight both this type of quest as well as the physical, emotional, and ethical perils that they faced.

The new lands to which the Europeans traveled were already inhabited by indigenous peoples. Europeans carried diseases to which the native populations had never been exposed, and this often decimated indigenous populations and allowed European colonizers to conquer these people and wrest control over their lands. Additionally, rival groups of indigenous peoples allied themselves with the Europeans, further opening opportunities for colonization and exploitation, including enslavement. Due to shortages of Europeans as well as indigenous peoples to work hard labor, often on sugar plantations, the Atlantic slave trade began in the early 1500s, resulting in the sale and transportation of an estimated 12. 5 million indigenous African people to Europe and the Americas over approximately three hundred years. The inhumane treatment of these people was rationalized under the Middle Ages Great Chain of Being hierarchy in which non-Europeans were thought to be somehow "lower" than human, an idea that played a role in the treatment of Caliban in Shakespeare's *The Tempest*.

The Age of Revolutions

The word "revolution" in this context means a major change—a sudden, dramatic, and/or fundamental change in the way we see or think about something. Throughout this period in western history, revolutions occured in nearly all areas of society and substantially shifted the ways that we live and our ways of thinking about who we are, how we make decisions, what we value, and how technology fits within our daily lives. It was a time of great upheaval, innovation, and change.

The Scientific Revolution: A Precursor

The Scientific Revolution serves as one of the major shifts between the medieval way of thinking about the world and the modern way of conceptualizing how we come to know and understand Truth. The Scientific Revolution starts with the discoveries of astronomers Copernicus, Kepler, and Galileo that contradicted Catholic Church teachings about the universe. Their work contributed to the invention of the scientific method in the 16th century, which relies on developing a hypothesis/theory, gathering empirical evidence (evidence that we can measure), determining the validity or truth of that hypothesis, and then being able to repeat the same experiment to be sure that the results are valid.

The Enlightenment: An Intellectual Revolution

What is enlightenment? Many people today immediately think of Eastern thought, especially the Buddha, the "enlightened one." But the term and ideal of enlightenment has a home in the west as well as the east, from about the middle of the 16th through the end of the 18th century. The European Enlightenment was not the enlightenment of single individuals, but the gradual displacement of ancient certainties rooted in tradition with scientific and philosophical research rooted in reason alone. The Enlightenment replaced the medieval faith in God with hope and trust in human reason. The 'light' of the Enlightenment was the light of reason. Because of this emphasis on human reason, this period is sometimes also called "the Age of Reason."

The idea of human freedom is central to the idea of enlightenment. Immanuel Kant (1724–1804), one of the Enlightenment's most important thinkers, wrote that enlightenment "is mankind's exit from its self-incurred immaturity." Enlightenment is the human race finally growing up, shaking off the old masters and trusting itself. The only thing needed to overcome the old immaturity, according to Kant, is hard work and courage:

Laziness and cowardice are the reasons why such a great part of mankind, long after nature has set them free from the guidance of others,... still gladly remain immature for life and why for others to set themselves up as guardians. It is so easy to be immature. If I have a book that has understanding for me, a pastor who has a conscience for me, a doctor who judges my diet for me, and so forth, surely I do not need to trouble myself. I have no need to think, if only I can pay; others will take over the tedious business for me. [1]

The Enlightenment was a time of hope for the future of humanity. Relying on human reason would solve problems, answer questions and, most of all, emancipate humanity from its dependence on the traditional authority of church and state.

Of course, Enlightenment thinkers had predecessors in the Renaissance. The scientific revolution was also a major precursor. After all, if human reason could accomplish so much in the natural and mathematical sciences, why not apply it to all spheres of human life? Enlightenment thinkers encouraged beginning again, or starting over from scratch. The German word for enlightenment, *Aufklärung*, is best translated as *clearing up*, and includes the sense of getting rid of the old, and starting over. This was also an age of political revolution. It was a time of new beginnings.

Many of the values we take for granted today have their origin in this intellectual revolution. These include the political ideals of freedom of speech and conscience, separation of church and state, the emphasis on seeking to understand ourselves and the world around us through well-grounded scientific research, and perhaps most of all, the idea that progress is intimately connected to freedom. In many ways we are still children of the Enlightenment.

René Descartes was an important forerunner to the Enlightenment. He rejected the older medieval philosophy and bravely started over from the beginning. He was an arch-rationalist, as the readings below clearly demonstrate. A rationalist believes that knowledge of the world comes through reason, rather than the senses. The belief that sense experience is the primary source of our knowledge of the world is called empiricism. Empiricism was also a major feature of Enlightenment thought. Both empiricism and rationalism were central to scientific advances throughout the Enlightenment, which included new discoveries in both natural and mathematical sciences.

---

1. Immanuel Kant, An Answer to the Question: What is Enlightenment? trans. James Schmidt, in James Schmidt, et al, What is Enlightenment? , (Berkeley, CA: University of California Press, 1996), 58.

The Enlightenment's most profound impact was on everyday people in Europe. The rejection of traditional elites in both church and state gave rise to political and cultural revolutions, culminating in the French revolution of 1789. It was political philosophy that laid the foundation for revolution. Philosophers like Thomas Hobbes, John Locke and Jean-Jacques Rousseau are representative of the radical new thinking about the legitimacy of political power. And in their thought kings and bishops do not figure at all.

At the end of his famous essay on enlightenment, Immanuel Kant claims that he was not living in an enlightened age, but that he was living in an age of enlightenment. Enlightenment is an ongoing project of human culture, one that requires continued effort and renewed commitment. Kant offers the following as a motto for enlightenment, "Dare to Know!" He implores us to "have the courage to use [our] *own* understanding."

The Industrial Revolution: Innovations in Technology

In the 1700s, another shift occurs in the ways that we think about the role of technology in our lives. The Industrial Revolution began in 1760 with the invention of the steam engine, which was used in the textile industry (clothing, cloth, and other fabrics) to increase production and conserve human labor. This created a major population shift from the country to urban areas and a corresponding labor shift from farming to factory work. Further innovations were required to transport both goods and people, so we see the beginning of the adaptation of steam engine technology to develop railroads and steam-powered ships. Every invention, from modern electricity, communication systems, the internet, our computers, and even our cell phones, starts with the Industrial Revolution. The social effects of this radical change in lifestyle are broad-reaching, creating poor labor conditions and unsanitary living conditions for the working-class poor, environmental challenges due to factory pollution, and shifts in social classes with the rise of a strong middle class for the first time in world history.

The American, French, and Latin American Revolutions: Social and Political Revolutions

As the Enlightenment ideals gain prominence in the ways that we think about our individual roles in society, we see these bold ideas influence broad groups of people. John Locke's ideals of "life, liberty, and the pursuit of property" gain traction in the American colonies and become a call for American independence from Britain.

Suddenly, we have the conditions necessary for democracy to thrive, which creates a new form of social contract between a leader and the people that leader serves. Inspired by the American Revolution, the French and Latin American revolutions, as well as other social and political reform movements, follow. The ways that we think about our roles as citizens in the modern world are all heavily influenced by these 18th and 19th century shifts in government and leadership.

Romanticism: A Literary, Artistic, and Philosophical Revolution

Not everyone, however, was pleased with modern technological innovation or our increasing dependence on technology. Romanticism was a philosophical and artistic movement that reacted strongly against the dominance of reason and scientific and technological innovations. Romantics argued that we can't ever entirely get away from our emotions and subjectivity, nor should we, as these are essential to our very humanity. Additionally, in part, the Romantics argued that our over-dependence on technology and industrialization resulting from the Industrial Revolution would lead to the downfall of civilization. Not coincidentally, democratic revolutions, particularly the American and French Revolutions, were already in progress as the Romantic period began, and the Romantics often strongly sympathized and empathized with the causes that encouraged these political revolutions.

Romantic philosophy argues that the universe is a connected whole and that reason, even the scientific method, cannot fully explain the universe by dissecting it into discrete parts and analyzing each part separately and independently. For the Romantics, emotion, subjective experience, and intuition are important aspects to understanding the world and to human creative expression. As a whole, the Romantics reacted against the Enlightenment's claims to civilization's infinite progress through technology and advancements. Rather, they believed that civilization corrupts humans and leads them astray from both human morality and individual freedom. Instead of seeking more and more progressive civilization, humans should return to the simple life in natural surroundings. Nature, for the Romantics, helps humans reconnect with themselves, with morality, and, for the American Transcendentalists, the divine.

The roots of philosophical Romanticism began with Swiss philosopher Jean Jacques Rousseau, whose ideas about the Social Contract we study in the Enlightenment period, and German philosopher Immanuel Kant. The philosophical movement was largely centered in Germany and included such philosophers as Johann Gottlieb Fichte, Friedrich Schelling, and Georg Wilhelm Friedrich Hegel. Their ideas spread across Europe to influence the literary Romantics first in England with writers William Wordsworth, John Keats, Samuel Taylor Coleridge, Lord Byron, and Percy Bysshe Shelley, the husband of Mary Shelley. From there, the movement spread to France, the United States, Russia, and other nations.

As we will see in *Frankenstein*, Mary Shelley was heavily influenced by the philosopher Jean-Jacques Rousseau as well as the English Romantics in her social circle.

Introduction to the Philosophy of René Descartes

The work and life of the French philosopher, mathematician and scientist René Descartes (1596–1650) is a good marker for the beginning of the modern age. Born in La Haye, France, Descartes was educated in the Roman Catholic Jesuit school La Flèche, where he was given liberal access to their very good library. He then went on to complete a law degree, serve for several years in the military, and retire early to devote himself to philosophical, mathematical and scientific pursuits.

Descartes made some of the most important and influential advances in mathematics and physics of the seventeenth century. He discovered analytic geometry, and the Cartesian coordinate system, which, with its x and y axis familiar to students of algebra even today, is named after him. His pioneering work in mathematics paved the way for the development of modern physics. Without Descartes, Newton's discoveries would not have been possible only a generation later.

His philosophical work was no less significant. Descartes' philosophical writing exemplifies the rationalism that characterized the Enlightenment. The *Meditations on First Philosophy* also exemplifies the Enlightenment emphasis on beginning again, on starting over with nothing but reason alone. In the first meditation he tears down the entire structure of his belief system by rejecting as though they were false any belief he holds that might be even slightly doubtable. In the second meditation he discovers one belief that is impossible to doubt, and proceeds to rebuild his system of belief on that new foundation. He approaches knowledge like a mathematician and works from that one certainty as an axiom for his whole system, as geometry derives all theorems from just five axioms.

The *Meditations* are a record of Descartes' quest for certainty. He discovers that he cannot doubt his own existence, and this is what he lays at the foundation of his system of knowledge and belief. Further, he defines the fundamental nature of the human being, or the essence of the human, as mind. For Descartes, to be a human being is to be a "thinking thing." This is a radically new conception of humanity, one that places the human subject, or the "ego," over against a world of objects. It would have been difficult for pre-modern people to understand, yet we have little difficulty with it. The Cartesian subject is the mark of the modern.

Meditations Questions

What is Truth? You might say that this is the guiding question of Descartes' life. He steadfastly refuses to accept anything as true unless he can be certain of it. That's a tall order. Certainty doesn't admit degrees. You can't be a little more or less certain. If you hold a belief and it's even the slightest bit doubt*able*, even if it is not really that doubt*ful*, even if it's *probably true*, that's not certainty. The standard is hard to meet. In *Meditations* Descartes resolves to doubt the truth of everything he believes—*everything*. In this way he thinks he might find something that it turns out he simply cannot doubt. His skepticism is only methodological, however. He's on a search for certainty by means of doubt.

In the first meditation, Descartes destroys all that he had believed to be true, since it seems that he could find some reason, no matter how far-fetched, to doubt his beliefs. Early in the second meditation, however, he finds what he was seeking, a truth that is so clearly and distinctly known that it is impossible to doubt: that he exists. That is to say that Descartes' first, and fundamental truth is the truth of the sentence: "I exist," at least, as he points out, any time he says it or thinks it. Earlier, in *Discourse on Method*, he had put it differently, though more famously, "I think, therefore I am. " But though much more famous, this way of putting his discovery can be confusing. He's not deriving the fact of his existence from the fact of his thought. Rather, if you read the relevant passage in the *Meditations* closely, he argues from the fact that it is impossible to doubt his existence that the sentence "I exist" is necessarily true. He then goes on to derive his essence, or *what* he is, from this foundational proposition.

What is Justice? While Descartes does not write directly about issues of justice in his work, he does address the importance of ethics, and its relationship to the rest of the "tree" of knowledge in his work *The Principles of Philosophy*, excerpted below. He likens the relationship of all of the human sciences to a tree, with the more general sciences lower down, and the more specific sciences up in the branches. The sciences above depend on knowledge of the sciences below them. The science of morals he places in the highest part of the canopy, as it is the "last degree of wisdom," and a good understanding of morality requires "an entire knowledge of the other sciences."

What does it mean to be human? Descartes' conception of what it means to be human is the modern conception of the human being. His work is among the first philosophical examinations of this developing conception of the human being. It is still the default self-understanding in the modern world. It is our self-understanding.

Descartes begins the *Meditations* on a quest for certainty. In the second meditation, he discovers one thing to be certain: his existence, or *that he is*. Immediately following this discovery, he inquires about his essence, or *what he is*. He briefly surveys the Aristotelian answer, so authoritative in the late middle ages, that the human being is a "rational animal. " He rejects this as just leading to more and more questions, as another scholastic rabbit hole, the kind of thing he is trying to avoid by starting afresh without any presuppositions.

Starting from the impossible-to-doubt truth of his existence, and building on that foundational truth as an axiom in his new system of knowledge, he derives a second one, that he is essentially his thoughts, that he is a "thinking thing," a mind. He arrives at this conclusion by a kind of game of "takeaway. " What is it that, if taken away, you would cease to be? Since he has already supposed that, for all he knows, he may not have a body, this is not essential. What about thought? Well, it seems that if he stopped thinking altogether, he would no longer exist. Therefore, thought is the essence of the human being. In the Cartesian model, we are all essentially minds, or thought boxes. Today we may say these boxes are our brains, but it's still an essentially Cartesian model of the human.

What is the Good Life? Descartes doesn't write very much about ethics in his work, and in the selections below he doesn't directly address the good life as such. Still, his dedication to the truth, and his methodological search for it in these works gives us some idea of the role that the search for knowledge plays in his ideal of the good life. Reason plays a key role, as does his emphasis on never accepting anything to be true unless he is absolutely certain. In the selections below we can infer his ethics of belief.

From *The Principles of Philosophy*[1]

In this passage from *The Principles of Philosophy* Descartes explains his conception of how all the sciences are connected with the metaphor of a tree. It also highlights his conception of the place of morality, or ethics, in the system of knowledge.

Then, when he has acquired some skill in discovering the truth in these questions, he should commence to apply himself in earnest to true philosophy, of which the first part is Metaphysics, containing the principles of knowledge, among which is the explication of the principal attributes of God, of the immateriality of the soul, and of all the clear and simple notions that are in us; the second is Physics, in which, after finding the true principles of material things, we examine, in general, how the whole universe has been framed; in the next place, we consider, in particular, the nature of the earth, and of all the bodies that are most generally found upon it, as air, water, fire, the loadstone and other minerals. In the next place it is necessary also to examine singly the nature of plants, of animals, and above all of man, in order that we may thereafter be able to discover the other sciences that are useful to us. Thus, all Philosophy is like a tree, of which Metaphysics is the root, Physics the trunk, and all the other sciences the branches that grow out of this trunk, which are reduced to three principal, namely, Medicine, Mechanics, and Ethics. By the science of Morals, I understand the highest and most perfect which, presupposing an entire knowledge of the other sciences, is the last degree of wisdom.

The Principles of Philosophy. Question for Discussion:

1. Consider this vision of science offered up in Descartes, and the place of ethics, or morality, in it. What do you think he meant by the claim that "an entire knowledge of the other sciences" is necessary for understanding the good life? What is your understanding of science and morality?

---

1. Selections excerpted from René Descartes, *The Method, Meditations and Philosophy of Descartes*, trans. John Veitch (Washington, D. C.: M. Walter Dunne, 1901), 303. The editor has added italics and boldface type, and deleted parenthetical notes by the translator as well as other minor grammatical changes.

From *Discourse on Method*

In the first of these two passages from *Discourse on Method*, Descartes lays out a set of four rules for proceeding in his quest for certainty and for rebuilding science on a new foundation. The second selection includes the most famous quotation from Descartes, "I think, therefore I am."

I believed that the four [rules] following would prove perfectly sufficient for me, provided I took the firm and unwavering resolution never in a single instance to fail in observing them.

The first was never to accept anything for true which I did not clearly know to be such; that is to say, carefully to avoid precipitancy and prejudice, and to comprise nothing more in my judgement than what was presented to my mind so clearly and distinctly as to exclude all ground of doubt.

The second, to divide each of the difficulties under examination into as many parts as possible, and as might be necessary for its adequate solution.

The third, to conduct my thoughts in such order that, by commencing with objects the simplest and easiest to know, I might ascend by little and little, and, as it were, step by step, to the knowledge of the more complex; assigning in thought a certain order even to those objects which in their own nature do not stand in a relation of antecedence and sequence.

And the last, in every case to make enumerations so complete, and reviews so general, that I might be assured that nothing was omitted.

* * *

While we thus reject all of which we can entertain the smallest doubt, and even imagine that it is false, we easily indeed suppose that there is neither God, nor sky, nor bodies, and that we ourselves even have neither hands nor feet, nor, finally, a body; but we cannot in the same way suppose that we are not while we doubt of the truth of these things; for there is a repugnance in conceiving that what thinks does not exist at the very time when it thinks. Accordingly, the knowledge, *I think, therefore I am*, is the first and most certain that occurs to one who philosophizes orderly.

Discourse on Method. Questions for Discussion

1. Do you really think it is possible for a human being to follow these four rules as strictly as Descartes thinks he can? What do these rules say about how Descartes thinks we should go about discovering truths?

2. Does there seem to be an implied value judgment about how to seek the truth in these rules Descartes has set for himself (and everyone else)?

3. Do these rules adequately reflect how modern science goes about seeking truth? Are they more appropriate to some sciences (like math or physics) than others (like biology or geology)?

From *Meditations on First Philosophy*

The *Meditations on First Philosophy* include six meditations in total. It is a record of Descartes' first-person search for certainty, his attempt to underwrite the whole system of human knowledge with a truth impervious to doubt. In the first meditation he tears down his beliefs, and in the second discovers the one thing impossible to doubt, and begins the task of retrieving all the beliefs he discarded in the first meditation. The selections below include all of the first meditation, and the most significant selections from the second.

MEDITATION I: Of the Things on Which We May Doubt

Several years have now elapsed since I first became aware that I had accepted, even from my youth, many false opinions for true, and that consequently what I afterward based on such principles was highly doubtful; and from that time I was convinced of the necessity of undertaking once in my life to rid myself of all the opinions I had adopted, and of commencing anew the work of building from the foundation, if I desired to establish a firm and abiding superstructure in the sciences. But as this enterprise appeared to me to be one of great magnitude, I waited until I had attained an age so mature as to leave me no hope that at any stage of life more advanced I should be better able to execute my design. On this account, I have delayed so long that I should henceforth consider I was doing wrong were I still to consume in deliberation any of the time that now remains for action. To-day, then, since I have opportunely freed my mind from all cares, and am happily disturbed by no passions, and since I am in the secure possession of leisure in a peaceable retirement, I will at length apply myself earnestly and freely to the general overthrow of all my former opinions. But, to this end, it will not be necessary for me to show that the whole of these are false—a point, perhaps, which I shall never reach; but as even now my reason convinces me that I ought not the less carefully to withhold belief from what is not entirely certain and indubitable, than from what is manifestly false, it will be sufficient to justify the rejection of the whole if I shall find in each some ground for doubt. Nor for this purpose will it be necessary even to deal with each belief individually, which would be truly an endless labor; but, as the removal from below of the foundation necessarily involves the downfall of the whole edifice, I will at once approach the criticism of the principles on which all my former beliefs rested.

All that I have, up to this moment, accepted as possessed of the highest truth and certainty, I received either from or through the senses. I observed, however, that these sometimes misled us; and it is the part of prudence not to place absolute confidence in that by which we have even once been deceived.

But it may be said, perhaps, that, although the senses occasionally mislead us respecting minute objects, and such as are so far removed from us as to be beyond the reach of close observation, there are yet many other of their presentations, of the truth of which it is manifestly impossible to doubt; as for example, that I am in this place, seated by the fire, clothed in a winter dressing gown, that I hold in my hands this piece of paper, with other intimations of the same nature. But how could I deny that I possess these hands and this body, and withal escape being classed with persons in a state of insanity, whose brains are so disordered: and clouded by dark bilious vapors as to cause them pertinaciously to assert that they are monarchs when they are in the greatest poverty; or clothed in gold and purple when destitute of any covering; or that their head is made of clay, their body of glass, or that they are gourds? I should certainly be not less insane than they, were I to regulate my procedure according to examples so extravagant.

Though this be true, I must nevertheless here consider that I am a man, and that, consequently, I am in the habit of sleeping, and representing to myself in dreams those same things, or even sometimes others less probable, which the insane think are presented to them in their waking moments. How often have I dreamt that I was in these familiar circumstances, that I was dressed, and occupied this place by the fire, when I was lying undressed in bed? At the present moment, however, I certainly look upon this paper with eyes wide awake; the head which I now move is not asleep; I extend this hand consciously and with express purpose, and I perceive it; the occurrences in sleep are not so distinct as in all this. But I cannot forget that, at other times I have been deceived in sleep by similar illusions; and, attentively considering those cases, I perceive so clearly that there exist no certain marks by which the state of waking can ever be distinguished from sleep, that I feel greatly astonished; and in amazement I almost persuade myself that I am now dreaming.

Let us suppose, then, that we are dreaming, and that all these particulars — namely, the opening of the eyes, the motion of the head, the forth-putting of the hands — are merely illusions; and even that we really possess neither an entire body nor hands such as we see. Nevertheless it must be admitted at least that the objects which appear to us in sleep are, as it were, painted representations which could not have been formed unless in the likeness of realities; and, therefore, that those general objects, at all events, namely, eyes, a head, hands, and an entire body, are not simply imaginary, but really existent. For, in truth, painters themselves, even when they study to represent sirens and satyrs by forms the most fantastic and extraordinary, cannot bestow upon them natures absolutely new, but can only make a certain medley of the members of different animals; or if they chance to imagine something so novel that nothing at all similar has ever been seen before, and such as is, therefore, purely fictitious and absolutely false, it is at least certain that the colors of which this is composed are real.

And on the same principle, although these general objects, viz, a body, eyes, a head, hands, and the like, be imaginary, we are nevertheless absolutely necessitated to admit the reality at least of some other objects still more simple and universal than these, of which, just as of certain real colors, all those images of things, whether true and real, or false and fantastic, that are found in our consciousness, are formed.

To this class of objects seem to belong corporeal nature in general and its extension; the figure of extended things, their quantity or magnitude, and their number, as also the place in, and the time during, which they exist, and other things of the same sort. We will not, therefore, perhaps reason illegitimately if we conclude from this that Physics, Astronomy, Medicine, and all the other sciences that have for their end the consideration of composite objects, are indeed of a doubtful character; but that Arithmetic, Geometry, and the other sciences of the same class, which regard merely the simplest and most general objects, and scarcely inquire whether or not these are really existent, contain somewhat that is certain and indubitable: for whether I am awake or dreaming, it remains true that two and three make five, and that a square has but four sides; nor does it seem possible that truths so apparent can ever fall under a suspicion of falsity or incertitude.

Nevertheless, the belief that there is a God who is all powerful, and who created me, such as I am, has, for a long time, obtained steady possession of my mind. How, then, do I know that he has not arranged that there should be neither earth, nor sky, nor any extended thing, nor figure, nor magnitude, nor place, providing at the same time, however, for the rise in me of the perceptions of all these objects, and the persuasion that these do not exist otherwise than as I perceive them? And further, as I sometimes think that others are in error respecting matters of which they believe themselves to possess a perfect knowledge, how do I know that I am not also deceived each time I add together two and three, or number the sides of a square, or form some judgment still more simple, if more simple indeed can be imagined? But perhaps Deity has not been willing that I should be thus deceived, for he is said to be supremely good. If, however, it were repugnant to the goodness of Deity to have created me subject to constant deception, it would seem likewise to be contrary to his goodness to allow me to be occasionally deceived; and yet it is clear that this is permitted. Some, indeed, might perhaps be found who would be disposed rather to deny the existence of a Being so powerful than to believe that there is nothing certain. But let us for the present refrain from opposing this opinion, and grant that all which is here said of a Deity is fabulous: nevertheless, in whatever way it be supposed that I reach the state in which I exist, whether by fate, or chance, or by an endless series of antecedents and consequents, or by any other means, it is clear (since to be deceived and to err is a certain defect) that the probability of my being so imperfect as to be the constant victim of deception, will be increased exactly in proportion as the power possessed by the cause, to which they assign my origin, is lessened. To these reasonings I have assuredly nothing to reply, but am constrained at last to avow that there is nothing of all that I formerly believed to be true of which it is impossible to doubt, and that not through thoughtlessness or levity, but from cogent and maturely considered reasons; so that henceforward, if I desire to discover anything certain, I ought not the less carefully to refrain from assenting to those same opinions than to what might be shown to be manifestly false.

But it is not sufficient to have made these observations; care must be taken likewise to keep them in remembrance. For those old and customary opinions perpetually recur—long and familiar usage giving them the right of occupying my mind, even almost against my will, and subduing my belief; nor will I lose the habit of deferring to them and confiding in them so long as I shall consider them to be what in truth they are, viz, opinions to some extent doubtful, as I have already shown, but still highly probable, and such as it is much more reasonable to believe than deny. It is for this reason I am persuaded that I shall not be doing wrong, if, taking an opposite judgment of deliberate design, I become my own deceiver, by supposing, for a time, that all those opinions are entirely false and imaginary, until at length, having thus balanced my old by my new prejudices, my judgment shall no longer be turned aside by perverted usage from the path that may conduct to the perception of truth.

For I am assured that, meanwhile, there will arise neither peril nor error from this course, and that I cannot for the present yield too much to distrust, since the end I now seek is not action but knowledge.

I will suppose, then, not that Deity, who is sovereignly good and the fountain of truth, but that some malignant demon, who is at once exceedingly potent and deceitful, has employed all his artifice to deceive me; I will suppose that the sky, the air, the earth, colors, figures, sounds, and all external things, are nothing better than the illusions of dreams, by means of which this being has laid snares for my credulity; I will consider myself as without hands, eyes, flesh, blood, or any of the senses, and as falsely believing that I am possessed of these; I will continue resolutely fixed in this belief, and if indeed by this means it be not in my power to arrive at the knowledge of truth, I shall at least do what is in my power, viz suspend my judgment, and guard with settled purpose against giving my assent to what is false, and being imposed upon by this deceiver, whatever be his power and artifice.

But this undertaking is arduous, and a certain indolence insensibly leads me back to my ordinary course of life; and just as the captive, who, perchance, was enjoying in his dreams an imaginary liberty, when he begins to suspect that it is but a vision, dreads awakening, and conspires with the agreeable illusions that the deception may be prolonged; so I, of my own accord, fall back into the train of my former beliefs, and fear to arouse myself from my slumber, lest the time of laborious wakefulness that would succeed this quiet rest, in place of bringing any light of day, should prove inadequate to dispel the darkness that will arise from the difficulties that have now been raised.

MEDITATION II: Of the Nature of the Human Mind, and that It is More Easily Known than the Body

The Meditation of yesterday has filled my mind with so many doubts, that it is no longer in my power to forget them. Nor do I see, meanwhile, any principle on which they can be resolved; and, just as if I had fallen all of a sudden into very deep water, I am so greatly disconcerted as to be unable either to plant my feet firmly on the bottom or sustain myself by swimming on the surface. I will, nevertheless, make an effort, and try anew the same path on which I had entered yesterday, that is, proceed by casting aside all that admits of the slightest doubt, not less than if I had discovered it to be absolutely false; and I will continue always in this track until I shall find something that is certain, or at least, if I can do nothing more, until I shall know with certainty that there is nothing certain. Archimedes, that he might transport the entire globe from the place it occupied to another, demanded only a point that was firm and immovable; so, also, I shall be entitled to entertain the highest expectations, if I am fortunate enough to discover only one thing that is certain and indubitable.

I suppose, accordingly, that all the things which I see are false (fictitious); I believe that none of those objects which my fallacious memory represents ever existed; I suppose that I possess no senses; I believe that body, figure, extension, motion, and place are merely fictions of my mind. What is there, then, that can be esteemed true? Perhaps this only, that there is absolutely nothing certain.

But how do I know that there is not something different altogether from the objects I have now enumerated, of which it is impossible to entertain the slightest doubt? Is there not a God, or some being, by whatever name I may designate him, who causes these thoughts, to arise in my mind? But why suppose such a being, for it maybe I myself am capable of producing them? Am I, then, at least not something? But I before denied that I possessed senses or a body; I hesitate, however, for what follows from that? Am I so dependent on the body and the senses that without these I cannot exist? But I had the persuasion that there was absolutely nothing in the world, that there was no sky and no earth, neither minds nor bodies; was I not, therefore, at the same time, persuaded that I did not exist? Far from it: *I assuredly existed, since I was persuaded. But there is I know not what being, who is possessed at once of the highest power and the deepest cunning, who is constantly employing all his ingenuity in deceiving me. Doubtless, then, I exist, since I am deceived; and, let him deceive me as he may, he can never bring it about that I am nothing, so long as I shall be conscious that I am something. So that it must, in fine, be maintained, all things being maturely and carefully considered, that this proposition I am, I exist, is necessarily true each time it is expressed by me, or conceived in my mind.*

But I do not yet know with sufficient clearness what I am, though assured that I am; and hence, in the next place, I must take care, lest perchance I inconsiderately substitute some other object in room of what is properly myself, and thus wander from truth, even in that knowledge (cognition) which I hold to be of all others the most certain and evident.

* * *

But as to myself, what can I now say that I am, since I suppose there exists an extremely powerful, and, if I may so speak, malignant being, whose whole endeavors are directed toward deceiving me? Can I affirm that I possess any one of all those attributes of which I have lately spoken as belonging to the nature of body? After attentively considering them in my own mind, I find none of them that can properly be said to belong to myself. To recount them were idle and tedious. Let us pass, then, to the attributes of the soul. The first mentioned were the powers of nutrition and walking; but, if it be true that I have no body, it is true likewise that I am capable neither of walking nor of being nourished. Perception is another attribute of the soul; but perception too is impossible without the body; besides, I have frequently, during sleep, believed that I perceived objects which I afterward observed I did not in reality perceive. *Thinking is another attribute of the soul; and here I discover what properly belongs to myself. This alone is inseparable from me. I am — I exist: this is certain; but how often? As often as I think; for perhaps it would even happen, if I should wholly cease to think, that I should at the same time altogether cease to be. I now admit nothing that is not necessarily true. I am therefore, precisely speaking, only a thinking thing, that is, a mind, understanding, or reason, terms whose signification was before unknown to me.* I am, however, a real thing, and really existent; but what thing? The answer was, a thinking thing. The question now arises, am I aught besides? I will stimulate my imagination with a view to discover whether I am not still something more than a thinking being. Now it is plain I am not the assemblage of members called the human body; I am not a thin and penetrating air diffused through all these members, or wind, or flame, or vapor, or breath, or any of all the things I can imagine; for I supposed that all these were not, and, without changing the supposition, I find that I still feel assured of my existence.

But it is true, perhaps, that those very things which I suppose to be non-existent, because they are unknown to me, are not in troth different from myself whom I know. This is a point I cannot determine, and do not now enter into any dispute regarding it. I can only judge of things that are known to me: I am conscious that I exist, and I who know that I exist inquire into what I am. It is, however, perfectly certain that the knowledge of my existence, thus precisely taken, is not dependent on things, the existence of which is as yet unknown to me: and consequently it is not dependent on any of the things I can feign in imagination. Moreover, the phrase itself, I frame an image, reminds me of my error; for I should in truth frame one if I were to imagine myself to be anything, since to imagine is nothing more than to contemplate the figure or image of a corporeal thing; but I already know that I exist, and that it is possible at the same time that all those images, and in general all that relates to the nature of body, are merely dreams or chimeras. From this I discover that it is not more reasonable to say, I will excite my imagination that I may know more distinctly what I am, than to express myself as follows: I am now awake, and perceive something real; but because my perception is not sufficiently clear, I will of express purpose go to sleep that my dreams may represent to me the object of my perception with more truth and clearness. And, therefore, I know that nothing of all that I can embrace in imagination belongs to the knowledge which I have of myself, and that there is need to recall with the utmost care the mind from this mode of thinking, that it may be able to know its own nature with perfect distinctness.

But what, then, am I? A thinking thing, it has been said. But what is a thinking thing? It is a thing that doubts, understands, conceives, affirms, denies, wills, refuses; that imagines also, and perceives. Assuredly it is not little, if all these properties belong to my nature. But why should they not belong to it? Am I not that very being who now doubts of almost everything; who, for all that, understands and conceives certain things; who affirms one alone as true, and denies the others; who desires to know more of them, and does not wish to be deceived; who imagines many things, sometimes even despite his will; and is likewise percipient of many, as if through the medium of the senses. Is there nothing of all this as true as that I am, even although I should be always dreaming, and although he who gave me being employed all his ingenuity to deceive me? Is there also any one of these attributes that can be properly distinguished from my thought, or that can be said to be separate from myself? For it is of itself so evident that it is I who doubt, I who understand, and I who desire, that it is here unnecessary to add anything by way of rendering it more clear. And I am as certainly the same being who imagines; for although it maybe (as I before supposed) that nothing I imagine is true, still the power of imagination does not cease really to exist in me and to form part of my thought. In fine, I am the same being who perceives, that is, who apprehends certain objects as by the organs of sense, since, in truth, I see light, hear a noise, and feel heat. But it will be said that these presentations are false, and that I am dreaming. Let it be so. At all events it is certain that I seem to see light, hear a noise, and feel heat; this cannot be false, and this is what in me is properly called perceiving, which is nothing else than thinking. From this I begin to know what I am with somewhat greater clearness and distinctness than heretofore.

But, nevertheless, it still seems to me, and I cannot help believing, that corporeal things, whose images are formed by thought which fall under the senses, and are examined by the same, are known with much greater distinctness than that I know not what part of myself which is not imaginable; although, in truth, it may seem strange to say that I know and comprehend with greater distinctness things whose existence appears to me doubtful, that are unknown, and do not belong to me, than others of whose reality I am persuaded, that are known to me, and appertain to my proper nature; in a word, than myself. But I see clearly what is the state of the case. My mind is apt to wander, and will not yet submit to be restrained within the limits of truth. Let us therefore leave the mind to itself once more, and, according to it every kind of liberty permit it to consider the objects that appear to it from without, in order that, having afterward withdrawn it from these gently and opportunely and fixed it on the consideration of its being and the properties it finds in itself, it may then be the more easily controlled.

* * *

But, meanwhile, I feel greatly astonished when I observe the weakness of my mind, and its proneness to error. For although, without at all giving expression to what I think, I consider all this in my own mind, words yet occasionally impede my progress, and I am almost led into error by the terms of ordinary language. We say, for example, that we see the same wax when it is before us, and not that we judge it to be the same from its retaining the same color and figure: whence I should forthwith be disposed to conclude that the wax is known by the act of sight, and not by the intuition of the mind alone, were it not for the analogous instance of human beings passing on in the street below, as observed from a window. In this case I do not fail to say that I see the men themselves, just as I say that I see the wax; and yet what do I see from the window beyond hats and cloaks that might cover artificial machines, whose motions might be determined by springs? But I judge that there are human beings from these appearances, and thus I comprehend, by the faculty of judgment alone which is in the mind, what I believed I saw with my eyes.

* * *

But, in conclusion, I find I have insensibly reverted to the point I desired; for, since it is now manifest to me that bodies themselves are not properly perceived by the senses nor by the faculty of imagination, but by the intellect alone; and since they are not perceived because they are seen and touched, but only because they are understood or rightly comprehended by thought, I readily discover that there is nothing more Easily or clearly apprehended than my own mind. But because it is difficult to rid one's self so promptly of an opinion to which one has been long accustomed, it will be desirable to tarry for some time at this stage, that, by long continued meditation, I may more deeply impress upon my memory this new knowledge.

Meditations on First Philosophy. Questions for Discussion

1. Descartes' method of doubt has been criticized as merely pretending to doubt, when, in fact, it's actually impossible to doubt these things in ordinary, everyday life. Even if this is true, does this mean that Descartes' method in the *Meditations* is not appropriate for human knowledge?

2. Descartes argues that we cannot be certain about our immediate experience of the world via the senses because we might be dreaming. What do you think? Could you actually have overslept, and be dreaming right now?

3. Descartes is starting over. In order to do this, he has to doubt all of his previous beliefs about the world. The "malignant demon" or "evil demon" argument threatens a global skepticism, i. e., that nothing he believes is certain. How does he overcome this in the second mediation? What does he find impossible to doubt, and why? Do you agree?

4. Descartes argues, in the second meditation, that the human being is essentially a mind filled with ideas that represent the world. If this is correct, what does it say about the possibility of a self-conscious computer? Do you think a computer could be a kind of artificial mind, an artificial intelligence? What do you think Descartes would think? Do you think the mind is like a computer?

5. If Descartes is right, we could be in a computer simulation, and our present experiences could be false, for all we know. If he is right, does it matter? Should we be concerned about these kinds of questions about the truth of our perceptions? Why or why not?

Introduction to the Social Contract:
Hobbes, Locke and Rousseau

The Enlightenment reliance on human reason over traditional authorities led Thomas Hobbes (1588–1679) to conceive of what would become one of the most influential and enduring political ideas from the Age of Reason to our own day. Very briefly, the idea of a social contract is an attempt to set limits to political legitimacy without an appeal to traditional authorities. The central question is simple to state, but difficult to answer: why, and when does the individual citizen have the obligation to obey political authorities?

From the perspective of Enlightenment values, it is far from evident just why we should obey the rulers, or what the moral force of the laws has on the individual. Is it merely an imposition of the power of the strong over the weak, or is there more to the nature of humanity and human community that morally binds the individual to obey the laws and legitimates political power? Social contract theory tries, in various ways, to ground the answer to these questions in human reason, and thereby provide a universal human foundation for the rule of law.

Thomas Hobbes (1588–1679) was a British philosopher. Born near the town of Malmesbury, he was referred to by his ecclesiastical enemies as "the monster of Malmesbury," for his unorthodox beliefs about religion. The son of an Anglican minister, Hobbes graduated from Oxford, and worked as a tutor for a noble English family, a job that gave him opportunities to travel and meet the leading intellectual figures of the day, including many in Descartes' circle, and Galileo. Although he wrote on many topics, his philosophical account of the logical origin of the state is one of his most lasting influences in philosophy. He was the first to elaborate a social contract theory.

Before the state, or as Hobbes would say, the *commonwealth*, existed, there was a state of nature. It is important, however, not to take this too literally. Hobbes is not positing an historical state of nature prior to the historical development of the state. Rather, the state of nature is logically, not necessarily historically, prior to the state. If there were no state, human beings would be in this state of nature. And this situation would be intolerable. He describes life in the state of nature in stark terms as "solitary, poor, nasty, brutish and short." Without the commonwealth overseen by a strong sovereign, human beings were radically equal. They were equal in the sense that each had the right to everything, provided one could take it. Hobbes refers to this situation without civil society as "the right of all to all." Human beings without civil society, motivated only by the desire to survive and the fear of death, would be hostile to one another; chaos would reign, and it would be, says Hobbes, a "war of every man against every man."[1]

This seems to imply a deeply cynical view of human nature, where egoism reigns in the hearts of the individual. Hobbes also thought, however, that human beings in a state of nature were subject to natural laws. A natural law is a "precept or general rule, found out by reason." We are subject to natural laws because we have the power of reasoning. Further, given that human beings' fundamental motivation is survival, the first natural law is an inference from that: to seek peace. The second natural law also follows logically from the first: if you want peace, you have to give up your rights (to everything) as long as everyone else is willing to do the same. This is the origin of the state, or commonwealth. It's a logical inference from the desire for survival on the part of each rational individual. Each has made a deal, has implicitly entered into a contract—a social contract—with every other member of society.

Logically, however, it seems like the transition from a state of nature to the commonwealth would depend on a lot of mutual trust between the individual members of the contract. Why would anyone trust the other to keep their end of the bargain? Hobbes reasoned that the commonwealth required a sovereign with sufficient power to psychologically compel individuals to fulfill their end of the social contract. The commonwealth, united under an absolute sovereign is *Leviathan*, the *Mortal God*, the state. Until such a sovereign reigns, human beings will remain in a state of nature.

John Locke (1632–1704) also graduated from Oxford University, and although he would later become a medical doctor, he devoted himself to philosophy. Locke was a very influential thinker, but his political work, *Second Treatise of Government*, has perhaps had the most lasting impact. He begins his account of the origin of the state with the same idea that Hobbes had, the state of nature, with one difference. Where Hobbes painted a fairly grim picture of this free-for-all of unfettered egotistical

---

1. Thomas Hobbes, *Leviathan*, (Oxford: Clarendon Press, (1651) 1909, 62, 110, 100.

individualism, Locke saw a much more humane situation. Locke's state of nature is more idealistic: rational beings living together in a common life, just without a sovereign. As he puts it in the *Second Treatise*, "men living together according to reason, without a common superior on earth with authority to judge between them is properly the state of nature." Similar to Hobbes, Locke thinks that human beings in a state of nature are subject to natural laws, but he has a much more expansive conception of natural law. For Locke, the natural law is not only an instrumental rational determination of what you should do if you wish to avoid death and survive, but a clear moral law that teaches every human being to respect one another's "life, health, liberty or possessions."[2]

While this is a much more optimistic view of human nature, it makes it difficult for Locke to account for the origin of the state, and to ground political authority. There doesn't seem to be sufficient motive for human beings in a Lockean state of nature to enter into a social contract and found a state. Part of Locke's answer is that not all human beings would use their stock of reason to determine natural law, and he reasoned that the natural rights, especially that of property, are better secured for the individual in a civil society. Locke also agreed that a civil society required a sovereign, or some coercive power strong enough to enforce the social contract. Unlike Hobbes, he argued that this power should reside in the legislature, and that the executive power is under the law.

Finally, we can round out our Enlightenment thinkers of the social contract with the philosopher and novelist **Jean-Jacques Rousseau (1712–1778).** Born in Geneva to a watchmaker and his wife, Rousseau was one of the most influential *philosophes* of the French Enlightenment. His book *The Social Contract* is his account of the legitimacy of state authority. Rousseau idealizes the human being in a state of nature more than Locke. For Rousseau, the human being in a state of nature is happy and free, a "noble savage." For Rousseau, the human being is not born corrupted by original sin, but is corrupted by society. In a state of nature, humans are non-rational and pre-linguistic, driven to preserve their own safety and natural sympathy for others. They are free, not only from dependence on others, but also from the opinion of others. For Rousseau, the state of nature is also a state of natural virtue. Reason and language are acquired in history upon entering into society, which thus fundamentally changes what it means to be a human being. The human being in society is no longer only motivated by drive to self-preservation, but is now concerned with the

---

2. John Locke, *The Works of John Locke*, vol. 4, *Economic Writings and Two Treatises of Government* (London: C. Baldwin, 1824), 348–349, 341.

opinion of others. It is not until human beings enter into the social contract that they are, as it were, corrupted and enslaved. "Man" says Rousseau, "is born free; and everywhere he is in chains."[3]

Rousseau argues that human beings came to live together as a matter of practical necessity. The problem arises in that the "noble savage" is forced to give up natural freedom when entering into the social contract, when joining civil society. Like Locke and Hobbes, Rousseau also thinks that the social contract requires a sovereign, but he places sovereignty not in the people through the legislature, but in the "general will," a term that refers to the common good, to what everyone would agree is the best for all, whether or not in practice the people actually give their consent. The sovereignty of the general will is not the same as democratic process for Rousseau. The will of the majority can, on Rousseau's account, differ from the general will. The general will is the will of each individual who, having entered into the social contract, has agreed to pursue the general good. In this account of things, breaking the law amounts to asserting one's natural freedom and breaking the social contract. By forcing individuals to obey the law, the state is merely requiring them to abide by the contract, and to enjoy civil freedom. As Rousseau puts it, they "will be forced to be free."[4]

Hobbes, Locke, and Rousseau Questions

What is Truth? All of these thinkers have abandoned traditional authorities (church and state), and demanded a role for reason. This means a role for truths uncovered by reason as the final arbiter of the truth of any claims, no matter how much they may outrage conventional wisdom.

What is Justice? Justice is an obvious central issue. If the exercise of state power is not grounded in reason, is it unjust? With respect to freedom in particular, the question is when, if ever, is the limitation of individual freedom justified? Social contract theory tries to answer these questions in terms of justice.

What does it mean to be Human? All three of the social contract theories above are rooted in a conception of human nature. But there are significant differences among them.

---

3. Jean-Jacques Rousseau, *Rousseau's Social Contract, etc.*, trans. G. D. H. Cole (London: J. M. Dent and Sons, 1923), 5.

4. Ibid, 18.

What is the Good Life? While Hobbes, Locke, and Rousseau differ considerably in their vision of what constitutes the good life, there are some important similarities. Individual liberty, in particular, appears to be necessary conditions for any truly good life.

Questions for Discussion

1. Hobbes, Locke, and Rousseau have very different ideas about the natural state of human beings. Which most accords with your own intuition about how human beings would live without the constraints of society? Justify your answer.

2. Hobbes, Locke, and Rousseau all propose some version of a "natural law" solution to the problem of how to legitimate government authority. Which seems to accord best with your own experience and intuitions? Justify your answer.

3. Rousseau, unlike Locke and Hobbes, argues that human beings are naturally good, and that society is a corrupting force. He even argues that advances in the sciences and the arts actually increased the separation of human beings from nature. Reflect on modern technology, and how it may impact modern ways of interacting with nature and our self-understanding. Consider specific examples of technology and explore their impact.

4. Natural law theory presupposes agreement about human nature, what it really means to be a human being. Which theory do you think best accords with your own sense of human nature? Offer concrete examples to justify your answer.

Introduction to Mary Shelley and
Frankenstein (1818)[1]

Mary Shelley (1797–1851)

From her early life, Mary Shelley was surrounded by major thinkers and writers of the day, and her work reflects those Romantic philosophical and literary influences. She was the daughter of Mary Wollstonecraft, a pioneer in the women's rights movement in the late 18th/early 19th centuries, and William Godwin, a philosopher, political activist, and novelist. Then, when she was still a teenager, she met and fell in love with British Romantic poet Percy Bysshe Shelley. Shelley was married at the time, but after his wife committed suicide under somewhat suspicious circumstances, Mary Godwin married Percy and became Mary Shelley.

Mary Shelley experienced great loss in her life. Not only did her own mother die just days after her birth, Shelley herself had a number of miscarriages and lost other children when they were young. In fact, only one of her children, Percy Florence, survived. Her husband Percy drowned in a boating accident in 1822.

While at the time, Percy Bysshe Shelley was a famous writer of his day and is still studied in English literature courses around the globe, the major work of his wife's creative life, *Frankenstein*, by far outlives his works in the popular imagination of today.

Frankenstein the novel

The story behind the novel *Frankenstein* is almost as interesting as the novel itself.

Mary Godwin was brought to Lake Geneva in 1816 by her lover, Shelley, to join a big party with a number of the British Romantic intellectuals of the day, including Lord Byron. It was a miserable cold and rainy summer, which was a freak of nature at the time, and everyone was getting bored. Lord Byron suggested a story competition—whoever could tell the scariest story would win the competition. Rumor has it that Mary had a nightmare that night, from which *Frankenstein* was born.

1. Students are required to purchase this book separately. See the course syllabus for additional information.

She was only 18 years old, the age of a traditional first-year college student, when she wrote the novel.

Mary Godwin Shelley was no scientist, so the novel is not a guidebook to the "hows" of creating life from scratch outside of a woman's body. However, the point of the novel isn't how we do it; it's whether we should try in the first place, and the "moral" of the story isn't exactly subtle or ambiguous. Additionally, there are more than a few *Frankenstein* scholars who analyze the novel from a psychological perspective linking Shelley's nightmarish experiences with miscarriage to the novel's and the creature's monstrous "birth."

Those of us in the modern age are often more familiar with the Frankenstein of the cinema, particularly the creature we call Frankenstein—the giant 9-foot monster with green skin and bolts in his neck. In the novel, the creature remains nameless, and while he is large in proportion and he is viewed as monstrous, particularly in his eyes and his size, his appearance isn't particularly well defined. His fictional creator, Victor Frankenstein, abandons him after creation and refuses to grant him his paternal name, or indeed any name. Our image of Victor Frankenstein, if we remember him at all, is of a scientist obsessed with ambition, who cannot see the consequences of his actions.

While Hollywood's film interpretations of Victor and his creature are extreme, the novel does critique the industrial age and question the proper role of science and technology in our lives. The novel also questions the role of individual ambition and accountability for our actions. Additionally the novel delved into the various ways we alienate those whom we perceive to be different from ourselves.

In the modern era, *Frankenstein* continues to be relevant to our thinking. As humanity has "cracked" the genetic code, created innovations that allow couples with infertility problems as well as same sex partners to have children, cloned a variety of animals in lab settings, and in at least one case even manipulated a fetus's genetic code so that to prevent the inheritance of the HIV virus, questions over the limits of science and technology are more important than ever. No one, really, wants to experience Victor Frankenstein's or his creature's fate.

The novel also poses a number of Romantic and Enlightenment ideas for us to consider, including our relationship with nature, philosophical beliefs about humanity's essential nature, and above all, what it really means to be human.

Frankenstein's Structure

The novel is set up as a series of embedded narratives with different storytellers. In part, this lends a feeling of authenticity to the events of the novel, which could well seem unrealistic to an audience without this series of "witnesses." It's all fiction, of course, but the idea is to make us think about events that might at the surface seem impossible until we witness them ourselves. Below is a chart that shows how this frame narrative works:

Robert Walton, the explorer, on his quest to be the first to reach the North Pole; writing letters to his sister Margaret Saville Prologue (letters I-IV)

> Victor Frankenstein in the northern regions telling his story to Robert Walton aboard the ice-locked ship

>> The creature telling Victor Frankenstein the story from his birth to the current moment when they meet on Mont Blanc

> Victor Frankenstein telling of the events following his meeting with the creature in the Alps

Robert Walton recounting Victor's story to his sister Margaret and its effect on his decisions regarding his expedition

---

Frankenstein Questions

What is Truth? The quest for truth in this novel is different for different characters. Robert Walton's quest to reach the North Pole and a Northwest Passage is a quest for geographical truth, as it was unmapped in the West. Victor Frankenstein's quest is to understand the origins of life and to be able, like a god, to recreate it on his own. The creature's quest is to understand his own origins and to seek some semblance of his own good life. Ultimate truths are somewhat hidden from us here, but we can make some determinations about how and why the characters seek truth in the ways they do, what they find, and then how that influences their future thinking and behavior.

What is Justice? There are at least three major ways of thinking about this question in relation to *Frankenstein*. The first is what does justice look like for the creature? To what degree is he responsible for his actions and to what degree is his "parent," Victor? Another is what does justice look like for Victor, who creates and then abandons his creation? Finally, we see the justice system in action, and it continually fails to fulfill justice because it lacks accurate information. So how, when we can never know the "full" and totally objective truth about an event, can justice ever be achieved?

What does it mean to be Human? Victor creates life out of body parts. The creature clearly doesn't look completely human, and yet most of him is constructed of human parts. In our quest for understanding humanity, this novel forces us to ask, where does humanity end and non-humanity begin? Is it physiological components, or is there something more, something that many of us might identify as a soul? Where does that come from? Can we reproduce it? And, much like Gilgamesh asked, what happens after death and how do we choose to handle our inevitable mortality?

What is the Good Life? For better or worse, Shelley, through her characters, answers this question for us, and not very subtly either. You may or may not agree with her answer, but the Romantics would have, and at least on the surface, it's hard to totally disagree with. As you read the novel, consider what Robert Walton, Victor, and the creature need to live a good life.

Frankenstein. Questions for Discussion

1. Only one chapter, early in the novel, is dedicated to Victor's process of creating his creature. Examine what Victor tells and what he doesn't tell about his motives, his process, and his perceptions of the result. What is he showing his audience, Robert Walton, about himself, whether consciously or not?

2. The creature's story in the middle of the narrative closely follows philosopher Jean-Jacques Rousseau's theories of both childhood development and civilization. Track these developments and consider then what Mary Shelley is trying to show about the creature, whether or not the creature's audience, Victor Frankenstein, understands it.

3. Victor Frankenstein commits several major crimes. Consider those crimes and whether and how justice is (or is not) served in the novel. Based on the evidence in the novel, which is more important in this case—the human justice system or an individual's own conscience?

4. Frankenstein's creature also commits several major crimes. Consider the creature's motives, actions, and crimes in context. Based on the evidence in the novel, where and how is the creature punished for his crimes? Do you think that justice is served in regards to the creature at the end of the novel? Why or why not?

5. The need for companionship, whether that's friendship or a romantic partnership, appears in a number of important ways: Victor and Robert Walton, Victor and Elizabeth, Victor and Henry Clerval, and the creature's quest for a friend and later companion. Why is this such an important focus and trend in this novel?

6. The quest for knowledge is discussed in many ways throughout the novel, from Victor's and Robert Walton's early passion for books to the creature's educational and literacy development to the desires to attain secret and specialized knowledge that others don't possess. What does the novel in the end have to say about the benefits and dangers of knowledge? Might we compare this to Prospero's sorcery in *The Tempest*, or is something different going on here?

7. Research some modern equivalents to Victor's scientific advance and ambition or Robert Walton's exploration and ambition. Consider animal cloning such as pet cloning, endangered or extinct species cloning, human cloning, genetic enhancement techniques using such tools as CRISPR, deep oceanic or space exploration, or other similar types of scientific exploration. For you, when are the ethical costs greater than the benefits of science?

Late Modernity

Late Modernity: Overview
(20th century CE-the Present)

The Twentieth Century

The lives of human beings changed more, and more rapidly, throughout the 1900s than during any other period of history. It was a century of two catastrophic world wars, totalitarianism, and genocide. Democracy began to take hold, not only in the West, but throughout the world. The world has become smaller through globalization, the economic, political and social interconnectedness and interdependency of everyone on the planet. By the end of the century it also became clear that human activity was impacting the very climate of Earth, and we were facing dangerous increases in average global temperatures that threaten the well-being of billions of people. It's difficult to find hope in this list of troubles. These were years of human devastation. They were also years of astounding progress. Never before in human history have such a large percentage of the global population enjoyed such high levels of well-being, and there is real hope that this progress will continue throughout the twenty-first century. The work still to be accomplished is staggering, but there is also genuine cause for hope.

The First World War

The First World War (1914–1918) began with the assassination of the Austrian Archduke Franz Ferdinand and his wife Sophie, Duchess of Hohenberg, by a Serbian nationalist who sought the reunification of his country with Bosnia-Herzegovina. Unlike any previous war, however, the resulting conflict between the Central Powers (led by Germany and Austria-Hungary) and the Allied Powers (led by Britain, France, and the United States) spread far beyond Europe. It was the first truly global war. When the war ended with the Allied victory over the Central Powers, more than twenty million people—soldiers and civilians—had been killed. The 1918 global influenza pandemic would add another fifty million lives to the already incomprehensible death toll.

The Rise of Totalitarianism

The decades following the First World War would see the return of militarism in Europe and the rise of totalitarian regimes. Totalitarianism is any form of government characterized by centralized authoritarian leadership, and the repression of all opposition to state power. Europe saw the rise of totalitarianism with the triumph of fascism, a form of populist political practices motivated by far-right nationalist ideology, in Germany, Italy and Spain. Russia succumbed to totalitarianism following the 1917 Communist revolution, and China would follow suit in 1949. These regimes rejected the Enlightenment political ideals of democracy, the rule of law, multi-party systems, limited government, respect for individual rights, and freedom of the press. Racism was also characteristic of government policy, and mass murder, terror and brutality were commonplace.

Communism

Communism is a social, political and economic ideology that strives for social equality by eliminating private ownership of the means of production (tools, facilities, raw materials, etc., that are used to produce goods). To achieve this goal of radical social equality, communist regimes have resorted to extreme brutality that resulted in great misery and the deaths of tens of millions.

The two major offenders were the Soviet Union under Joseph Stalin and the People's Republic of China under Mao Zedong. Both of these communist leaders were ruthless in their pursuit of absolute power and communist social and economic objectives. As premier of the Soviet Union from 1927 until his death in 1953, Stalin ruled the Soviet Union with absolute power. His policy of rapid industrialization and forced collectivization of farming resulted in the deaths, through execution or starvation, of tens of millions of peasants. He also brutally eliminated the least hint of opposition or dissent through several 'purges' in which innocent people suspected of disloyalty were found guilty in "show trials" after the elicitation of false confessions through torture. Many were executed, or sent to the so-called 'gulags' (concentration camps) where millions died from poor living conditions. Mao Zedong, who led the People's Republic of China from 1948 until his death in 1976, also pursued brutal policies of radical social and economic reform that resulted in tens of millions of deaths and misery on an incomprehensible scale.

The Second World War

The rise of fascist militarism, especially in Germany after the rise to power of Nazism and Adolf Hitler in 1933, was one of the leading political causes of the second major conflict of the century, the Second World War. The death toll for this conflict was staggering. More people died as a result of this war than any other in history, more than seventy million people in six years, from 1939–1945.

The war was fought between the Axis Powers (led by Nazi Germany and the Japanese Empire), and the Allies (led by Britain, the United States, France, and the Soviet Union). On June 6th, 1944, the Allies landed in German occupied France at Normandy, with the largest amphibious (water-to-land) invasion in history. This ultimately led to victory over the Axis Powers in Europe, with the unconditional surrender of Nazi Germany on May 8th, 1945. The United States used two atomic bombs against Japan, destroying the city of Hiroshima on August 6th, followed by a second attack that destroyed the city of Nagasaki on August 9th. This resulted in more than 130,000 deaths and the end of the war in the Pacific with the surrender of the Japanese Empire on September 9th.

The Holocaust

Genocide is the deliberate attempt to destroy an entire ethnic or national group. The term was coined in response to the mass murder and attempted destruction of the Jewish people of Europe by the Nazi regime during the Second World War. Nazism was fundamentally anti-Semitic, that is, anti-Jewish. During the course of the war, Jewish people were forced out of public life, stripped of citizenship, forced into slave labor, and had their property confiscated.

This was only preliminary persecution, however, that soon escalated to outright genocide, resulting in the death of two-thirds of the Jewish population in Europe, around six million people. Jewish men, women and children were forced into extermination camps and systematically murdered, many by means of poison gas. The mass murder of European Jews by the Nazis and their collaborators is referred to as the Holocaust, or the Shoah. The Nazis also targeted other groups, including the Roma people and homosexual men. People with mental or physical disabilities were also systematically euthanized.

After the German surrender, the Allied Powers brought many leading Nazis to trial for crimes against humanity, and executed many, including members of the Nazi high command who had survived the war.

The Cold War

After the Second World War the United States and the Soviet Union emerged as dominant world powers. They entered into a so-called "cold war" since there were no "hot" battles, but only an escalating tension with the constant threat of all-out nuclear war, since these two countries had both become armed with devastating nuclear weapons. They followed a national security policy of "mutually assured destruction," the idea that war could best be avoided if the destruction of both combatants was the assured outcome. This led to a nuclear arms race, with both nations and their allies competing for the largest and most destructive arsenal of nuclear weapons. The arms race came to an end with the collapse of the Soviet Union in 1991.

Climate Crisis

Beginning in the 1970s it became increasingly clear to scientists studying climate that there was an alarming increase in the average temperature of Earth. Further, this was clearly the result of the exponential increase in carbon emissions that begin with the industrial revolution. Global warming is primarily the effect of certain gases, especially carbon dioxide (CO_2), called "greenhouse gases," or GHGs. These GHGs allow sunlight to enter Earth's atmosphere but prevent heat from escaping, very much like a greenhouse. Today the best science is unequivocal: the temperature of Earth has been increasing due to human activity, and action on a global level is necessary to mitigate the negative effects.

Global warming is already a global crisis, which impacts the well-being of people all over the planet. If the current trend in global warming continues unabated, the impact on human well-being will be catastrophic. Severe flooding and extreme weather events, such as Hurricane Katrina, or Superstorm Sandy, will continue to be more severe, more common and less predictable. Sea level increases could threaten major centers of coastal populations, such as New York City, Shanghai, and Dhaka. Biodiversity will decrease, especially as the bleaching of coral reefs causes Earth's oceans to become more acidic due to the absorption of excess CO_2. This is only a partial list of foreseen consequences of climate change; there are sure to be as yet unforeseen consequences as well.

The Twenty-first Century: Entering the Anthropocene

The Holocene began about ten thousand years ago. It is the geological age beginning with the end of the last major ice age, and has been particularly mild for human beings, allowing our species to flourish. Geologists and other earth systems scientists now argue that we have entered a new geological era. The era is known as the Anthropocene, from the Greek term for human being, *anthrōpos*, since the dominant force driving Earth's environmental changes, including but not limited to climate, is humanity.

One of the four big questions is "What does it mean to be Human?" The advent of the Anthropocene makes this a very pressing question. At the beginning of the twenty-first century, human beings are increasingly forced to reevaluate their relationship and responsibility to Earth, and to their fellow human beings across the globe.

The easy answer to the question is that we are *homo sapiens*, the product of biological evolution through natural selection. But there are other answers in different registers. Sophocles, in the first choral ode of *Antigone* has the chorus of old men sing, "There are many strange and wonderful things / but nothing more strangely wonderful than man." The word here translated "strange and wonderful" is *deinos* in Greek. It poses a difficulty for translators. Its range of meaning can include strange, full of wonder, clever, or dreadful. Our species is unlike any other in Earth's history. We are strange, and we are also dreadful, as the political history of the twentieth century and environmental devastation of Earth clearly demonstrates. We are also clever and wonderful.

Looking back at the beginning of the third decade of the twenty-first century there is still more than ample reason to hope. In spite of death and destruction, humanity now has more to look forward to than at any other time in history. Human life and well-being is more secure for a greater percentage of the global population now than in any other period of human history. New developing technologies and changes in lifestyle promise to reduce human greenhouse gas emissions. A higher percentage of the global population enjoys liberty and individual rights than in any other period of history. The end of extreme poverty is a real possibility. So in spite of real and persistent problems—the devastation of war, global poverty, over-dependency on fossil fuels, and global warming—this is still the best time in history to be a human being.

We face a daunting task to ensure a livable planet and a high level of well-being for our children and their children. It is our duty to pass on the blessings of happiness that many take for granted in the developed world to as many future generations as possible. What the Anthropocene will mean for human beings is impossible to predict, but there are good reasons to hope that we will meet the challenges ahead.

Introduction to the Philosophy of Friedrich Nietzsche

Friedrich Nietzsche (1844–1900), a startling and controversial philosopher, was born into a religious family in Prussia. His father, a Lutheran pastor, died when Friedrich was five years old, and he was raised by his mother, elder sister, and an aunt. An outstanding student, Nietzsche received his PhD in Classical Philology, the study of ancient Greek and Latin literature, and was given a full professorship at the University of Basel in Switzerland at the age of 24, the youngest person ever to attain such a position. His career as a classical philologist, however, did not meet the expectations of his early supporters.

Although Friedrich Nietzsche died in August 1900, his philosophy would have its greatest impact in the twentieth century. His work had a profound impact on the intellectual life of the period, influencing major thinkers in psychology, philosophy, literature, and politics. Many of his ideas become part of the wider culture by the end of the twentieth century. His doctrine of the "death of God" might be seen in the increasing secularization of Western culture. His radical individualism, the charge that each person must accept the obligation to "become who you are" through projects of self-creation, is often reflected in popular culture. Some argue that his cynicism about human nature and morality, including his subjectivism about truth, was a precursor to our "post-truth" era. His work continues to help diagnose the ongoing challenges faced by the human race in the twenty-first century.

Nietzsche failed to make his mark as a scholar of Greek literature and philosophy, and his first book, *The Birth of Tragedy*, met with considerable criticism from leading scholars. The book's style and approach to Greek culture did not meet the expectations of the rather stuffy world of German classical philology of the 19th century. Plagued by ill health, especially debilitating migraine headaches all his life, Nietzsche actually taught very little during his nine years as a professor. He retired on a state pension in 1878 and spent the rest of his life writing the many works that would make him famous (and infamous). In 1889 Nietzsche had a severe mental collapse, possibly caused by advanced syphilis. Although he briefly regained consciousness, he later slipped into a comatose state, remaining unconscious until his death in August of the first year of the 20th century.

Nietzsche Questions

What is Truth? Objective truth is the idea that a true statement is objectively true because of the way the world is, independently of our subjective state of mind, or perspective. Nietzsche rejects objective truth. For Nietzsche, human beings can only ever have a perspective, and there's no ultimate way to determine whose perspective is true in an absolute sense. We might think of Nietzsche's approach here as putting scare quotes around the word; he only believes in "truth. "

His subjectivism is especially clear in his rejection of any objective sense of morality. Right and wrong for Nietzsche are radically subjective, and simply dependent on the culture one happens to live in; he's a cultural relativist.

What is Justice? Nietzsche also rejects justice in any substantive sense. Justice is merely convention, whatever our culture happens to call just. There is no objective truth of the matter as to what is just or unjust, right or wrong, good or bad. Thus, Nietzsche offers a genealogy of morality, a psychological-historical account of the genesis of our present systems of values. Nietzsche argues that our present moral value judgments (good and evil) develop out of the historical struggle of weakness and resentment, especially as this is expressed in religion. In his reading, the Judeo-Christian tradition was really a deeply suppressed resentment of the weak against the strong, what he calls "Slave Morality," and contrasts with "Master Morality. " His critique of the Judeo-Christian tradition extends to the morality of the Enlightenment, to ideas such as equality and social justice. For Nietzsche, Enlightenment moral principles are simply a secular version of the original religious ideas. He sees the emphasis on human dignity, for example, as rooted in the Christian idea that we are all children of God.

What does it mean to be Human? Nietzsche is decidedly critical of humanity. This is particularly clear in the very idiosyncratic novella, *Thus Spake Zarathustra*. For Nietzsche, humanity is something to be overcome, and he sets individual human beings the goal of overcoming what he takes to be human weakness, and to become Übermenschen, or supermen (literally overmen). The superman is not a person who is necessarily physically big and strong, like the cartoon character, but an individual who has overcome the essential meaninglessness of existence by becoming a creator of meaning, or value for her or his own life. This is in contrast to a person finding meaning for their life through a body of shared knowledge and traditions.

Nietzsche sees the weakness of human beings especially in their reliance on religion for meaning. He thought that religion, especially Christianity and Platonic philosophy, were really just sophisticated ways of avoiding the meaninglessness of existence by positing an "other world" of genuine meaning, truth, beauty and goodness. This is also understood to include a negative evaluation of the worth of this life, or "The Earth. " Unlike Christianity and Platonism, Nietzsche's superman is able to overcome nihilism by embracing an aesthetic or artistic approach to life. As Nietzsche puts it, the superman remains "true to the Earth" and gives "style" to her or his life. The life of the superman is difficult, and most people, Nietzsche thinks, will always choose comfort over the struggle to overcome their humanity.

What is the Good Life? The good life for Nietzsche is one that overcomes the meaninglessness of human existence by imposing individual subjective values on an otherwise meaningless existence. In short, it is to become a superman, or Übermensch. Life, for Nietzsche, should be a work of art, an individual's greatest work of art. This is not what Nietzsche considers to be the easy, blind self-deception of religion that denigrates life in contrast with an imaginary perfect "other world," nor is it what Nietzsche views as the comfortable blindness of the atheist who avoids the problem through distraction with pleasure in life.

From *The Birth of Tragedy*[1]

Comment: *In this selection from The Birth of Tragedy, or Hellenism and Pessimism, Nietzsche sets up the problem of nihilism, or the meaninglessness of human existence, and sketches the Greek (Hellenic) response, so different in his eyes from modern responses. He admired the Greeks for the way they could embrace tragedy, not only on stage, but in the whole of human life. In a sense all life is tragic, yet the Greeks were able to overcome this through art. In this way they transform the "wisdom of Silenus" and are able emphatically to say "Yes" to life in spite of what Nietzsche understands to have no underlying purpose or meaning.*

---

1. Selected excerpts from Friedrich Nietzsche, *The Birth of Tragedy, or Hellenism and Pessimism*, trans. William Haussmann (London: George Allen & Unwin, 1910). The selections from Nietzsche have been slightly modified. British spelling has been silently changed to standard American spelling, unnecessary em-dashes have been eliminated, and Nietzsche's parenthetical comments on the Greek have been moved to the footnotes.

Whosoever, with another religion in his heart, approaches these Olympians and seeks among them for moral elevation, even for sanctity, for incorporeal spiritualization, for sympathetic looks of love, will soon be obliged to turn his back on them, discouraged and disappointed. Here nothing suggests asceticism, spirituality, or duty: here only an exuberant, even triumphant life speaks to us, in which everything existing is deified, whether good or bad. And so the spectator will perhaps stand quite bewildered before this fantastic exuberance of life, and ask himself what magic potion these madly merry men could have used for enjoying life, so that, wherever they turned their eyes, Helena, the ideal image of their own existence "floating in sweet sensuality," smiled upon them. But to this spectator, already turning backwards, we must call out: "depart not hence, but hear rather what Greek folk-wisdom says of this same life, which with such inexplicable cheerfulness spreads out before thee." There is an ancient story that king Midas hunted in the forest a long time for the wise *Silenus,* the companion of Dionysus, without capturing him. When at last he fell into his hands, the king asked what was best of all and most desirable for man. Fixed and immovable, the demon remained silent; till at last, forced by the king, he broke out with shrill laughter into these words: "Oh, wretched race of a day, children of chance and misery, why do ye compel me to say to you what it were most expedient for you not to hear? What is best of all is for ever beyond your reach: not to be born, not to *be,* to be *nothing.* The second best for you, however, is soon to die."

How is the Olympian world of deities related to this folk-wisdom? Even as the rapturous vision of the tortured martyr to his sufferings.

Now the Olympian magic mountain opens, as it were, to our view and shows to us its roots. The Greek knew and felt the terrors and horrors of existence: to be able to live at all, he had to interpose the shining dream-birth of the Olympian world between himself and them. The excessive distrust of the titanic powers of nature, the Moira[2] throning inexorably over all knowledge, the vulture of the great philanthropist Prometheus, the terrible fate of the wise Oedipus, the family curse of the Atridae which drove Orestes to matricide... To be able to live, the Greeks had, from direst necessity, to create these gods: which process we may perhaps picture to ourselves in this manner: that out of the original Titan thearchy[3] of terror the Olympian thearchy of joy was evolved, by slow transitions, through the Apollonian impulse to beauty, even as roses break forth from thorny bushes. How else could this so sensitive people, so vehement in its desires, so singularly qualified for *sufferings* have endured existence, if it had not been exhibited to them in their gods,

2. This means fate

3. "Thearchy" means rule by the gods. In Greek mythology the Titans were gods older than the Olympian gods.

surrounded with a higher glory? The same impulse which calls art into being, as the complement and consummation of existence, seducing to a continuation of life, caused also the Olympian world to arise, in which the Hellenic[4] "will" held up before itself a transfiguring mirror. Thus do the gods justify the life of man, in that they themselves live it—the only satisfactory Theodicy![5] Existence under the bright sunshine of such gods is regarded as that which is desirable in itself, and the real *grief* of the Homeric men has reference to parting from it, especially to early parting: so that we might now say of them, with a reversion of the Silenian wisdom, that "to die early is worst of all for them, the second worst is—some day to die at all." If once the lamentation is heard, it will ring out again, of the short-lived Achilles, of the leaf-like change and vicissitude of the human race, of the decay of the heroic age. It is not unworthy of the greatest hero to long for a continuation of life, ay, even as a day-laborer. So vehemently does the "will," at the Apollonian stage of development, long for this existence, so completely at one does the Homeric man feel himself with it, that the very lamentation becomes its song of praise.

The Birth of Tragedy. Question for Discussion:

1. Based on this reading, how would you characterize Nietzsche's admiration for the Greeks? What is it about early Greek culture that he seemed to think was important?

From *The Joyful Wisdom*[6]

Comment: The first two passages here from The Joyful Wisdom include Nietzsche's famous (or infamous) declaration of the death of God, by which he means that the idea of Judeo-Christian God no longer anchors morality and meaning for Western culture as a whole, and has already become unworthy of belief, especially since the advance of the sciences, and the rejection of religious authority in morality during

4. Hellenic means Greek.

5. Theodicy means a justification, or explanation of the existence of evil and suffering in the world, in spite of the goodness of God or gods.

6. Selections excerpted from Friedrich Nietzsche, *The Joyful Wisdom*, trans. Thomas Common, Paul Cohn, and Maude Petre (London: T. N. Foulis, 1910).

the Enlightenment. It's important to see that, although Nietzsche is undoubtedly an atheist, that is not the point of these passages. He's commenting on the almost imperceptible decline in the efficacy of the idea of God as an anchor of value. Notice that he has his "madman" bring the news of God's death to a group of atheists, who ridicule him. Nietzsche thinks the death of God is a very significant "event" indeed.

108. *New Struggles.* After Buddha was dead people showed his shadow for centuries afterwards in a cave,—an immense frightful shadow. God is dead: but as the human race is constituted, there will perhaps be caves for millenniums yet, in which people will show his shadow—And we—we have still to overcome his shadow!

125. *The Madman.* Have you ever heard of the madman who on a bright morning lighted a lantern and ran to the market-place calling out unceasingly: "I seek God! I seek God!"—As there were many people standing about who did not believe in God, he caused a great deal of amusement. Why! is he lost? said one. Has he strayed away like a child? said another. Or does he keep himself hidden? Is he afraid of us? Has he taken a sea-voyage? Has he emigrated? —the people cried out laughingly, all in a hubbub. The insane man jumped into their midst and transfixed them with his glances. "Where is God gone?" he called out. "I mean to tell you! *We have killed him,*—you and I! We are all his murderers! But how have we done it? How were we able to drink up the sea? Who gave us the sponge to wipe away the whole horizon? What did we do when we loosened this earth from its sun? Whither does it now move? Whither do we move? Away from all suns? Do we not dash on unceasingly? Back-wards, sideways, forewards, in all directions? Is there still an above and below? Do we not stray, as through infinite nothingness? Does not empty space breathe upon us? Has it not become colder? Does not night come on continually, darker and darker? Shall we not have to light lanterns in the morning? Do we not hear the noise of the grave-diggers who are burying God? Do we not smell the divine putrefaction? —for even Gods putrefy! God is dead! God remains dead! And we have killed him! How shall we console ourselves, the most murderous of all murderers? The holiest and the mightiest that the world has hitherto possessed, has bled to death under our knife,—who will wipe the blood from us? With what water could we cleanse ourselves? What lustrums, what sacred games shall we have to devise? Is not the magnitude of this deed too great for us? Shall we not ourselves have to become Gods, merely to seem worthy of it? There never was a greater event,—and on account of it, all who are born after us belong to a higher history than any history hitherto!"—Here the madman was silent and looked again at his hearers; they also were silent and looked at him in surprise. At last he threw his lantern on the ground, so that it broke in pieces and was extinguished. "I come too early," he then said, "I am not yet at the right time. This prodigious event is still on its way, and is travelling,—it has not yet reached men's ears. Lightning and thunder need time, the light of the stars needs time, deeds need time, even after they are done, to be seen and heard. This deed is as yet further from them than the furthest star,—*and yet they have done it!*"—*It* is further stated that the madman made his way into different churches on the same day, and there intoned his *Requiem aeternam deo*[7]. When led out and called to account, he always gave the reply: "What are these churches now, if they are not the tombs and monuments of God? "

126. *Mystical Explanations.* Mystical explanations are regarded as profound; the truth is that they do not even go the length of being superficial.

> *Comment: In this passage Nietzsche elaborates on his ideal of living a radically individualistic life as though you were creating a work of art, his aesthetic analogy of a good life.*

290. *One Thing is Needful.* To "give style" to one's character—that is a grand and a rare art! He who surveys all that his nature presents in its strength and in its weakness, and then fashions it into an ingenious plan, until everything appears artistic and rational, and even the weaknesses enchant the eye—exercises that admirable art. Here there has been a great amount of second nature added, there a portion of first nature has been taken away: in both cases with long exercise and daily labor at the task. Here the ugly, which does not permit of being taken away, has been concealed, there it has been re-interpreted into the sublime. Much of the vague, which refuses to take form, has been reserved and utilized for the perspectives: it is meant to give a hint of the remote and immeasurable. In the end, when the work has been completed, it is revealed how it was the constraint of the same taste that organized and fashioned it in whole and in part: whether the taste was good or bad is of less importance than one thinks,—it is sufficient that it was *a taste!*—It will be the strong imperious natures which experience their most refined joy in such constraint, in such confinement and perfection under their own law; the passion of their violent volition lessens at the sight of all disciplined nature, all conquered and ministering nature: even when they have palaces to build and gardens to lay out, it is

7. May God rest in peace.

not to their taste to allow nature to be free. —It is the reverse with weak characters who have not power over themselves, and *hate* the restriction of style: they feel that if this repugnant constraint were laid upon them, they would necessarily become *vulgarized* under it: they become slaves as soon as they serve, they hate service. Such intellects—they may be intellects of the first rank—are always concerned with fashioning and interpreting themselves and their surroundings as *free* nature—wild, arbitrary, fantastic, confused and surprising: and it is well for them to do so, because only in this manner can they please themselves! For one thing is needful: namely, that man should *attain to* satisfaction with himself—be it but through this or that fable and artifice: it is only then that man's aspect is at all endurable! He who is dissatisfied with himself is ever ready to avenge himself on that account: we others will be his victims, if only in having always to endure his ugly aspect. For the aspect of the ugly makes one mean and sad.

The Joyful Wisdom. Question for Discussion:

1. What do you think of Nietzsche's charge to live your life with "style"? Is this the meaning of life, or do you think there needs to be something more? Why or why not? If you think there must be more to life, what might that consist of?

Comment: *This passage illustrates Nietzsche's subjectivism about truth. All meaning and value, for Nietzsche, must be created by individuals themselves. All meaning, value, and truth is dependent on individual subjective projection.*

301. *Illusion of the Contemplative.* Higher men are distinguished from lower, by seeing and hearing immensely more, and in a thoughtful manner—and it is precisely this that distinguishes man from the animal, and the higher animal from the lower. . .

It is we, who think and feel, that actually and unceasingly *make* something which did not before exist: the whole eternally increasing world of valuations, colors, weights, perspectives, gradations, affirmations and negations. This composition of ours is continually learnt, practiced, and translated into flesh and actuality, and even into the commonplace, by the so-called practical men (our actors, as we have said). Whatever has *value* in the present world, has not it in itself, by its nature,—nature is always worthless:—but a value was once given to it, bestowed upon it and it was *we* who gave and bestowed! We only have created the world *which is of any account to man!*—But it is precisely this knowledge that we lack, and when we get hold of it for a moment we have forgotten it the next: we misunderstand our highest power, we contemplative men, and estimate ourselves at too low a rate,—we are neither as *proud nor as happy* as we might be.

Comment: In this strange passage Nietzsche poses a "thought experiment," a radical conjecture, and a colorful one, too. The supposition that our life would be lived over and over innumerable times, and exactly the same way down to every conceivable detail, is usually referred to as Nietzsche's doctrine of "The Eternal Return of the Same." Note that it's not at all like doctrines of reincarnation in Eastern philosophy, or the transmigration of souls in classical Greece. As a thought experiment, it controls for the possibility that there's nothing of value outside your life, and challenges the reader to say "Yes," to life. Saying "Yes" means that your life would be lived in such a way that one could will the eternal return, could radically affirm each and every individual action, every decision that that makes up a human life. There's no room for regret for one who says "Yes" to the demonic prophet of the Eternal Return.

Illusion of the Contemplative. Question for Discussion

1. Is all meaning and value purely subjective? Can you just choose in all cases what is meaningful, worthwhile, or valuable? What about love? Can you just choose to love?

---

341. *The Heaviest Burden.* What if a demon crept after thee into thy loneliest loneliness some day or night, and said to thee: "This life, as thou livest it at present, and hast lived it, thou must live it once more, and also innumerable times; and there will be nothing new in it, but every pain and every joy and every thought and every sigh, and all the unspeakably small and great in thy life must come to thee again, and all in the same series and sequence—and similarly this spider and this moonlight among the trees, and similarly this moment, and I myself. The eternal sand-glass of existence will ever be turned once more, and thou with it, thou speck of dust!"—Wouldst thou not throw thyself down and gnash thy teeth, and curse the demon that so spake? Or hast thou once experienced a tremendous moment in which thou wouldst answer him: "Thou art a God, and never did I hear anything so divine!" If that thought acquired power over thee as thou art, it would transform thee, and perhaps crush thee; the question with regard to all and everything: "Dost thou want this once more, and also for innumerable times?" would lie as the heaviest burden upon thy activity! Or, how wouldst thou have to become favorably inclined to thyself and to life, so as *to long for nothing more ardently* than for this last eternal sanctioning and sealing?

The Heaviest Burden. Questions for Discussion

1. What would you say to this challenging set of questions? Would you say yes to your life, would you desire to live it over exactly as it has been and will be lived?

2. This thought experiment posits an afterlife, so to speak, exactly like your current life. It effectively takes heaven or any reward beyond life out of consideration. Without some more robust afterlife, what makes your life matter, what gives it meaning? Can life be meaningful without heaven, or an 'otherworld'? And what about the suffering of so many? What is the meaning of suffering without heaven or nirvana, or something like that?

Comment: *In this passage Nietzsche sets out the importance of the death of God and also explains its potential dire consequences. He also explains how the "philosophers and free spirits" can still rejoice in the coming moral apocalypse in the West. In spite of the struggle to come, Nietzsche finds the destruction of the old anchor of value and meaning exhilarating, since the opportunity to begin again, to start over from scratch, is now a genuine possibility.*

343. *What our Cheerfulness Signifies.* The most important of more recent events—that "God is dead," that the belief in the Christian God has become unworthy of belief—already begins to cast its first shadows over Europe. To the few at least whose eye, whose *suspecting* glance, is strong enough and subtle enough for this drama, some sun seems to have set, some old, profound confidence seems to have changed into doubt: our old world must seem to them daily more darksome, distrustful, strange and "old." In the main, however, one may say that the event itself is far too great, too remote, too much beyond most people's power of apprehension, for one to suppose that so much as the report of it could have *reached* them; not to speak of many who already knew *what* had taken place, and what must all collapse now that this belief had been undermined,—because so much was built upon it, so much rested on it, and had become one with it: for example, our entire European morality. This lengthy, vast and uninterrupted process of crumbling, destruction, ruin and overthrow which is now imminent: who has realized it sufficiently to-day to have to stand up as the teacher and herald of such a tremendous logic of terror, as the prophet of a period of gloom and eclipse, the like of which has probably never taken place on earth before? ... Even we, the born riddle-readers, who wait as it were on the mountains posted 'twixt to-day and to-morrow, and engirt by their contradiction, we, the firstlings and premature children of the coming century, into whose sight especially the shadows which must forthwith envelop Europe *should* already have come—how is it that even we, without genuine sympathy for this period of gloom, contemplate its advent without any *personal* solicitude or fear? Are we still, perhaps, too much under the *immediate effects* of the event—and are these effects, especially as regards *ourselves,* perhaps the reverse of what was to be expected—not at all sad and depressing, but rather like a new and indescribable variety of light, happiness, relief, enlivenment, encouragement, and dawning day? ... In fact, we philosophers and "free spirits" feel ourselves irradiated as by a new dawn by the report that the "old God is dead"; our hearts overflow with gratitude, astonishment, presentiment and expectation. At last the horizon seems open once more, granting even that it is not bright; our ships can at last put out to sea in face of every danger; every hazard is again permitted to the discerner; the sea, *our* sea, again lies open before us; perhaps never before did such an "open sea" exist.

What our Cheerfulness Signifies. Questions for Discussion

1. What do you think of the claim that God is dead, and that we (our culture in the West since the Enlightenment) have "killed" him? What evidence for this do you find in our culture today?

2. Nietzsche is writing this in the late 19th century. To what extent has his prognosis, or prediction, for Western culture come true? What evidence for your answer can you list?

From *The Genealogy of Morals*[8]

Comment: *In this passage and the following one from The Genealogy of Morals, Nietzsche explains his account of the origin of the Western way of thinking of morality in terms of the valuation set, "good and evil." He contrasts this with an older valuation set, "good and bad." His account is both psychological and historical. That is, his explanation of the origin of the Christian and Enlightenment vision of morality is rooted in the psychology of a certain kind of person that predominates over the course of Western history. All too briefly, the psychological mechanisms are two: the will-to-power and resentment. Because one type of person, "the slave," desires power and harbors resentment for the strong (the "Masters"), a system of morality arises that is in the interest of the weak. The older morality, Master Morality, is focused on character, and the basic valuations are good and bad, applied to individual character. The new morality, however, focuses on evaluating actions in terms of good and evil, depending on whether they are in the interest of the weak. Needless to say, these are ideal types, and no individual or culture perfectly exemplifies them. Nevertheless, Christianity and Judaism is the primary historical example of what Nietzsche calls "Slave Morality" and the Vikings or Homeric Greeks (not the Classical Greeks, they're too Platonic) are pretty close to what he has in mind for examples of "Master Morality."*

Needless to say, this is a harsh, some might say outrageous, account of the psychological motives behind Christianity. In his reading, the Gospel of love is really the expression of a sublimated hatred.

10. The revolt of the slaves in morals begins in the very principle of *resentment* becoming creative and giving birth to values—a resentment experienced by creatures who, deprived as they are of the proper outlet of action, are forced to find their compensation in an imaginary revenge. While every aristocratic morality springs from a triumphant affirmation of its own demands, the slave morality says "no" from the very outset to what is "outside itself," "different from itself," and "not itself": and this "no" is its creative deed. This volte-face of the valuing standpoint—this *inevitable* gravitation to the objective instead of back to the subjective—is typical of "resentment": the slave-morality requires as the condition of its existence an external and objective world, to employ physiological terminology, it requires objective stimuli

8. Selected from Friedrich Nietzsche, *The Genealogy of Morals: a Polemic*, trans. Horace Samuel (London: T. N. Foulis, 1913).

to be capable of action at all—its action is fundamentally a reaction. The contrary is the case when we come to the aristocrat's system of values: it acts and grows spontaneously, it merely seeks its antithesis in order to pronounce a more grateful and exultant "yes" to its own self;—its negative conception, "low," "vulgar," "bad," is merely a pale late-born foil in comparison with its positive and fundamental conception (saturated as it is with life and passion), of "we aristocrats, we good ones, we beautiful ones, we happy ones."

When the aristocratic morality goes astray and commits sacrilege on reality, this is limited to that particular sphere with which it is *not* sufficiently acquainted—a sphere, in fact, from the real knowledge of which it disdainfully defends itself. It misjudges, in some cases, the sphere which it despises, the sphere of the common vulgar man and the low people: on the other hand, due weight should be given to the consideration that in any case the mood of contempt, of disdain, of supercil-iousness, even on the supposition that it *falsely* portrays the object of its contempt, will always be far removed from that degree of falsity which will always characterize the attacks—in effigy, of course—of the vindictive hatred and revengefulness of the weak in onslaughts on their enemies. In point of fact, there is in contempt too strong an admixture of nonchalance, of casualness, of boredom, of impatience, even of per-sonal exultation, for it to be capable of distorting its victim into a real caricature or a real monstrosity. Attention again should be paid to the almost benevolent *nuances* which, for instance, the Greek nobility imports into all the words by which it distin-guishes the common people from itself; note how continuously a kind of pity, care, and consideration imparts its honeyed *flavor*, until at last almost all the words which are applied to the vulgar man survive finally as expressions for "unhappy," "worthy of pity."[9] The latter two names really denoting the vulgar man as labor-slave and beast of burden)—and how, conversely, "bad," "low," "unhappy" have never ceased to ring in the Greek ear with a tone in which "unhappy" is the predominant note: this is a heritage of the old noble aristocratic morality, which remains true to itself even in contempt.[10]

9. Nietzsche's parenthetical comment here: "Compare δειλο, δείλαιος, πονηρός, μοχθηρός."

10. Nietzsche's parenthetical comment here: "Let philologists remember the sense in which ὀιζυρός, ἄνολβος, τλήμων, δυστυχεῖν, ξυμφορά used to be employed."

The Genealogy of Morals. Question for Discussion

1. Nietzsche offers a critique here of the origin of the Judeo-Christian worldview, which includes the Enlightenment ideals of equality, justice, and human dignity, etc. . He argues that the origin of these ideas is the resentment of the weak and their will to power. Is this a plausible story?

2. Nietzsche is clearly calling for a new set of values and denigrating the older values in the West rooted in Christianity and the Enlightenment. What do you think of his critique? What do you think might replace the older values, and is this desirable? Why or why not?

From *Beyond Good and Evil*[11]

260. In a tour through the many finer and coarser moralities which have hitherto prevailed or still prevail on the earth, I found certain traits recurring regularly together, and connected with one another, until finally two primary types revealed themselves to me, and a radical distinction was brought to light. There is MASTER-MORALITY and SLAVE-MORALITY,—I would at once add, however, that in all higher and mixed civilizations, there are also attempts at the reconciliation of the two moralities, but one finds still oftener the confusion and mutual misunderstanding of them, indeed sometimes their close juxtaposition—even in the same man, within one soul. The distinctions of moral values have either originated in a ruling caste, pleasantly conscious of being different from the ruled—or among the ruled class, the slaves and dependents of all sorts. In the first case, when it is the rulers who determine the conception "good," it is the exalted, proud disposition which is regarded as the distinguishing feature, and that which determines the order of rank. The noble type of man separates from himself the beings in whom the opposite of this exalted, proud disposition displays itself he despises them. Let it at once be noted that in this first kind of morality the antithesis "good" and "bad" means practically the same as "noble" and "despicable",—the antithesis "good" and "EVIL" is of a different origin. The cowardly, the timid, the insignificant, and those thinking merely of narrow utility are despised; moreover, also, the distrustful, with

11. Excerpted from: Friedrich Nietzsche, *Beyond Good and Evil*, trans. Helen Zimmern (New York: Macmillan Company, 1907).

their constrained glances, the self-abasing, the dog-like kind of men who let them-selves be abused, the mendicant flatterers, and above all the liars: it is a fundamental belief of all aristocrats that the common people are untruthful. "We truthful ones"—the nobility in ancient Greece called themselves. It is obvious that everywhere the designations of moral value were at first applied to MEN; and were only derivatively and at a later period applied to ACTIONS; it is a gross mistake, therefore, when historians of morals start with questions like, "Why have sympathetic actions been praised? " The noble type of man regards HIMSELF as a determiner of values; he does not require to be approved of; he passes the judgment: "What is injurious to me is injurious in itself;" he knows that it is he himself only who confers honor on things; he is a CREATOR OF VALUES. He honors whatever he recognizes in himself: such morality equals self-glorification. In the foreground there is the feeling of plenitude, of power, which seeks to overflow, the happiness of high ten-sion, the consciousness of a wealth which would fain give and bestow:—the noble man also helps the unfortunate, but not—or scarcely—out of pity, but rather from an impulse generated by the super-abundance of power. The noble man honors in himself the powerful one, him also who has power over himself, who knows how to speak and how to keep silence, who takes pleasure in subjecting himself to severity and hardness, and has reverence for all that is severe and hard. "Wotan placed a hard heart in my breast," says an old Scandinavian Saga: it is thus rightly expressed from the soul of a proud Viking.

Such a type of man is even proud of not being made for sympathy; the hero of the Saga therefore adds warningly: "He who has not a hard heart when young, will never have one." The noble and brave who think thus are the furthest removed from the morality which sees precisely in sympathy, or in acting for the good of others, or in DESINTERESSEMENT[12], the characteristic of the moral; faith in oneself, pride in oneself, a radical enmity and irony towards "selflessness," belong as definitely to noble morality, as do a careless scorn and precaution in presence of sympathy and the "warm heart. "—It is the powerful who KNOW how to honor, it is their art, their domain for invention. The profound reverence for age and for tradition—all law rests on this double reverence,—the belief and prejudice in favor of ancestors and unfavorable to newcomers, is typical in the morality of the power-ful; and if, reversely, men of "modern ideas" believe almost instinctively in "progress" and the "future," and are more and more lacking in respect for old age, the ignoble origin of these "ideas" has complacently betrayed itself thereby. A morality of the ruling class, however, is more especially foreign and irritating to present-day taste

12. This French term means "selflessness."

in the sternness of its principle that one has duties only to one's equals; that one may act towards beings of a lower rank, towards all that is foreign, just as seems good to one, or "as the heart desires," and in any case "beyond good and evil": it is here that sympathy and similar sentiments can have a place. The ability and obligation to exercise prolonged gratitude and prolonged revenge—both only within the circle of equals,—artfulness in retaliation, RAFFINEMENT[13] of the idea in friendship, a certain necessity to have enemies (as outlets for the emotions of envy, quarrelsomeness, arrogance—in fact, in order to be a good FRIEND): all these are typical characteristics of the noble morality, which, as has been pointed out, is not the morality of "modern ideas," and is therefore at present difficult to realize, and also to unearth and disclose.

It is otherwise with the second type of morality, SLAVE-MORALITY. Supposing that the abused, the oppressed, the suffering, the unemancipated, the weary, and those uncertain of themselves should moralize, what will be the common element in their moral estimates? Probably a pessimistic suspicion with regard to the entire situation of man will find expression, perhaps a condemnation of man, together with his situation. The slave has an unfavorable eye for the virtues of the powerful; he has a skepticism and distrust, a REFINEMENT of distrust of everything "good" that is there honored—he would fain persuade himself that the very happiness there is not genuine. On the other hand, THOSE qualities which serve to alleviate the existence of sufferers are brought into prominence and flooded with light; it is here that sympathy, the kind, helping hand, the warm heart, patience, diligence, humility, and friendliness attain to honor; for here these are the most useful qualities, and almost the only means of supporting the burden of existence. Slave-morality is essentially the morality of utility. Here is the seat of the origin of the famous antithesis "good" and "evil": power and dangerousness are assumed to reside in the evil, a certain dreadfulness, subtlety, and strength, which do not admit of being despised. According to slave-morality, therefore, the "evil" man arouses fear; according to master-morality, it is precisely the "good" man who arouses fear and seeks to arouse it, while the bad man is regarded as the despicable being. The contrast attains its maximum when, in accordance with the logical consequences of slave-morality, a shade of depreciation—it may be slight and well-intentioned—at last attaches itself to the "good" man of this morality; because, according to the servile mode of thought, the good man must in any case be the SAFE man: he is good-natured, easily deceived, perhaps a little stupid, un *bonhomme*[14]. Everywhere

13. This French term means "refinement."

14. This French term means "good natured," or "easy-going person."

that slave-morality gains the ascendancy, language shows a tendency to approximate the significations of the words "good" and "stupid."—A last fundamental difference: the desire for FREEDOM, the instinct for happiness and the refinements of the feeling of liberty belong as necessarily to slave-morals and morality, as artifice and enthusiasm in reverence and devotion are the regular symptoms of an aristocratic mode of thinking and estimating. —Hence we can understand without further detail why love AS A PASSION—it is our European specialty—must absolutely be of noble origin; as is well known, its invention is due to the Provencal poet-cavaliers, those brilliant, ingenious men of the "gai saber," to whom Europe owes so much, and almost owes itself.

Beyond Good and Evil. Questions for Discussion

1. One of the more radical things about Nietzsche's work is that he offers a naturalistic, even psychological, origin for morality. This means that morality is relative to culture and history. What do you think about this idea? Can right and wrong change from one society to the next, or from one period to the next? Can we legitimately criticize other societies, or our own past culture, for practices that we now think are wrong? On what basis?

2. What is the difference between the values of the "masters" and the values of the "slaves"? Do we see this division in our own culture? Are there people in our culture better described as one or the other category? Note that Nietzsche doesn't think anyone perfectly fits any type here, but rather they're ideal categories. Which way do you think our culture is going today?

From *Thus Spake Zarathustra*[15]

Comment: *This is from the very strange novella that Nietzsche often remarked was the fullest expression of his philosophy. In this translation Thomas Common has used language reminiscent of the King James, or Authorized version of the Christian Bible. This is somewhat in keeping with Nietzsche's German, since he intentionally makes allusion in his style to Luther's German translation, which was similar to the King James Bible in its cultural impact (at one time). And of course, Nietzsche is writing a secular, even atheistic scripture. In this passage the title character, Zarathustra, is preaching about the coming of the "superman."*

When Zarathustra arrived at the nearest town which adjoineth the forest, he found many people assembled in the market-place; for it had been announced that a rope-dancer would give a performance. And Zarathustra spake thus unto the people:

I TEACH YOU THE SUPERMAN. [16] Man is something that is to be surpassed. What have ye done to surpass man?

All beings hitherto have created something beyond themselves: and ye want to be the ebb of that great tide, and would rather go back to the beast than surpass man?

What is the ape to man? A laughing-stock, a thing of shame. And just the same shall man be to the Superman: a laughing-stock, a thing of shame.

Ye have made your way from the worm to man, and much within you is still worm. Once were ye apes, and even yet man is more of an ape than any of the apes.

Even the wisest among you is only a disharmony and hybrid of plant and phantom. But do I bid you become phantoms or plants?

Lo, I teach you the Superman!

The Superman is the meaning of the earth. Let your will say: The Superman SHALL BE the meaning of the earth!

I conjure you, my brethren, REMAIN TRUE TO THE EARTH, and believe not those who speak unto you of superearthly hopes! Poisoners are they, whether they know it or not.

Despisers of life are they, decaying ones and poisoned ones themselves, of whom the earth is weary: so away with them!

15. Excerpt from Friedrich Nietzsche, *Thus Spake Zarathustra: a Book for All and None*, trans. Thomas Common (New York: The Macmillan Company, 1914).

16. The German term here translated as "superman" is Übermensch, which has the connotation of strength which our "superman" evokes, but also the sense of "overcoming" and "beyond," which "superman" doesn't really capture.

Once blasphemy against God was the greatest blasphemy; but God died, and therewith also those blasphemers. To blaspheme the earth is now the dreadfulest sin, and to rate the heart of the unknowable higher than the meaning of the earth!

Once the soul looked contemptuously on the body, and then that contempt was the supreme thing:—the soul wished the body meagre, ghastly, and famished. Thus it thought to escape from the body and the earth.

Oh, that soul was itself meagre, ghastly, and famished; and cruelty was the delight of that soul!

But ye, also, my brethren, tell me: What doth your body say about your soul? Is your soul not poverty and pollution and wretched self-complacency?

Verily, a polluted stream is man. One must be a sea, to receive a polluted stream without becoming impure.

Lo, I teach you the Superman: he is that sea; in him can your great contempt be submerged.

What is the greatest thing ye can experience? It is the hour of great contempt. The hour in which even your happiness becometh loathsome unto you, and so also your reason and virtue.

The hour when ye say: "What good is my happiness! It is poverty and pollution and wretched self-complacency. But my happiness should justify existence itself!"

The hour when ye say: "What good is my reason! Doth it long for knowledge as the lion for his food? It is poverty and pollution and wretched self-complacency!"

The hour when ye say: "What good is my virtue! As yet it hath not made me passionate. How weary I am of my good and my bad! It is all poverty and pollution and wretched self-complacency!"

The hour when ye say: "What good is my justice! I do not see that I am fervor and fuel. The just, however, are fervour and fuel!"

The hour when ye say: "What good is my pity! Is not pity the cross on which he is nailed who loveth man? But my pity is not a crucifixion."

Have ye ever spoken thus? Have ye ever cried thus? Ah! would that I had heard you crying thus!

It is not your sin—it is your self-satisfaction that crieth unto heaven; your very sparingness in sin crieth unto heaven!

Where is the lightning to lick you with its tongue? Where is the frenzy with which ye should be inoculated?

Lo, I teach you the Superman: he is that lightning, he is that frenzy!

Thus Spake Zarathustra. Questions for Discussion

1. Do you think the Superman would be an advance or a regression for civilization, based on the description here? Why or why not?

2. Do you think the Superman, as here described, is possible? Would you want to become such a person? Why or why not?

3. Do such persons as this Superman exist today? Can you think of examples of human beings who are close, or on the road? What about you?

4. How do you think the daily life of such a person as this Superman would be different from others?

5. Is this really a good answer to the problem of nihilism, the meaninglessness of lives in the modern world without (real) belief in God? Explain your answer.

Introduction to Aldous Huxley and
Brave New World (1932)[1]

Aldous Huxley (1894–1963)

Aldous Huxley was a British writer who wrote over 47 books in his lifetime, but he is most known for the novel *Brave New World*. Like his ancestors, he was extremely interested in science from a young age, but due to a serious eye ailment that left him partially blind, he moved away from science into literary writing, an occupation that ran in his mother's family line. He spent much of his later life in the United States, including California and the desert Southwest, particularly Northern New Mexico, which plays a pivotal role in *Brave New World*.

Huxley was an intellectual, novelist, and essayist who thought seriously about social, economic, technological, scientific, governmental, and religious/mystical systems and problems. As a way of exploring the unknown, he also experimented with hallucinogenic drugs in his later life, which he describes in the also famous*Doors of Perception* that has had a cult following since its publication in 1953.

Brave New World

Brave New World is a post-apocalyptic, dystopian novel. You've probably read or watched some post-apocalyptic works: the *Mad Max* movies, *The Hunger Games*, or *The Walking Dead* series. Dystopian stories are always intended to show us more about ourselves and our own society by stretching out our desires, motives, and actions to extreme levels, and they do so with the goal of warning us against our worst selves and maybe even our best motives.

In the novel, which is set far into the future, a historical event of mass destruction resulted in a complete restructuring of the entire global social and economic system into "The World State. "This remaking allowed a kind of re-boot, so that the resulting governmental and social systems are consciously and systematically constructed to create what the founders believe to be an ideal world, or a utopia, out

1. Students must purchase this text separately. See course syllabus for additional information.

of the ashes of civilization's literal self-destruction. While most of the people in the World State believe that their world is a utopia, our main characters are outsiders who question the basic premises of the World State, allowing us to see both the ways that the general population views the society and the ways that critics of the social structure help us see its underlying problems.

Brave New World takes place far into the future in two main settings: the World State in New London, representing "civilization," and the "Savage Reservation" in what was once (as it is now) northern New Mexico, around Taos/Santa Fe. The first half of the novel portrays the World State's society as it wants to be seen, as an improvement over the "old days" that we as readers recognize as our current society. The second half of the novel reveals the uglier underbelly of the society that shows what important values are sacrificed and why. In the end, the novel requires us to consider our own values and way of life, and perhaps shocks us into reevaluating and possibly altering the directions that our society is pursuing.

Huxley was, particularly in this novel, quite a visionary. He described aspects of his World State that are far more true of 21st century America and England than they were at the time that he wrote and published the novel in the 1930s, including contraception and reproductive technologies, automation of virtually all aspects of our lives, technologies that are designed to allow us to live lives of leisure, the use of drugs and anti-depressants as forms of social control, and even large scale commercialization and the rise of controlled obsolescence—technologies that are built to fail within a certain time so we'll constantly buy more, newer, "better" goods.

The World State is a disturbing world, and Huxley intends for us to be shocked and even revolted by its moral standards. By the middle of the book, the dark secrets of this utopia have become clear to some characters and most definitely to modern readers.

The assumptions that the novel poses about class, social conditioning, accepting one's pre-destined, pre-defined role in society, and even conformity to social expectations, need examining in light of not only how we want to live our individual lives but also what would make the world better, if not "perfect." As a novel of its place and time, *Brave New World* also includes several stereotypical and racist references to people of color. Additionally, women are limited to lower castes and thus non-leadership positions. In this way, the novel reveals the author's limitations in conceptualizing difference even as he tried to advocate for individualism and critical thought. In the 21st century, we can read with a more critical eye towards 21st century conceptions of ethnicity and difference as we consider what our new and better world might look like in the near future.

The title, *Brave New World*, is an allusion to William Shakespeare's *The Tempest*, and elements of the play, including several key characters, run throughout the novel. Although you don't have to know Shakespeare's work to appreciate the novel, it absolutely makes the reading experience richer when you do.

John the Savage, like Caliban, is treated as an "Other" because he is different both from the indigenous people he's grown up with on the Savage Reservation and from the World State citizens whom he meets. Ironically, John is also the Miranda character who speaks Miranda's lines at several key points in the novel.

While there are some allusions to magic in *Brave New World*, it is quite clear from the outset that modern technology is the "magic" that empowers a select group of people and disempowers the rest of the people across the planet. And yet ultimately it is superior knowledge rather than technological expertise that dominates the power structure of the novel. In that respect, Mustapha Mond, one of the twelve World Controllers, is our "sorcerer," and it is his access to the world's great books that in part grants him such powerful knowledge that only World Controllers possess—or even know exists.

Unlike Shakespeare, though, Huxley did not intend to create a fantasy; rather, he was trying to represent a vision of what might happen to our "real world" if we don't heed his warnings, and indeed, there are warnings here that we must consider in the 21st century.

Brave New World Questions

What is Truth? You'll find that the citizens of the World State are actively prevented from thinking about our four big questions. They are raised ("conditioned" is the word used in the novel) not to think critically at all, much less think critically about big abstract questions. In that sense, we are back to Plato's "Allegory of the Cave. "Is ignorance bliss, or will the truth set us free? The novel constantly asks us to think about this, and the answer isn't particularly comfortable—leading us to more questions if we're willing to keep thinking about it instead of finding a convenient and oversimplified answer.

What is Justice? There is virtually no crime and no need for a complex judicial system in the World State. Does that mean that they have a just society? When everyone (or almost everyone) knows their place and feels that their place is exactly where they want to be, then the question of justice doesn't come up in the minds of the people. It is assumed to exist. Why is this a problem? Why do we have to continue asking this question? What, in the end, does justice look like for those who break the rules?

What does it mean to be Human? Humanity has been fundamentally and permanently altered in *Brave New World* from conception to birth, to childhood, to adulthood, and even to death. Do we consider the citizens of the World State to be fully human? Or is there something fundamentally missing? When we think of the ways that we are altering humanity and/or that we are considering altering humanity, does the result make us less human? What is Huxley trying to show us is most valuable about our humanity? How do we keep our worst selves from destroying that humanity?

As satire, *Brave New World* presents a world of people who believe that they are living the good life when we as readers are supposed to see that they are not living what the author believes to be the good life. One of the mantras of the World State is that "Everybody's happy now. "[2] And they are happy precisely because they have been trained to believe that they are happy. Does that make them happy? Does that lead to the good life? And if so, what sacrifices must be made for that to always be so? Is that what we are supposed to want for ourselves? Why or why not?

Brave *New World.* Questions for Discussion

1. Consider how the World State defines utopia. What do they value? What are they willing to sacrifice to achieve their utopia? Consider the following:

A. Governmental Structure or alternative: What are the guiding principles or rules of the community? How will decisions get made about and for the community? Why?

B. Judicial system:How does the society deal with people who break the rules? Who enforces the rules? What is the system of crime and punishment that this community agrees to abide by?

C. Economic Structure:How are goods and services exchanged within and between communities, and why? What kind of economic system is in place and what is the justification for that system?

D. Social/Cultural/Religious Structures: How do people interact with one another and form a sense of community? What are the guiding principles

2. Aldous Huxley, *Brave New World* (NY: Perennial Classics, 1946), 75.

of those communities, from family units to small groups to national/international groups?

2. Consider how you would define utopia. What do you value? What would you be willing to sacrifice to achieve your utopia?

A. Governmental Structure or alternative: What are the guiding principles or rules of the community? How will decisions get made about and for the community? Why?

B. Judicial system:How do you deal with people who break the rules? Who enforces the rules? What is the system of crime and punishment that your community agrees to abide by?

C. Economic Structure:How does the system of exchange for goods and services work within and between communities, and why? What kind of economic system functions best and what is the justification for it?

D. Social/Cultural/Religious Structures: How do people interact with one another and form a sense of community? What are the guiding principles of those communities, from family units to small groups to national/international groups?

3. Individuality in the World State is considered dangerous. However, most of the significant characters not only have names but also have individualized personalities and character traits. Consider how and why characters like Bernard Marx, John the Savage, Helmholtz Watson, Lenina Crowne, and Mustapha Mond are both unusual and at times pose a potential or direct threat to the balance of society. What is done to ensure the continuance of stability, which is one of the three pillars of the World State's motto?

4. The title, *Brave New World*, comes directly from Shakespeare's *Tempest*, and like Miranda, John the Savage says the lines first naively and ironically and then over time the words begin to haunt him in various ways. The phrase is often used today, particularly in relation to advancements in technology, sometimes beautiful and exciting ones and at other times terrifying ones. What does this novel show us about intended and unintended consequences of technology and how we might re-assess our dependence on it?

5. The ending of *Brave New World* haunted Aldous Huxley for the rest of his life. He returned to the idea ina new foreword in 1946 stating that he wished he had ended it differently, and published a "sequel," *The Islands* in 1962, which was

"what *Brave New World* should have been," according to Huxley's stepson. Huxley also wrote *Brave New World Revisited*, a collection of essays examining the book against the times of the 1950s. Do you think that the novel could have ended differently and still remained consistent with the rest of the plot and the principles of the World State? Why or why not? How would you choose to end the novel?

Introduction to George Orwell and
1984 (1949)[1]

George Orwell (1903–1950)

George Orwell, whose birth name was Eric Arthur Blair, was a British writer of fiction and non-fiction. Although he was born in Bengal, a province in India at the time and close to the border of Nepal, Orwell was a British citizen whose father worked in the opium regulation industry there. In his early adulthood, Orwell spent a significant amount of time in Burma (now Myanmar, located in between India and Thailand) as part of the Burmese Indian Imperial Police. His famous essay, "Shooting an Elephant," appears in many textbooks and highlights Orwell's criticism of imperialism. Orwell was a passionate political advocate both in his life and in his writing for those who were economically disadvantaged and/or oppressed. Both his fiction and non-fiction advocate for better working conditions, stronger protections for those living in poverty, and better government. He wrote two famous satires, *Animal Farm*, published in 1946, followed by the dystopian novel *1984*, which was published in 1949.

1984

The most famous line from *1984* that you've probably heard is "Big Brother is watching you."Big Brother here refers to the state, in other words the government. In this novel, England has merged with a number of other countries andbecome a totalitarian state (called Oceania) ruled by Big Brother, whom no one ever sees but is nonetheless an *omnipresent* (all-present) character in their lives. The rest of the world is divided into two other very large states: Eastasia and Eurasia.

Oceania follows a form of socialism called INGSOC (or English Socialism). Socialism is broadly defined as "a way of organizing a society in which major industries are owned and controlled by the government rather than by individual people

---

1. Students are required to purchase this book separately. See the course syllabus for additional information.

and companies. "In this society, all individuals work for the government, regardless of what they do.

While we often think of socialism as not having economic classes, there are classes in the state that depend on how close they are to the central government or Big Brother:the Inner Party (an upper class, closest to Big Brother, who receive benefits both social and economic), the Outer Party (like the middle class), and the Proles (commoners). Our main character, Winston, from whose perspective the novel is told, is an Outer Party member.

We learn quite a lot, too, about the various ministries, or government agencies, that people work for. In British society, a ministry is a government office or department, like the Department of the Interior or the Department of Transportation. There are four main ministries with ironic names that are described in the novel:

Ministry of Truth (also called minitru): controls all media, including news and
    entertainment of all types, as well as education
Ministry of Peace: handles international affairs, primarily war
Ministry of Love: controls law and order
Ministry of Plenty: handles the economic affairs of the state

The plot of *1984* revolves around Winston, who works in the Ministry of Truth, discovering that truth is being covered up in the ministry and therefore in the government. As he determines what to do with this knowledge and how to uncover the truth both for himself and for the larger society of Oceania, the plot unfolds.

The fictional world we enter is intentionally confusing, and there are a few concepts that are worth understanding before they appear in the novel.

Thought Police (Thinkpol) and thoughtcrime: In Oceania, the Thought Police are a secret police force that monitors the thoughts of all its citizens. Don't overthink how this works; instead imagine how every thought you have could be tracked by an outside secret police force and you could be punished accordingly.
Doublethink: Doublethink is a way of holding in your mind two totally contradictory beliefs at the same time. Famous examples from the novel are "War is Peace," "Freedom is Slavery," "Ignorance is Strength." While we can clearly see that these are ironic and paradoxical (and impossible), it's also true that we often engage in this practice, called "cognitive dissonance," without fully recognizing it.
Newspeak: a "new" way of speaking that is in the process of being perfected in Oceania. The dictionary is intentionally being limited in vocabulary and many words are being eliminated in favor of simpler ways of speaking that then limit un-

derstanding and ultimately intelligence. For example, "uncold" replaces "warm."There are many interesting examples that you'll find as you read—like "unperson" for a person who has been "eliminated" (i. e. assassinated or murdered) by Big Brother.

1984 Questions

What is Truth? This is perhaps the most troubling of the four big questions in the novel, because Winston goes on a quest for the Truth in a place where it's dangerous for him to do so and where all the odds are against him. How can we know what the truth is if we're being fed untruths, fake news, and downright lies? With the advent of fake news, of doctored images and videos, of people actively trying to spread disinformation, the novel as a whole makes us examine the consequences of not fighting for truth.

What is Justice? 1984 is not exactly subtle in its critique of totalitarian governments and the effects of tyranny on those who are not in power. If we allow a small group to take power away from the people, how can justice be served?

What does it mean to be Human? Generally, we consider individuality and autonomy, the capacity to determine our own destiny, as essential to our humanity. At what point do we cease to be human when those things are taken away from us? How do we prevent that outcome?

What is the Good Life? As satire, 1984 presents a world of people who are led to believe that they are living the good life and that they are happy precisely because they have been trained to believe that they are happy and that they have all that they need. Does that make them happy? Does that mean they are really living the good life? And if so, what sacrifices must be made for that to always be so? Is that what we are supposed to want for ourselves? Why or why not?

1984. Questions for Discussion

1. Identify three or four examples of Newspeak and/or doublethink that exist in our world today and explain how and why we use them and why this is beneficial and/or dangerous.

2. Examine the ways that conspiracy theories work in *1984* and how we understand them to be true or false. Then, research a conspiracy theory that has taken hold in modern America and consider where and how that might damage our quest for the truth.

3. If you were Winston Smith, the main character in *1984*, what could you do if you were convinced that you were being oppressed by an authoritarian dictatorship that was feeding you lies to such a degree that truth was impossible to determine, and that that government was using you to create fictional histories and "alternative facts"? Imagine at least two or three different possibilities.

4. If you found yourself in Winston's situation in the novel, what would you do to expose the government's corruption? Given what we know about the world of Big Brother in *1984*, what do you think would happen to you and/or to society as a result of your actions?

5. If you were Winston, what *wouldn't* you do? Given what we know about the world of Big Brother in *1984*, what do you think your life and the lives of those around you would be like as a result of your inaction?

6. What do you see as the one or two biggest problems/trends in our society today that could, if continued, lead us down the path of *1984*? What can we as individuals and/or as an American society do to avoid the fate of *1984* in terms of the problems that you have identified?

Afterword

Afterword
Looking Forward

As the readings in the "Late Modernity" overview suggest, both humans and our planet are at something of a crossroads. We are moving from the Holocene Age, which started with the decline of the last ice age nearly 12,000 years ago, into what many are calling the Anthropocene, which breaks down into "anthropo"—meaning human—and cene—meaning "new." This unofficial geological term starts at the time when humans became the dominant influence on the planet, as e adapting it to meet our needs and thus have altered it, particularly its climate, rather than adapting ourselves to our surroundings.

This Anthropocene designation requires that we acknowledge how our thoughts and actions have had a direct and massive impact on how we live, which in turn has had a direct and long-lasting if not permanent influence on the planet we all call home.

So what is it that drives our understanding of ourselves and our home places? As a species, humans place significant emphasis and value on history, and while that includes our greatest advances and achievements, it also includes our greatest weaknesses and failures. How does this knowledge inform, or influence, who we are as individuals and who we become as societies and as a species?

Throughout this course, we have seen in literature and philosophy from Plato's "Allegory of the Cave" all the way into *Brave New World* and *1984* that knowledge can feel like an overwhelming burden. In *Frankenstein*, the knowledge of the inhuman ways humans treat other humans sends Victor's creature spiraling into emotional and existential angst. But without knowledge, we run the risk of acting without recognizing the consequences of those actions and/or of being controlled, without being aware of it, by those who are more powerful and more knowledgeable than ourselves. We become human pawns, not unlike the characters Prospero controlled like puppets on the island in *The Tempest*, the members of the *Brave New World* World State, or the *1984* proles.

That might seem like a stretch of the imagination, as *The Tempest* has a number of fantasy elements, and our 20th century dystopian novels are wildly speculative.

However, while the World State arose only after a nearly apocalyptic war, there are elements that are frighteningly modern:

We are addicted, as a species, to modern technologies; for example, two-thirds of the planet's population own a mobile device, and automation is becoming increasingly popular in industry for all kinds of reasons.

We have the capacity to genetically alter species and even to clone them. Much of the planet's corn comes from genetically modified crops.

People are now able to clone their favorite pets.

Scientists have artificially created human "model embryos"[1] in a lab setting that comes close to a 14-day maximum for experimentation on human embryos.

We have nuclear technology that creates the threat of "mutually assured destruction."

And while England did not become the Big Brother totalitarian state that Orwell feared by the year 1984, there are frightening elements that ring true in today's democracies:

The rise of "alternative facts" and efforts to undermine the media have become a problem that we in the United States face daily. Others work hard to manipulate us every day over social media and other platforms.

According to a Morning Consult Poll, "26% of the U. S. population qualified as highly right-wing authoritarian.[2]

How do we keep from being crushed under this burden of the past and the threats of the present in order to create a better future, for ourselves as individuals but also for society and for the planet? While knowledge carries great responsibilities for us, and while information without context can be dangerous, it is also that which brings us out of Plato's cave and into the light of wisdom.

To engage in that level of self-reflection about our own lives, as well as the history of our culture and even species, is difficult, and often painful. Critical thinking is the key to ensuring that even if life outside of Plato's cave may be more challenging than life inside the cave, it is worth the costs in that you then have the opportunity to live a fuller and richer life in which you, at least in part, control your own destiny.

1. Rob Stein, "Scientists Create Living Entities In The Lab That Closely Resemble Human Embryos," *All Things Considered*, March 17, 2021, https://www. npr. org/sections/health-shots/2021/03/17/977573846/scientists-create-living-entities-that-closely-resemble-human-embryos.

2. Quoted in Jennifer Rubin, "The Truth About Many in the GOP Base: They Prefer Authoritarianism to Democracy," *Washington Post*, June 29, 2021, https://www. washingtonpost. com/opinions/2021/06/29/truth-about-gop-they-prefer-authoritarianism-democracy/.

It's difficult, too, to gain perspective outside of our own brains in our quest for knowledge and understanding. Neuroscience as a field is barely scratching the surface of what is hard-wired inside our brains that influences and even controls our behaviors without our awareness. And that all comes before socialization and acculturation create layers of influence on our attitudes, values, and behaviors that are so ingrained that they seem "natural" to us. Unpacking and decoding those influences is vital to determining who we are, both in terms of our best and even our worst selves. For those of us whose first love is the humanities, these are questions worth asking, and literature, history, and philosophy help us ask the questions, examine our own lives, and consider how to live a truly good life.

In the closing poem of this anthology, "The Algorithm of I," Jack Crocker ponders these questions within his own life. If you read carefully, you can find elements of all of our four big questions working together as he strives to articulate his purpose and meaning, and even joy, in the quest.

The Algorithm of I[3]
Jack Crocker

If chance is the companion of birth, is birth the ancestral
Prison where the brain arranges the "I" of self? And freedom
From the random sentence of life is found only in death?

Can we make glorious the art of joy and grief, proclaim
Victory—not in the promised rewards of myth—but breath
By breath in daily revolt—step by completed step?

I suppose "I" interrogating the brain is the tail chasing
The cat. After all, I'm locked in its cells of being.
(Can the 1s and 0s trapped in its folds and troughs

Trick me into believing I'm free?) Or, Ventriloquist,
Is it telling me what to say, just as the spiral chains
Of the double helix shackled me from the beginning?

3. Jack Crocker, "The Algorithm of I," *The Algorithm of I* (Silver City, NM: Mimbres Press of Western New Mexico University), 1–7.

Yet, how does the brain explain the mind? Is it a
Rogue angel exiled from the cerebellum but allowed to
Pal around with its buddies in the playground of the

Neocortex? Is the enfant brain like a jukebox, preloaded,
Until the mind kicks in—tuning in to a new playlist,
Singing its own songs, dancing to a different beat?

And then there's gut feeling—an intuitive spark
That catches the brain looking the other way? And
All the organs that serve emotions, the irascible spleen

And glorious heart—the fertile cause of love and all
Its fallible effects (not to forget the exalted private parts
And whatever explodes when beauty is perceived).

Did reason come first, or faith? Perhaps once upon a time
A committee of brains failing to reason themselves out of
Death spread the tale of eternal life to save face and keep

Power with faith for savior against doubt. (Knowledge
Pitted god against man. Animal nakedness was lost to
Shame. Sacrifice became the cost of salvation and nations

Surrendered to the pulpit conspiracies of fear.) (Or, is this
The brain's power play to hide responsibility in the rule of those
Who cannot reason beyond the utility of religion?)

(And faith is the spiritual mantra the neurons make, the brain's
Choir, harmonizing to the big bang frequency of the universe?)
I don't know how out of our chemical innocence guilt came, but it's

Kin to spirit and soul—ghosts the brain gives as pablum
For the unexplainable? Are the neuron glitches that gave us
Mozart and serial killers random, or of the same intent?

Why is the brain so defensive about itself? Dining on
perceptions and sunning on the algorithm of need, does it
Amuse itself with hints and labyrinthine leads, partial truths

And dead ends? Is it afraid of its alien siblings gestating
In the lab-wombs of god-brains creating a new digital Eden? Or
Is it addicted to its own self-deception, distracting itself

From the only word that completes the sentence of life?
Lately, it's letting itself be called a predictive error machine.
(I still answer no to the robot question, though captchas give

Me grief.) Entertaining perhaps, but doing battle with
The brain I can't win. Programmed between the contradiction
Of predestination and hubris of free, there's one last

Trick to play: I turn to imagination, the sweetest dream
That thinking knows, and stand mentally naked before
The mirror of I am, was, and cannot help but be:

Cell
A genetic comma surviving the tidal pool
Translations of nature's phrases.

Primitive
Married to the universe in a union of senses
Until consciousness fell in love with itself.

Homo sapiens
Moving across trade routes of survival
Exchanging Neanderthal genes.

Human
Learning to sign my own name against
The power of systems that would sign for me.

Mule
Arrogantly posing as the climax
Of evolutionary intent.

Hunter
Raised by the rifle,
Outgrowing the nature to kill.

Athlete
Tracing the arc of instinct toward
The void of the eternal hoop.

Believer
Accepting that gods do not exist
Except in the need for belief.

Atheist
Reasoning with the passion of faith that heaven
And hell exist only as hope and fear.

Individualist
Putting new tattoos
On old arms of tradition.

Citizen
Living in the social soup of custom and cant
Voting on which spoon to use.

Existentialist
Taunting the absurd by stopping for snacks
On the way back down to where the boulder waits.

Capitalist
Descending the high-rise of profit
To where enough is getting ahead.

Consumer
Cajoled by cleavage to invest in dreams—
A new pair of cowboy boots the only gain.

Taoist
Dissolving self in burning sage to breathe
The vapors of Yin and Yang.

Musician
Planted in Country, rooted in Blues,
Branched out in Rock-n-roll.

Gambler
Shooting the dice of orgasms
In the roulette beds of one-night-stands.

Dreamer
Going to sleep with scripts
Of unreal possibilities . . . .

Realist
Firmly ignorant of much,
Skeptical of the truth of truths.

Hedonist
Thinking vomit reveals the inner life
Of last night's binge.

Delusionist
Lured to the comfort of convenient lies
When scraps of truth are not enough.

Optimist
Lifting to vertical each morning
Knowing death is the only thing we own forever.

Pessimist
Leaving a light on at night,
To mimic counterfeit eternity.

Insomniac
Sweat-awakened at 3:00 a. m. to the hounds of terror
Unleashed into the future's urgency.

Anemic
Believing words are vitamins
To hold decomposition at bay.

Rhetorician
Slick-tongued agent of language
Pulling joy out of the hat of grief.

Artist
Devising gifts of light in exchange
For the dark promise of empty canvases.

Lover
From the first touch of Lynda Boykin's lips
Addicted to the fate of female mercy.

Husband
Hell was Baptist for those who would not wait.
Marriage, then, was the heaven of lust.

Mississippian
Suffering the 2016 election,
Emmett Till exhumed to be killed again.

Southerner
Birth by chance battling the birthmark of
A past that lives in the future again and again.

Hiker
Using trailheads for entry as next
Of kin into Nature's reunions.

Environmentalist
Moved to mountains from the apocalyptic beach,
As if altitude could prevent catastrophe.

Seeker
Neuronal collisions with truth
At the crossroads of beliefs and dreams.

Scholar
Not of footnotes and learned critiques,
But receptor of feelings, mentor of thought.

Tourist
Believing anonymity of place
Is a way to learn the lies of maps.

Wino
Uncertified sommelier of soil and sun,
Addict of the grape's momentary truth.

Alien
Gravity-browsing the boulevards
Of galactic neighborhoods.

Historian
Staring through the window's reflections
To imagine what the panes have seen.

Philosopher
Of black holes schooled in darkness
Of the mind seeking the light of pretend.

Futurist
Imagining beyond the present's cage
As far as the past can see.

Poet
Pushing the limits of words
To go beyond what they are.

Father
Love, finally, asking forgiveness from Jessi and Will
For coming so late to Jodi.

Questions for Discussion

1. How does this poem ponder issues of Truth? Does it seem like the speaker believes in an absolute, eternal truth, and if so what is it? If not, then how do you think the speaker of the poem defines Truth?

2. Select several couplets that clearly call into question issues of justice. Based on what you see in the poem, how do you think that the speaker would answer the direct question, what is Justice? What facets of justice does he emphasize, and where and how might that lead to a better future?

3. Much of the poem revolves around what it means to be human. To what degree does it seem that the speaker thinks that we as humans have free will and self-determination? To what degree does it seem that he thinks that we are bound by social convention, our brain chemistry, and possibly even fate? Based on what you've read in this poem, what do you think the speaker considers most valuable and valued about humanity?

4. Friedrich Nietzsche said that the truly good life is one that seems as if it were destined to be exactly as it was, and that the person having lived that life would look back on it without regret. Based on this poem, do you think that the speaker believes in Nietzsche's "amor fati" and that he believes, at least up to this point, that he has lived a truly good life? Why or why not?

5. Consider how the speaker sees the relationship between science and the humanities, and then consider what connections you can make across the various disciplines (for example, Liberal Arts, science and mathematics, social and behavioral sciences, business) as you work through your individual program.

6. Try out the speaker's "Trick to play" (line 52) and using your imagination, "stand mentally naked before /The mirror of I am, was, and cannot help but be" (lines 53–54) and create an imitation poem that portrays who you are, were, and cannot help but be.

Index

CPSIA information can be obtained
at www.ICGtesting.com
Printed in the USA
LVHW020914140722
723431LV00001B/6